DOG BITES WITH STEVE BROOKS

STEVE BROOKS (C.P.D.T.-K.A.)

Certified Professional Dog Trainer

DOG BITES
Written by Steve Brooks www.SteveBrooksK9U.com
Edited by Serena Tarica www.SerenaTarica.com
Cover Design & Photos by Steve Brooks

This edition published by

Dog Ear Publishing

4010 W. 86th Street, Ste H

Indianapolis, IN 46268

www.dogearpublishing.net

Library of Congress Cataloging-in-Publication Data

Brooks, Steve
Dog Bites with Steve Brooks
ISBN: 978-145753-132-3

Contents...

Introduction

Steve Brooks is a world-renowned Certified Professional Dog Trainer (CPDT-KA), Dog Behavioral expert and talented cook who will show you how to make amazing, healthy human meals for you and your family that you can safely share "bites" of with your dog and use as rewards for good behavior.

In this book, Steve shares how to cook delicious meals that you can prepare for your family and yes, even share *dog bites* with your dog! He will also incorporate using food as a training tool. Keep in mind, just because a certain food may not be toxic to dogs, doesn't mean it's necessarily safe. As recommended throughout this book, if you have any doubts about feeding your dog human food, always check with your Veterinarian first.

As many **STEVE BROOKS K9U** (http://www.SteveBrooksK9U.com) clients will attest, Steve practices a training method that uses food as just one of the many real-life training rewards because food is fun! Reward your dog with *dog bites...* small bites of human food that you cook for yourself and share bites of with your dog.

*Discover what is safe and unsafe to feed your dog while learning
how to modify your favorite meals to share with your pup!*

Dog Bites will demonstrate how to make homemade, gourmet human recipes that can be modified to share with your K9. While Steve is cooking, he is not only training dogs, he is teaching YOU the owner how to train your dog. This is not about how to cook meals for your dog that you would not want to eat yourself. In fact, Steve will show you how to modify meals that are safe and delicious for K9 consumption. He will also demonstrate the health benefits and dangers of many human foods and show you how to use food correctly to train your dog with lasting results.

Discover how to train your dog for life!

Steve Brooks' philosophy of *"dog training for the real world"* holds that every dog should know a set of real-life manners using positive reinforcement without the use of threats or force. In this book, he will be sharing over 20 years of invaluable dog training tips that could save your dog's life in an emergency; Steve's philosophy that dog training should be a part of everyday life; and most of all… that training should be fun for you and your dog! Steve will show you how to use food correctly to remedy a myriad of behavioral problems. Discover how to teach your dog cool tricks that will blow your friends away and even teach your pooch how to become your Sous chef!

Steve teaches dogs a plethora of good manners… not only while cooking in the kitchen, but greeting behaviors when your guests arrive for everything from a Thanksgiving dinner to an intimate meal with impeccable table manners while you and your guests enjoy. Steve also shares how to socialize your dog in the real world… including how to take your dog on a walk, to a friend's house, or to a coffee shop and request him into a "down/stay" position while the waiter walks by with a tray of food or even when someone on a skateboard whizzes by!

Dog Bites provides K9 (canine) health tips not to be missed including: digestion tips; what your dog should *never* eat; how to avoid poisonous foods; feeding tips for puppies, adults, seniors, and over-weight dogs; exercise tips; what to do if your dog is choking; how to minimize their chance of getting bloat and other maladies. You will learn to teach your dog a fool-proof "down/stay" while preparing a gourmet human meal…even if you accidentally drop BBQ ribs right in front of your dog's nose your dog should stay and your baby backs will not be touched!

Steve Brooks is a master at creative, positive, science-based reward training methods with teeerrrific results without the use of force or threats.

The goal is to have a healthy, well-behaved dog…especially any time they are around food. Let's face it, food is one of many great rewards and food is fun! Try cutting back about 10 percent of your dogs regular dog food and adding a few delicious *dog bites* during the week for training. Think about it… if you were a dog, you would be pretty bummed if all you ever ate your whole life was the same old boring food. Guess what? Your dog does too! So enjoy this book and be sure to note your dog's favorite recipes.

This book is called *Dog Bites* because we are using small "bites" of food as a reward to train pooches. You will discover how to modify behavior problems; how to get your dog accustomed to other dogs; how to reduce the chance of food guarding and other types of aggression… even how to teach your dog to take food *gently* right out of the palm of your hand! The key is to build trust with your dog and one way to do this is with lots of love and yes, even food treats! Contrary to popular belief, FOOD can be the best way to build trust and bond with your four-legged friend. Steve's dog changed his life, and he believes yours will too!

DISCLAIMER: While there are vast arrays of delicious, nutritious foods that are safe, many human foods are not safe or recommended for canine consumption. This book only *suggests* that safe human food (in moderation) be used in addition to your dog's regular dog food. A list of unsafe foods is included in this book, but by no means is this list intended to be inclusive of all possible food hazards. Always check with your Vet before changing your dog's diet. If your dog gets sick from eating human food, immediately call: **Animal Poison Control Center (ASPCA) 1-888-426-4435** or go to your nearest Veterinary Emergency Hospital. Write your local Emergency Vet Hospital name and number here:

____

REWARD-BASED TRAINING

Dog bites are payment for a job well done!

Historically, dogs have been "man's best friend" for over 30,000 years. In fact, as far back as the 15th century, dogs were trained with Reward-Based Training and wore head collars like the leaders and halters dogs wear today. The kennel workers were only about seven- or eight-years-old and if the kennel workers were mean to the dogs, *they* would be punished, not the dog! While I don't advocate punishing kennel staff, the reason I share this story is to let you know that Reward-Based Training has been around for centuries and has been used with great success, which is why it is the method I advocate.

I always say, 'I don't work for free so why should a dog?' Dogs, like humans, are motivated by incentives. For us it might be money, a promotion or praise for a job well done. Motivating payment for a job well done may include treats or what I call *dog bites* (small bites of amazing, tasty leftovers or modified human food or dog treats). Other rewards include favorite toys, games, walking and praise.

What motivates one dog may not motivate every dog, so you need to find out what motivates *your* individual dog. Some of the rescue dogs I've trained are so beaten down it's hard to find anything to motivate them. Others may not have had an adequate amount of socialization as a pup so they might be afraid or may not even know what a toy is.

I work for a paycheck, so why can't my dog?

In my experience… most dogs after joining a loving home "get complacent" within the first few months and expect everything in life to be free. I wouldn't work very hard either if everything in life was free! I have to work for a living and money motivates me. Having a job makes me feel good about myself; it gives me purpose. So when a dog gets everything for free, why would they want to work? The reality is they can become scatter-brained, confused or just plain lazy if they don't have structure, rules and training.

Dogs have been bred as workers and herders for thousands of years. In fact they are happier when they have a job, a purpose, structure and leadership. It's easy to say, "My dog is hyper, dominant, has Attention Deficit Disorder (ADD), or is not food motivated." But to me, those are excuses for a dog that really doesn't know what *you* want them to do or hasn't been trained. It is important to understand the difference between being a "leader" and thinking you need to be a pack leader. You don't need to be the alpha leader and dominate your dog in order to be effective. And you certainly don't need to kick, threaten or intimidate by pinning them on their backs, poking, making a *"psssstt "*sound, punching in the neck, yanking with a chain, or pinching with prongs…all of which you've probably seen on TV. Those methods will only destroy your dog's trust, and *trust* is what we are trying to build in order to train.

Being a leader means you are influencing behavior. I like to influence my dog's behavior with positive real-life rewards. You will see way more fallout like aggression from forceful methods than you will by using positive reward-based methods. Harsher methods may work sometimes, but they are only a Band Aid; they don't get to the underlining problem and fix it. They also don't change your dog's emotional feelings towards something… like fear to joy!

I want my dog to listen because they want to, not because they have to.

The trick is to become the problem solver in your dog's eyes. I want to become more exciting than a squirrel to my dog! According to scientists, dogs wouldn't survive very long on this planet without humans. Whether this is true or not, I want the dog to realize that *good things* come from me, especially in the beginning stages of training. One way to do that is to limit your dog's freedom until they know the rules solid as a rock. It's the same idea as a child having a crib, playpen, baby gate, nanny-cam or a swimming pool cover. Children aren't free to do whatever they want until they learn the rules. Once your dog knows the rules they can be like the famous Rough Collie named *Lassie* (1954-74); they can have more freedom then any dog on the block!

All dogs are different. You've got to find what motivates your individual dog.

Imagine that your dog is a gambler and you are a slot machine… If you are the slot machine you want to mostly pay out the dog a low enough value reward that will keep him playing. For a human gambler, a "low-value" reward might be a pay out on a Vegas slot machine of $5. For a dog, an equal reward could be dry kibble and a pet on the head. As long as the reward is motivating enough to the dog, work off the low-value rewards on your list. Then, just when the "doggy gambler" is getting bored and ready to go to another machine, you might surprise your dog with a liver treat or something off the "medium-value" list. This would be the equivalent of $50 to the human gambler. If your dog gets ready to go to another casino, surprise them with a juicy bite of chicken or something off the "high-value" list. This would be $500 to the human gambler!

REAL-LIFE K9 REWARDS

I suggest creating a list of real-life rewards for training purposes and categorize them into three groups: high-value, medium-value, and low-value.

- ✓ **Favorite Foods (in order of preference)**
- ✓ **Favorite Toys**
- ✓ **Favorite Places To Be Pet or Touched**
- ✓ **Favorite Places To Go; Things They Like To Do There**
- ✓ **Favorite Phrases That Make Your Dog Happy**
- ✓ **Verbal Praise**
- ✓ **Sniffing Outside**
- ✓ **Going Potty**
- ✓ **Going Out A Door For Exercise**
- ✓ **Coming In A Door For Shelter**
- ✓ **Going To Their Bed For Rest**
- ✓ **Swimming**
- ✓ **Playing with Other Dogs**
- ✓ **Retrieving**
- ✓ **Running**
- ✓ **Games**
- ✓ **Water**

NOTE: Water as a reward doesn't mean you should ever deprive your dog from drinking. What it means is if your dog is thirsty after a walk, or if their bowl is empty, then maybe you can ask your dog to do a sit/stay for ten seconds while you freshen up their bowl and send them off to drink when you are ready. Having them work for all these things and accepting baby steps will help your dog realize that you are influencing their behavior and not the other way around, which in turn, will make you a leader in your dog's eyes. You can become a leader by controlling resources… not by using force.

Food is a great reinforcer for dogs.
If used properly it can produce excellent results!

Some dogs are motivated by food more than any other factor because dogs need food for survival. So why not make food both nutritious and educational? Think about it… your dog literally depends on you for food every single day – they don't have thumbs so they can't open a can of food or drive to the store and buy a bag of kibble. Food works better for some dogs; toys work better for others. You've got to find out what motivates your individual dog. You can use any real-life reward off your list and keep trying until you find something that your dog cares about.

I recommend that you keep your dog on the diet that your Veterinarian recommends and ask your Vet if you can supplement about 10% of their regular diet for small *dog bites* of healthy non-toxic people food. All dogs are individuals; some are more sensitive to certain foods than others (the same way we are), so when giving your dog something new to eat, always start small. Never take a chance feeding your dog human food if you are not 100% certain that it is safe. I bet your Vet will say that's its fine as long as there are no underlining medical problems. I like to use food to train new behaviors, and then I wean the dog back using food less, and incorporating other real-life rewards. I'm always ready to surprise my dog with a tasty *dog bite* when they least expect it in order to help maintain what I have trained.

When left outside on their own or in the wild, canines forage about 80 percent of the time. What that tells me as a trainer is that dogs like to eat small amounts throughout the day – which is actually healthier. Keep in mind that feeding randomly throughout the day may interfere with potty training. In other words, you don't want to feed Fido a large meal right before bed because that means you have to get up at 3 am. to walk him.

- If you're afraid that giving your dog people food will create a beggar, be aware that it might if you don't practice self-control exercises with your dog. You can also look at it this way: if a dog is begging that means they are motivated, and when a dog is motivated, that's the best time to train!
- Use food for training. It's used for zoo animals, so why not dogs?
- Dogs are social animals. If socialized and trained, most dogs love to be pet and praised, and if you really dig deep, connect with them, and mean it when you

praise your dog, you'd be surprised how far some good verbal and physical praise can go!

If you're having fun, training is fun – make training a game for your dog! Soon they too will have fun and you won't need to be so dependent on food.

When using food rewards, a few things have to happen all at once:

1. The dog has to take the reward "gentle" with their front teeth, not rough with their K9 teeth. They also can't just knock it out of your hand and run off with it.
2. They must exercise self-control; four paws on the ground or sitting.
3. Take your sunglasses off when training. You want your dog to see your face and eyes to be aware of your emotions. You want the dog to *see* that you're happy; their tail should wag.
4. Be sure to pair petting with delivering the food (if the dog allows it).

Dogs are smart… If they know you have something yummy in your hand, they might only listen when they *see* you holding the food. Be creative. Use slight-of-hand magic tricks. Keep them guessing! Maybe the treats in the right hand; maybe in the left hand…maybe the treats in both hands, or maybe it's not in your hands at all! If your dog will only work if he sees you holding the food first, avoid letting them see it. Request or cue the desired behavior, or capture the desired behavior, then mark it instantly with a click, "good dog" or "yes"! Deliver the food immediately (within two seconds) and don't forget to pair food with pets, the dog taking it gentle, exercising self-control on the dog's part, and eye contact.

More dog bites (the good kind) means more opportunity to train!

Here's where many people fail when using food… they give too big a piece. You want to start with the smallest piece of kibble or food that will work. If you are feeding with dry kibble and the type of kibble allows for it, break the kibble into even smaller-sized pieces. If your dog is a large breed you may use bigger pieces. I start by hand-feeding the dog the same amount normally put into their bowl but I put it in a treat pouch instead and feed throughout the day. I usually do this around breakfast and dinnertime.

MEALTIME TRAINING

Training works best when it coincides with feeding.

I feed in many small sessions throughout the day, usually between 7:00 - 9:00 am. and 5:00 - 7:00 pm. What I've discovered is that dogs seem to be more receptive to training at dusk and at dawn. Training during meals is very effective. When I first start training, I actually don't use a bowl to feed. I feed as a reward for positive behavior by hand. If the dog did well on a walk or whatever training task I'm trying to achieve, I might give him the balance of his meal in a bowl. I always try to get the dog to show enthusiasm for dry boring kibble out on a walk before I go to the good stuff because if I start with the good stuff, then I have nowhere to go. I use food to train where the dog is slacking the most. For instance, if the dog is not coming when called, I will use about 90 % of their food to work on different come exercises until that problem is resolved and I might give the other 10 % in a bowl. Sometimes I will feed my dog meals stuffed into a Kong™ toy.

- If you stuff a Kong™ toy and leave it with your dog when you leave the house, it may keep them busy for a while, but keep in mind that they may also get thirsty and have to go potty before you get home.
- There are hundreds of ways to feed your dog if you get creative. (You will find many more ways to feed throughout this book).
- In my opinion, it's boring for a dog to get the same thing out of the same bowl every day for life.

Q: My dog is a finicky eater. How can I get her to work for food?

There are dogs that will only eat kibble (dry dog food) on the way home from a walk, while others may only eat it by the front of your house or in your driveway. Some will only eat inside; others only outside. Some will only eat kibble in the shade, others only in the sun, and others only out of your hand; some will only eat off the ground… Many dogs will only eat the kibble if you break it in half under their nose, while others want to take the kibble away and play with it. Some will even bury it like they do a bone so it will be there for later!

Maybe your dog is full and has already eaten? Many dogs won't eat if they are full so you better check with the rest of your family, neighbors… and even dog walkers to see what else your dog is getting into. There is also concern when a dog won't eat that they may have eaten something that they shouldn't have that may be blocking them up. When in doubt, or if the protesting of food persists, always check with your Vet. They may need to take x-rays to check for an intestinal obstruction.

When I start training a new behavior, I like the dog to work for low-value food first like dry dog kibble. If they reject the kibble, wanting chicken instead, they will have to wait until they love the kibble before getting little bites of chicken again. Once the dog is happily working for dry kibble, I'm ready to start using tiny bites of better, more amazing foods, and yes, even human foods! What do you think dog food is anyway? It's people food made into little pieces of dry kibble. Of course, you have a better chance of getting your dog to repeat a desired behavior if you use high-quality, gourmet beef than you will if you use dry boring kibble but I prefer to save the good stuff for when I really need it. When you do give a bite of good stuff, it has to be tiny crumb-size pieces.

Dry kibble is the easiest to use on a walk. If I start with the good stuff, I will have nowhere to go from there. You need to be in control. The dog can't be manipulating you and only eat the good stuff. I want them to lure or follow my hand, even if it's just an inch for a finicky dog or three feet for a food hound. Many dogs will take dry kibble and like it, then when I surprise them with something better, they love it! But when I go back to dry kibble, they spit it out thinking, "Why would I eat kibble when I smell hot dog on you?" That's when you have to play hardball and mean it…

When a dog is scared, they can shut down and may not eat.

A dog will perform better with some food in their stomach. If you have a dog that won't eat, sometimes you have to let them win the battle and give in. Some dogs might eventually eat after a day of protest. But then when they do eat, they eat a lot so you're back to square one. It's a balancing act – keep trying and believe me I know it can be hard if your dog won't take the food. Just try to play hardball but never starve your dog and never willingly skip more than one meal. The key is to gain the dog's trust and make them feel comfortable and they will usually eat.

Even though my facility is Feng Shui with aromatherapy and classical music playing like at a spa… and all the other dogs are chill – the fact is some dogs just take a while to adjust. Eventually, they will eat. My goal is that when they do eat, it comes from my hands using a technique called Luring (see Luring). Even if they move just one inch for a bite, I'm happy. Because once you start getting them to take baby steps… you know there is hope!

One trick I use to get a finicky dog to like kibble as a reward is to put bits of cheese or lunch meat in the kibble container to give it that aroma. I smash a crumb of cheese, lunch meat, a bit of tuna or sardine juice onto a few pieces of kibble – keeping a mixture of flavored and unflavored kibble in my hand. This helps to get the dog happier to work for kibble without filling them up on heavy treats. Another reason dogs won't eat is if they have been abused, as is often the case with rescues (see Cheryl Tiegs' story). If you have a finicky dog that won't eat, it makes it worse if you try too hard and constantly shove the food in their face, so don't overdo it. Try a little then take a break and maybe try again in a different environment or observe your dog's body language, and when you see them relax a bit, try the food again.

One reason dogs may fear training is if they previously have had harsh training with choke chains, pinch collars, or shock collars. Let's say you are trying to feed them a hot dog, and, at the same time, using a shock collar to discipline. What will happen is, the dog may have a fearful association with hot dogs and never eat them again. If a dog has had a negative experience with training that uses forceful methods, it may take time, even with the best of reward-based trainers, to make progress. You need to keep experimenting and find what motivates your dog. Using food is a great way to train a new behavior, and also to bond with your pup, but you don't want to solely rely on food. You want to use it because it's fun, not because you have to. When I'm training with food, I want to use the majority of it where the dog's behavior is slacking the most, until I make progress with that behavior, and then I will do the same with the next behavior problem, training request, or trick I need to work on.

USING FOOD ON A WALK

First, you need to have easy access to get to the treats; you don't necessarily want the dog to know that you have them. I don't recommend using small plastic baggies or holding your purse filled with treats when training. You don't want to be fiddling around with the treats; you want to be organized quick and smooth. You have to have your hands free on a walk, and it helps if you take that poop bag holder off the end of your leash too! It gets in the way… just carry the poop bag in your pocket. The best way to feed while training is to use a treat pouch (to keep your hands free). I like to keep my treat pouch on my right side and the dog on the left when walking so they're not as apt to jump up and grab. Also, if I have food in my hand, I will hold it up high enough that the dog won't jump up and grab it from my hands. If you walk at a brisk pace, your dog will not be as apt to jump.

When feeding dogs by hand, food-aggressive dogs may get exuberant and excited and try to "bite the hand that feeds" or grab aggressively, especially over high-value foods. You need to read your dog's body language and watch your fingers – if you have any trepidation, talk to a Veterinary Behaviorist (ACVB Certified Professional Dog Trainer (CPDT), Certified Applied Animal Behaviorist (CAAB or ACAAB) or an experienced Force-Free Trainer from the Pet Professional Guild. In these instances, food must be delivered very carefully.

When I have a dog that grabs food hard out of my hand here's what I do… I keep the treat in a closed fist or even two closed fists touching each other and glued to my leg (the bigger the target, the less likely the dog is going to bite your finger). I don't deliver the treat until the dog backs off a little. Then, the second he backs off, I give him the treat to reward that behavior. Never just give the treat for grabby or aggressive behavior. Some dogs might get protective over their human carrying a treat pouch full of tasty *dog bites*. It's possible that carrying a treat pouch can cause or increase protective, territorial, and guarding-type aggression. I find this very rare, but if you see any signs of your dog getting aggressive over the treat pouch, get help before proceeding with training.

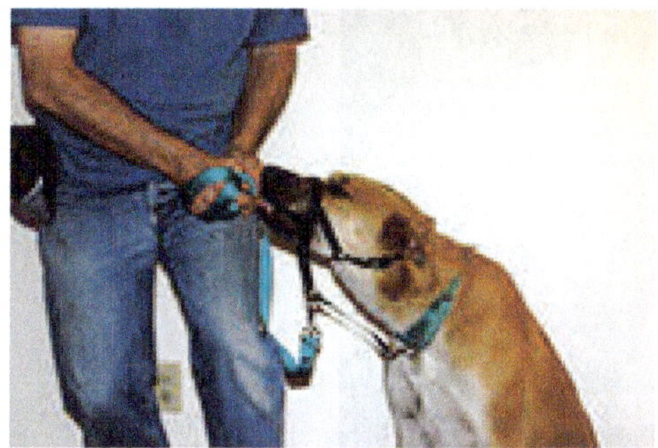 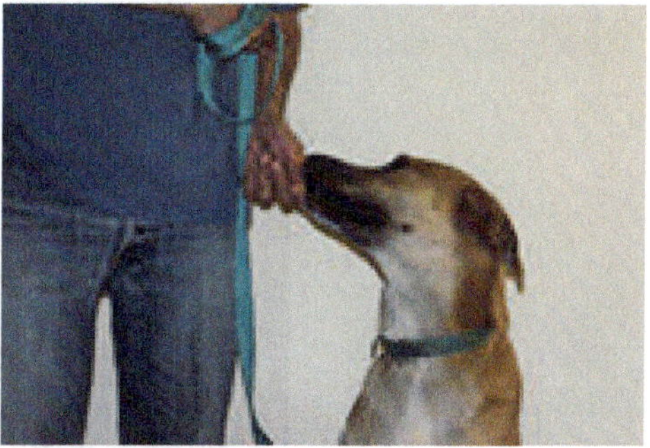

Here's a little trick that I use if I don't want to get my hands dirty while training, or if I'm training a dog that takes food rough out of my hand. I also use this technique if I don't want to fill my dog up too quickly. I take a non-toxic garden hose (you can usually find them at boating or RV stores); if you're shopping for a hose at a hardware store, look for lead-free as some garden hoses still contain led. Cut a four- to five-inch piece of hose. Cut a hot dog lengthwise and stuff it into the hose so it sticks out about an inch on each side. You can also stuff the hose with my Salmon Pâté (see recipe), peanut butter, cream cheese, or string cheese. Feed the dog on a walk by letting them lick the hose filled with a treat to redirect attention when passing big distractions or to curtail barking.

Recently, I was hired for a wedding where I had to teach the dog to be the ring bearer. This dog had separation distress and would bark like crazy whenever he would see his mom and couldn't get to her. He was also aggressive with certain strangers and there were going to be 300 people at the wedding! During the ceremony, I walked the dog down the aisle and stood with the dog as the couple said their vows. It was a complete success! How did I do it? A stuffed piece of garden hose full of sticky, yummy *dog bites* discretely fed to the dog was all it took to keep him quiet. It's hard to bark with a mouthful of goodness!

I can think of hundreds of ways to feed a dog…

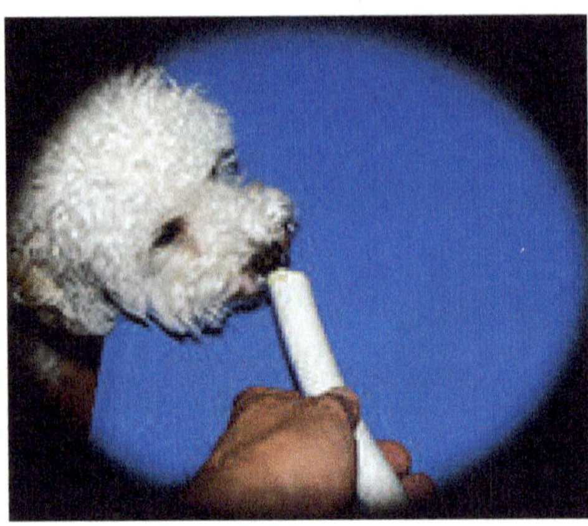

I would much rather put food in an interactive dog toy or hand-feed during training sessions and surprise my dog for good behavior when they least expect it! Just when your dog thinks you don't have anything; then, boom! You've got something hidden behind your back. Sleight of hand… a magic trick… Your dog sees your empty hand and then all-of-a-sudden there's a treat in it! I like to use food when I first start training a new behavior. Once the dog knows it well, I start to wean down, sometimes even during the first lesson. Eventually, they might get *dog bites* just some of the time.

So why not stop using food treats all together? Well, using food with your dog is both fun and motivating. The way I see it, I work for a paycheck and a dog should too! How would you like to go to work tomorrow and have your boss say, "You have been doing such a good job I decided not to pay you anymore?" Would you go back to work the next day and keep working? I don't think so! Practice training in different environments. Just because your dog will listen and respond to treats in the kitchen, doesn't mean they will listen on a busy street. A human can learn something in one room and be able to perform that behavior anywhere, whereas a dog has to practice in low-distraction areas first and then move to different areas.

I sometimes start weaning down treats on the first session, but I never like to completely wean off food entirely because training with food is fun, if you do it correctly. To cut back food rewards, it helps if you pair petting or massage with the delivery of a food treat or toy. Usually, I deliver the treat *only* if the dog does the desired behavior perfectly. But sometimes, you might be asking too much of the dog too soon, so you have to slow down and deliver treats for the smallest of baby steps.

Your dog may be overwhelmed, stressed, or fearful. If this is the case, you may have to lower your criteria and build slowly. As the dog gets better at what you are teaching, you can start asking for a chain-of-behaviors before you deliver the treat. For instance, requesting your dog to perform a set of behaviors: "sit", "stay", "come", "down", "roll over"…and *then* giving the reward paired with a pet. Whenever you pet your dog as a reward, you have to dig deep within yourself to let your dog know that you really mean it! You can't just say "good dog" in a monotone voice and pet half-heartedly. They know when you're faking, trust me. Be aware that many dogs don't like being pet on the head and others don't like being hugged, so petting on the chest might be safer. Some dogs can be taught to like being pet if food is paired at the same time and done in a calm, controlled manner.

Steve Brooks' K9U Golden Rules:

1. Be alert; be in tune with your dog. Be proactive. Manage your dog and the environment so your dog can't practice making mistakes.
2. Train a solid foundation of good manners to override any behavior issue.
3. Learn reward-based Behavior Modification techniques ~ change your dog's emotional feelings from fear to joy!
4. Make training part of everyday life with your dog.
5. Let your dog know when they do something right! Praise with feeling; Dig deep and really mean it!
6. Become a problem solver in your dog's eyes.
7. Become more exciting than a squirrel!
8. Make training itself your dog's reward; use food to help reach the training goal.
9. Be happy with baby steps your dog offers and don't be afraid to lower the criteria to make the task easier for your dog to succeed. In the long run, they will blossom!
10. Be clear, concise, and consistent! Don't clutter their heads with a bunch of jib-jab.
11. As a general rule: don't pair food with fear; put the food away. When the fear subsides, try again.
12. It always helps to have a goal before each training session. Even if you change your goal once you start, it's better than not having a goal at all.
13. Believe in yourself and be the type of dog owner who relishes in training.
14. Have fun so both you and your dog enjoy a happy, healthy companionship!

POSITIVE TRAINING TACTICS

Training your dog is essential to a happy, healthy relationship for life!

When it comes to changing your dog's emotional feeling towards something, I recommend using Behavior Modification: the process of transforming a negative emotion into a positive one. I have found it highly effective in training thousands of dogs, which is why I advocate that every owner learns and practices what I call "positive training tactics". In this book, you will discover an understanding of the process of modifying behavior as it relates to effectively training your dog for life!

When a client first brings their dog to me for training, I assess the K9's weight, coat, eyes, energy, emotions, and overall health. Dog training is not an isolated thing; it actually works in-tandem with health and fitness. People always ask me if I can train any dog at any age and I always say, "as long as they are in good health". I have always made tremendous progress training each and every dog, no matter the breed or size, but I'll let you in on a little secret; it's also my job to train the owners just as much as the dog!

STEVE BROOKS K9U DOG TRAINING (stevebrooksk9u.com) consists of three essential components: Management, Training, and Behavior Modification.

MANAGEMENT

Management is the first tier of training and
resolving behavior problems.
The second is teaching a solid foundation of Dog-mandments;
The third is Behavior Modification.

Management is learning how to prevent your dog from practicing bad behavior in the first place. It's being proactive, being alert, and thinking one step ahead of your dog. The two most essential behaviors when it comes to training that can save your dog's life are to come when called and to stay. These requests have to be solid, which means your dog will come and stay – even with huge distractions. If and when you feel confident that your dog will come and stay, then you can allow them more freedom. Once your dog knows the rules, using techniques in this book, then they will get more freedom than any dog on the block!

Whenever I have a new dog-in-training, I want to know what they are doing at all times. This is where management comes into play. They can have a recess if and when I allow it (in a fenced yard), but I am the playground monitor. This way, I don't let them practice bad behavior because I am keeping an eye on them. If they find that chewing on my lawn furniture is fun, I'm right there with something even more fun to replace that behavior. It's important, as an owner, that you practice management. Managing a dog means setting them up to *win* and not allowing opportunities to practice bad behavior until they know the rules solid as a rock.

Management can be having a leash on your dog (even in the house), holding it or letting them drag it, or tethering your dog to your hip or a hook in the wall. (Never keep a leash on or tie your dog unattended for safety reasons.) Management can mean crating your dog for a short while when you are not able to watch him or using a baby gate in the doorway of your kitchen, using a dog run, playpen, closing doors, putting the trash and kid's toys out of reach, using a head harness, a muzzle, to name a few…

Until a dog is trained, I want each dog to be doing something specific like chewing a bone, napping in their dog bed, or enjoying a short recess in the yard. I want to know *where* they are and *what* they are doing at all times until they know the rules. What I don't want is for them to be off in another room when my back is turned. I don't ever want to wonder, "Where's the dog?" Sure, I will let them wander the house freely, as long as I am proactive. In other words, I might let a dog explore off leash in a safe area, but I am observant of their body language; I am focused and observant of what they are doing. The second I see them give up on whatever they are into – for instance, staring at a bird outside the window – the second they give up on the bird even just a little bit…turn their head away or when their ears or tail relaxes, breathe easier, yawn, sit…the *second* they give up, I mark it with a "good boy" or "good girl" or a click sound and I call the dog back to me for some love and yes, maybe even a tasty dog bite! I always want my dogs to know that I'm more fun then everything else out there.

TRAINING ESSENTIALS: SBK9U DOG-MANDMENTS

Dog-mandments (as I call them) are behaviors every dog is taught to know and understand, solid as a rock. As a Certified Professional Dog Trainer, I would like to share the manners or Dog-mandments that I teach all the dogs I train in order to give them a solid foundation. These requests are essential to training and hold the *secret* to success. In fact, I have taught these vital behaviors with great success at Steve Brooks K9U to thousands of dogs and their owners! Teaching a solid foundation is at the heart of every training program at Steve Brooks K9U.

1. **SIT**
2. **DOWN**
3. **STAY**
4. **COME**
5. **WALK WITHOUT PULLING ON THE LEASH**
6. **A MARKER WORD: "YES"! "GOOD DOG" OR "CLICK"**
   SO THE DOG KNOWS WHEN THEY DID SOMETHING CORRECTLY
7. **DOG'S NAME = LOOK AT ME**

Also very important is "Don't Potty in the House!" You will also need to teach them not to be destructive when left alone. Everything else is icing on the cake! As simple as it sounds, knowing these requests can save your dog's life! Most people think their dog already knows these basic commands, but I believe an owner should be responsible for making sure their dog is well-versed in any situation. Steve Brooks K9U's human clients learn how to use voice, hand-signals and body language to issue Dog-mandments successfully. When your dog knows all seven, is potty-trained, and can be left alone without being destructive, then they can be the dog of your dreams and hopefully, have more freedom than Lassie!

It's also important is to teach your dog to retrieve, which means to go get an item and then bring it back and drop it in your hands. If your dog picks up a dangerous item in their mouth, it can be life-saving if your dog has been taught to "Leave it" or "Drop it."

Q: What is Clicker Training?

Clicker training, developed by Karen Prior, uses a "mark" sound (the click sound) that tells the dog what he did right the *instant* he performs the desired behavior. The sound of the "click" means to the dog that a reward will be delivered any second. When you catch your dog doing a desired behavior, *mark it* with a "click" and reward that behavior (within two seconds or as soon as possible). You can use a clicker or a verbal click sound, a verbal "good dog, good boy or good girl", or a verbal "yes". The clicker sound is quicker then saying "good boy" but when using your voice instead of a clicker, you can use inflections in your voice. So if the dog does something you really like, you can increase the enthusiasm in your voice. I personally use a clicker, but most of the time; I just use my voice to emulate the sound that a clicker makes. I then follow it up with a verbal "good boy/girl". This way, it frees my hands up so I can be organized while dealing with holding the leash, toys, petting, and feeding and training properly.

Sequence & Timing: The Two-Second Rule

Let me explain sequence. When you say your dog's name that means: "look at you". Next in the sequence is a behavior request, cue, or what I call a Dog-mandment. This can be done with your voice, a hand signal, or both. If the dog follows your cue or signal, you should immediately reward them within what I call the "two-second rule"; two seconds of the dog listening and responding (or as quickly as possible). The reason for rewarding within two seconds is, if you wait too long, the dog will have no idea what they are getting that reward for. We have to teach the dog what behaviors we want first: Dog's Name, Come, Sit/Down, Stay, and Don't Pull on a Leash, to name a few….

Timing is key when it comes to effective training. Rewards, especially food rewards, have to be delivered at the right time to reinforce behavior. The food or toy also has to be paired with self-control on the dog's part – which means they can't be jumping out of control grabbing and they have to take the toy or food gently with their front teeth, not K9 teeth. You also want a tail wag on the dog's part and eye contact between you and to dog. I also suggest pairing a pet on the chest or head with the food or toy.

1. **Say dog's name**
2. **Request a behavior**
3. **If they listen, mark it.** Mark the fact that the dog listened with a clicker, a verbal click sound, a verbal "good boy", "good girl" or "yes". I want the dog to know that I'm happy and they did the behavior correctly.
4. **Reward immediately with something off their real-life reward list.**
5. **Release the dog with the word "okay" or "free."**

When it comes to training, everything has to happen within two seconds or as quickly as possible for the dog to make a connection between their action and the consequence. Association with the Dog-mandment must be immediate for it to be effective. You must be clear and concise.

COME

Come means to come when called. Come is a position for the dog to be facing in front of you. There are many ways to teach a dog to come. Here are just a few… Start in a contained area with no big distractions. One way I teach a dog to come is to turn my back and play hard to get. You want the dog to look for your front. I like to teach the ending of this behavior first, which means I need them to find my front. Start out by saying, "Where's the puppy?" Pretend you can't find your dog and talk baby talk. They usually come around to your front to see where you are. Once they do, lower your body and lure them in toward your shins and say "come". Label the word come *when they are in motion*, coming towards you with enthusiasm, when they're almost to your front. Make sure you pair the word with the action. Think of it as you are teaching them to "find your front". Praise like crazy when they get to you. Once the dog is trying hard to find your front, you can start asking them to come first instead of labeling it. Eventually, you can call them from a distance.

I also teach dogs to come by luring them to my front. I lure from a heel position, which is on my left side, to a come position, which is to be standing or sitting in front of me, and back and forth. By teaching them this pattern, it will come in handy when you start to stretch out on the sidewalk during daily walks. Say you're on a walk and you pass an aggressive dog... If your dog has practiced this pattern, it will become second nature for your dog to turn around and face you when you back up and say "come". Walk forward once the other dog passes – if you've practiced this pattern, your dog should flip back to your left side and walk forward with you. You can back up into a driveway or between two trash cans when you see another dog approaching if you need to. When the other dog passes, you can walk forward and your dog will flip right back to your left side. Alternate from "heel" to "come" on walks… it will keep your dog on their toes!

"Wait, why don't you hang out a bit longer?"

Once the dog has a concept of what come and heel means, you can try working them off-leash in a secure yard. If you need to, for safety purposes use a 20-30 foot leash. (Never use a retractable leash as they are dangerous and never leave a leash on unattended.) If you're feeling lucky and you think your dog will come, call them in a happy voice using the word 'come.' You want to be crystal clear, bend your elbow, bring your hand to your chest, get low and open your arms; be inviting. Once they run to you, reward and praise them like crazy!

The next thing I do, once they come with enthusiasm, is to run back into the house, leaving the dog to think, "Wait, why don't you hang out a bit longer?" After a couple of minutes I go to another door of the house and yell "come". Do this five or six times; each time they come, praise them like crazy! When you are ready to let them back in the house, surprise them about 50% of the time with another amazing tasty *dog bite* or the balance of their meal. Soon they will start to trust you and want to come.

If the dog doesn't come because he's distracted by a squirrel, go back in the house and shut the door. Go straight to your fridge and get the best leftover you can find (even a whole roast chicken). Go back out into the yard with the whole chicken, but don't go towards the dog…walk to the other corner of the yard and play hard to get. Act smug, sit with your butt on the ground. If you have a hoody, cover and lower your head. Act mysterious, quietly talk baby talk to yourself and pretend you are eating the best food in the entire world or pretend you are playing with a little puppy. Avoid looking at your dog.

Have faith, because nine out of ten times, your dog is going to stop whatever it is they are doing and come running over to you to see what's so interesting. When the dog shows up, carefully show them the food but don't give them any. Say "Sorry, you could have had some of this, but you're too late," and walk right back into your house. They will probably scratch at your door and feel a bit devastated thinking, "How could you have that whole roast chicken and not even give me one bite?" Eventually, they will wander away. The second they do, call them back with an enthusiastic "come" and this time, give them a little bite (no bones and not the whole chicken). I bet the next time you call with a crystal clear "come" they will come a lot quicker!

Another way I teach dogs to come is by playing hide-and-seek. Each family member will hold a portion of the dog's meal. You can divide the food into separate bowls or put it in your hands. Everyone hides in a different room. Have one person say "come". When the dog comes, have the person praise like crazy, pet, and deliver the treat… then *ignore* the dog. The first person will cue the next person to say "come." One at a time, each of the other people do the same thing. The dog runs from room to room, responding to the word "come" and eating his meal. Kids love this game!

Another exercise involves using a leash in a safe area. While walking your dog and when your dog least expects it, drop the leash on the ground and run *away* from the dog. Then yell "come." This teaches the dog that chasing you is a really fun game. I have a client who says their dog just won't come no matter what. Well, I discovered that the client chased the dog as a form of play. Of course the dog won't come if they think running away from you is a game. You never want to chase your dog; you want them to chase you!

Exercise: How to Get Your Dog to Come in Mid-Run

- ➢ Start in a room of your house with a door that has an inch of space under it. Sit at the other end of the room with a handful of boring kibble with an A-list treat hidden behind your back or on a shelf within reach. Throw the kibble towards the door and tell your dog to "go get it".
- ➢ When the dog runs a few feet and eats the kibble, say "come" and feed them another piece of kibble for coming. Then throw another piece of kibble closer and closer to the door and repeat the above steps.
- ➢ On the 5th or 6th time, throw the treat *under* the door so he can't get to it. That's when you yell "come". When they come back to you, give them the A-list treat that you had hidden. This will teach your dog to come in mid-run because you could always have something even better!

Here's another version using a toy… First you need to find out which toy is your dog's favorite. The way to find her favorite is to put several toys in a pile and say "go get it". The dog will pick her favorite A-list toy. Do it again to find their second or B-list toy favorite. Now, take the favorite A-toy and hide it behind your back. Take the B-toy and play retrieve with it. Throw the B-toy across the yard and have someone step on it so the dog can't get it. Now you yell for her to come to you. She should respond because the first toy thrown is impossible to get, and when she does, give her the A-list toy. She will be amazed! This is how they learn to come in mid-run; *you* are always a better bet.

Exercise: "STEAL the DOGGIE"

"Steal the Doggie" is an effective technique inspired by John Rogerson and designed to teach a dog to come. It helps the dog build speed and learn to come in a straight line right to you.

> ➢ Have a friend or family member sit in a chair with an amazing, tasty leftover *dog bite* in their hand (or in a treat pouch). Show the dog the food – let him smell it and maybe even let them taste a small bite. Then have them say, "Look what I've got, puppy!" in baby talk. Note: During this game is one of the only times I will use food as bribery. You don't want to bribe; you want to surprise the dog!

> ➢ *Have* another person hold the dog on a leash (for this exercise it's best if the dog is wearing a harness). As the dog is sniffing the treat from the person sitting in the chair, the person holding the leash will slowly walk the dog *away* toward the other end of the room. The dog will be pulling on the leash to get at the person holding the treat, which is just out of reach.

> ➢ As soon as the leash is tight, have the person holding the leash drop the leash. The second they drop the leash and the dog is running to the person with the food is when they say "come" in a crystal-clear voice. Say it as the dog's *in motion*! Give them a bite and pet enthusiastically once they do. Repeat 5 or 10 times (switching roles as well.) Then try it in different chairs and different rooms around the house.

Emergency TIPS: Getting Your Dog to Come

> o Get low or sit on the ground (don't yell the word "come" in a mean voice or act intimidating, remember to get low and be positive and inviting)
> o When your dog least expects it and when you're feeling lucky, ask your dog to "come" and surprise them with something amazing! Repeat at least several times a week.

- o Shake a pill bottle or Tic-Tac container to make a rattling sound or try a high-pitched trill in your voice
- o Blow a whistle or shake your car keys
- o Bring another dog who knows how to come (to show them how)

LURING: TEACH SIT & DOWN / STAY

Sit and down mean your dog remains in the position until released. Luring is the most common way to teach a sit and down. First, put a treat in your hand (in a closed fist) and place it near the dog's nose so they can smell it.

For sit: slowly raise your fist between their eyes and lure their head upward. This will cause their butt to lower to the ground. If a dog's head goes up, their butt usually goes down. The second their butt hits the ground, and for down, the second they hit the deck, I bring the treat up to my face first before I deliver so they can see my eyes. Then I deliver the treat paired with a pet on the head or chest. This way we have eye contact, self-control on the dog's part, and I pet the dog at the same time as the treat is delivered. Then I quickly release the dog with an "okay" when I am ready. I try to get the dog to realize that I'm the reason they get out of the down/stay. I don't want them to get up until I release them. I'm happy with a five-second down/stay at first and I will build from there and keep them in the sit or down position a little longer each time.

Once I am sure they have a good concept of sit and down, I try luring *without* having food in my hand. The food treat now comes from another area (slight-of-hand) as a surprise so they don't think it's always in your hand. For down: lure from under their nose toward their toes. During the next training session I reduce the effort of my motions until luring is just a small movement or a little inflection and then I use my voice or hand signals to get them to sit or lie down.

Another way I teach down is to lure them under my leg (while I'm sitting on the floor) and gently lower my leg a little lower to the ground as they try to get the treat from my hand. Usually, I don't deliver the treat until they are all the way down, but sometimes you have to be happy with baby steps and treat for little efforts until they are all the way down. Don't put pressure and push your dog down, just make them realize that if they lay down you will let them get the treat.

I don't ask a dog to sit or lie down at first. If I don't think they know it, I label it when they're about 95% into the sit or down position, and that's when I add the word "sit" or down *as it is happening*. Once I think the dog has a concept of sit or down, then I will start asking it first (see Sequence).

Sequence to Teach Sit and Down:

1. **Say dog's name**
2. **Ask him/her a sit or down with voice or hand signals, or both**
3. **If the dog listens, instantly say "good boy/girl" or click to mark that you are pleased**
4. **Get eye contact and connect with your dog**
5. **Self-control on the dog's part**
6. **Praise and reward**
7. **Release him/her on your terms**

SHAPING & TARGETING TO TEACH SIT & DOWN

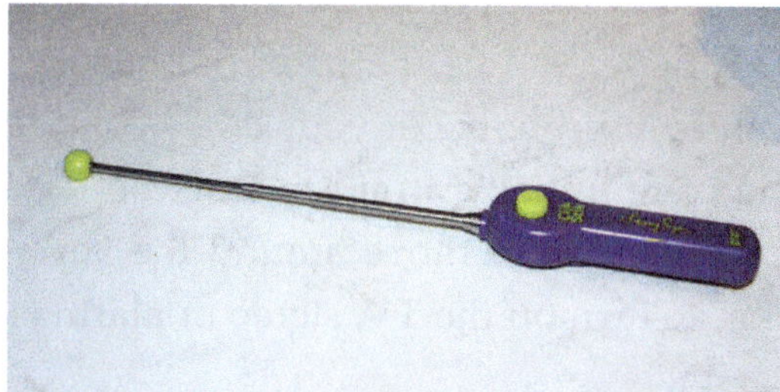

Target Stick

I teach "sit" using a technique called Targeting by holding a target stick (pictured above) or my hand above their head. As they raise their head to touch the target with their nose, this will cause their butt to lower. Accept and be happy with incremental baby steps until they are all the way into a sit position. If they don't move into a sit position, you can gently penalize them for non-compliance by ignoring, walking away, closing your treat pouch, or putting them calmly back in their crate (not as punishment) and trying again in a few minutes. You don't want them to be able to wander off and find something else more fun than training. Limit their options through management so you become more fun than anything else.

You can use this same method to teach "down" and instead of holding the target above their head, try slowly lowering it from under their nose toward their toes until they go all the way down. When they touch the target, I click or say "good dog" and treat. Be happy with baby steps until they are all the way down.

Targeting is teaching your dog to touch a target in order to move the dog into certain positions without using force. A dog is usually taught to target using their nose or paw to touch a target. A target can be the palm of your hand, a target stick, or any type of stick. Targeting can be used to boost your dog's confidence. I've used targeting to teach fearful dogs, who were initially afraid to walk on unfamiliar surfaces or were noise sensitive, how to play piano and move around the keys. I taught my Love Dog, Sven, when he was a senior, to turn off the TV, stereo or alarm clock, to name a few… by the use of targeting.

And recently, I taught my new puppy, Uni, to come using targeting. Targeting is used by many movie trainers to get a dog to hit a certain spot or a mark. Hold the target stick or your hand a few inches from your dog's nose and eventually, hold it further and further away and when the dog touches it, which they usually do out of curiosity, then you click and treat. Reward with the other hand instantly or toss the treat in their mouth or on the ground.

Exercise: The Tie Method - Teaching Sit & Down

1. Using a harness, tie the dog with a leash to a door (always attended)
2. Have them go to the end of leash
3. Put a tasty *dog bite* on the ground just out of reach
4. This frustrates the dog; they will try to get you to give them the treat
5. Ignore other behaviors they may offer except sitting or lying down
6. As soon as they sit or flop on the ground (because they can't stand forever) slide the treat between their feet and say "down" in a calm tone or calmly reward
7. If they get up before you get there with the treat, give them a look of disappointment or a worried look (but not a threatening look) and walk away

Dogs are great at reading facial expressions and discover that if they stay lying down or sitting…good things will happen!

TIPS: Teaching "Down"

- You don't want to have to bend every time you ask your dog to lie down. It's okay at first, but wean away from bending. If your goal is a down, you (the trainer) stand up as the dog is dropping to the down position so the dog knows to stay down and eat a few bites when you are up. You want the dog to think that treats keep growing from the ground between their legs so they stay there.
- It helps to capture the behavior as it happens using the word "down." Say down slowly with body language using an open hand toward the ground.
- Release the dog after a few seconds. Build from there and keep them in the sit or down position a little longer each time.
- Make sure you have eye contact and you are the reason they get up out of the down position.
- For down: always try to get the dog's hip into a comfortable position so they are relaxed, not ready to bolt or dive at any moment.
- Using the Tie method works great because you don't have to ask the dog anything and you don't have to correct behavior, just capture the dog doing

what you want, label it and reward. Ignore everything else, but if you ask your dog to stay, then be willing to stop whatever it is you are doing and gently place them back into the same spot and same position they were in before. If you let them have an inch, they will take a mile!

- o It helps if sit and down also mean stay. You can add the word "stay" if you like but don't say it over and over again. The less words used, the less likely you are cluttering the dog's head.
- o Teaching down is always easier if you practice when your dog is tired.
- o It helps to practice teaching down /stay on a soft surface.

STAY

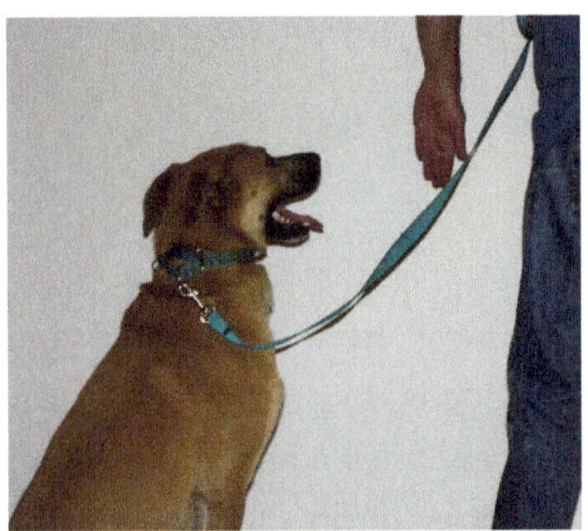

Stay means do not move until released. The dog should sit or lie down when asked and stay until released even if your back is turned – even if you drop a whole roast chicken in front of their nose! Your dog should stay at the far end of the kitchen whether you are cooking oatmeal or a gourmet meal. Your dog should stay outside the dining room while you enjoy a holiday dinner, not hang around under the table.

The best time to teach a stay is after a walk. After you get back from the walk, keep the leash on for a while and guide the dog onto a dog bed or mat and ask for a sit or down (or let them stand). Just don't let them off the mat. Say "stay" in a confident, firm but non-threatening voice. You can use a hand signal as well by showing them the palm of your hand like an upside-down stop sign. As long as they stay, that's the most important thing. It's more comfortable and they can stay longer if they lie down and stay with their hip relaxed on one side. If they get up out of the stay, then immediately and gently put them back in the exact spot you had them in before. Don't get angry; don't let the dog see you get frustrated or upset.

You will practice by sitting six feet away at the end of the leash so they are not touching you or underfoot. You don't want what I call a "Velcro Dog;" you don't want a dog lacking confidence and self-control. If you ask the dog to stay and they get up, it's best if they can't have other options. I will put them back in that stay position by either using the leash to gently walk them back or I will guide or lure them back to the spot they were in. You can even pick them up and gently set them back in the spot and pet them once they are back in their spot. Don't get into a wrestling match with your dog…if you're not having success, take a break and try again later.

When it comes to training a dog, as Dr. Ian Dunbar says, "You don't want to be forceful, but you want to be persistent." The second they relax and stay, let them see your happy facial expression and notice your body language relax. Use an open hand motion like an upside-down stop sign to indicate a request to stay. Then walk back to your chair and sit. If they get up, use the leash and gently walk them back to the spot again. If they won't stay, use the techniques in the Tie Method above or try again later.

I practice stay everywhere… not to prove that I am the "alpha" (because to believe that is just silly) but for safety and manners. Before they go in and out of the door, I have them sit at a doorway…before they get in the car, at a curb, at the gate… I go through the door first and ask them to stay. If they follow me before I release them, I gently close the door on them and try again. Of course be careful; don't crush your dog in the door. You can also practice stay before they sniff and go potty outside. If they sit and stay the reward is they get to sniff freely. You can also practice stay before you feed them. Place the food bowl 10 feet away. Walk back to your dog. If they stay, say "go get it" and increase the distance each time. I also practice stay before I release them to get a toy. At the park, you can practice stay before you let them play with other dogs.

YES / GOOD BOY/GIRL / or a CLICK

These words mark a behavior the dog performs that you like or when they listen to the desired request, and you should mark it the instant they do it. If the dog follows your behavior request you should immediately click or say, "Yes, good dog!" and reward them. A reward should happen within what I call the two-second rule; or as quickly as possible. The reason for rewarding within two seconds is, if you wait too long, the dog will have no idea what they are getting that reward for. OKAY is used to release your dog; said in a mellow tone.

WALK WITHOUT PULLING ON THE LEASH/LOOSE-LEASH WALKING /WALK AT ATTENTION / (HEEL)

I try to walk my dogs a minimum of twice a day!

How often you should walk your dog depends on your dog's breed, age, and health. I encourage people to walk their dogs at least twice a day; even if it's just 10 - 15 minutes to go potty and for exercise. The walks are also a great time to feed them meals during training sessions. You have to feed your dog dinner anyway, so why not take advantage of killing two birds with one stone? Try feeding your dog for good behavior on their walk while incorporating behavior modification techniques in this book.

The word "heel" is an old-school term used to teach a dog to walk on a person's left side. Legend has it this was first done in the Military because soldiers' guns were on the right and dogs were on the left to stay out of the way of the gun. The soldier would kick the dog with spurs on their heels and say, "Heel". I prefer to think of heel as a position. The dog should be positioned on your left side and walk without pulling on the leash. The leash should be slack, or what is called loose-leash walking, which is not as formal as show heeling. I just want a pleasant loose-leash walk.

Training Goal: Don't pull when the leash is on. Don't pull no matter what the distraction – even if you are passing three dogs, a bike, a bus, a stroller, and a skate board! You want a slack leash at all times. Knowing this can also save your dog's life!

Here are a few ways to train your dog *not to pull on the leash* during a walk:

I like to practice a bit with the dog off leash and a little with the dog on a leash. My preference is a six-foot nylon leash, but cotton or leather is fine too. I do not recommend using retractable leashes or chains as they can be dangerous. I like a Martingale collar (without the chain) that fits around the neck (you should be able to fit two fingers underneath) preventing the dog from trying to back out of it. Your goal shouldn't be to rely on any gadget; it should be to teach your dog that they should *want* to walk next to you because it's more fun than all other options.

I also like head collars because they loop around the dog's snout and behind the back of his neck and control the dog's head like reigns guide a horse. Head collars are not meant for yanking – you can cause serious damage to your dog's neck! If your dog accepts wearing one, they can give you more confidence and control when walking. Introduce the head halter by having the dog place their nose through the head halter in order to get a tasty dog bite (the good kind!) so they start to associate good things with the new gadget. Make sure it fits snug behind their neck and that they can open their mouth all the way, but not so much that it will easily fall off. Keep some slack in the leash; you want to keep a candy cane shape in the leash below their mouth. If you're not paying attention, and the leash is tight under their neck, the dog will not like the head collar. You need to find the one that best fits your dog.

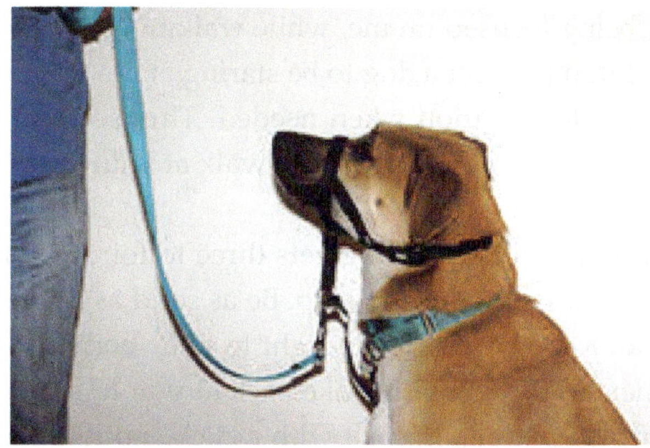

There are many brands of head collars including: Gentle Leader, Halti, Holt, Snoot Loop or Walk and Train, and remember dogs wore these types of collars thousands of years ago. A regular body harness can be used for walks too, but be sure to find a brand and size that fits properly and won't fall off. If your dog is overly aggressive or if they lunge at joggers or bikes, then a body harness will not give you the control that you need. But for a trained dog or a dog with a sensitive trachea like a yorkie, pug, or poodle… a body harness is better than having something around their neck.

One reason for a collar is so you have a place to put your dog's ID tags and pet license in the event they are lost. Be sure the tags don't hang so low that your dog can chew on it. K9 necks are just as sensitive as humans; you would not want to have someone pulling you by the neck, trust me. I always advise my clients when walking their dog to be mindful not to pull or yank the leash. As I have said previously in this book, I do not advise *ever* using prong, chain, choke, or electric shock collars. Beware… a loose collar on a dog in a metal crate can get caught in the bars.

I like to first start out by teaching them the heel position. To do this, I capture the moment they find my left side with a click to let them know that's what I like and then reward with a tasty dog bite or I will lure to my left. Once they find my left side, they need to know that good things will happen there! Even if I walk around the house, whenever a dog finds my left side, I reward and praise. I also hold a slack leash with the dog on my left side. Before I even take a step, I stand still and connect with the dog. If I can get some eye contact, I will explode with excitement and praise the dog so he realizes the left side is where he should be. Then I take about three steps and deliver another treat. I try to get in a rhythm of 1, 2, 3 steps and treat; then repeat. I aim for 10 steps, with the dog being focused on me, while walking and treating. Eventually, it will be every 10 houses. I don't expect a dog to be staring at me the entire walk; I just want to be able to call my dog to attention when needed. This helps to teach the dog the heel position, because how can you expect them to walk at your side if they don't even know what it is you want?

When you start on a walk, if the dog gets three to four feet ahead and starts to pull on the leash, the first thing you do is to stop. Be as solid as a tree; try not to sway. Don't let your arms extend. Keep your arms in tight to your body. Go ahead and let her pull but don't react. When the dog finally looks back at you to see why you aren't reacting, or when she gives up on pulling, mark it with a click and lure her back to your left side, which is the heel position, and praise. Have a moment of peace, relax for about three breaths and resume walking, but if they pull, stop again and repeat. You may have to stop 20 times on the first walk. Always remember to lure them back to the heel position and each day it will lessen until they walk without pulling.

Lefts, Rights & U-Turns

When training a dog, especially in loose-leash walking, it helps to have a variety of techniques so that if they get hip to one, you throw another at them until they finally realize that pulling sucks! I like to keep the dog guessing and I want the dog to want to catch up to me when I turn because it's a fun game. If they start to pull on the leash during a walk, one method is to turn left and gently cut them off.

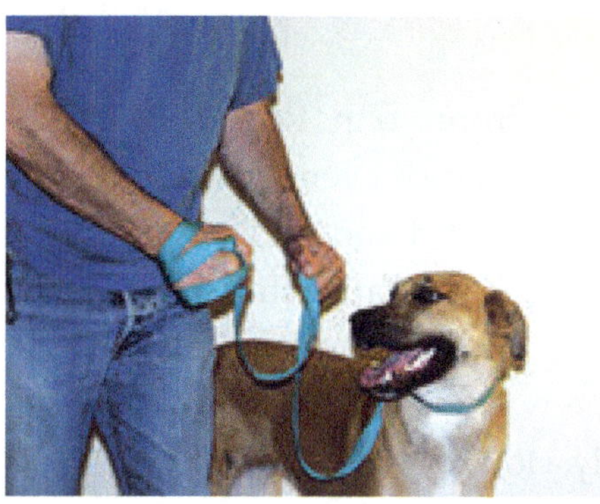 

- <u>For a left turn</u>: with both hands holding the leash (the dog on your left side) take your left hand and reach, with the leash in your hand, toward your back pocket or reach toward the middle of your back, then turn 180 degrees or 360 degrees and pivot to the left. Mix it up and keep them guessing. This will cut them off… You will both turn left together.
- <u>For a right turn</u>: when the dog starts to pull, let go of the leash in your left hand so the dog thinks they are free but hold the bulk of the leash around your right hand, then turn 180 degrees right and run one step in the other direction.
- Never pull the dog, just be so much fun that the dog will want to turn with you; you both turn right together.
- Elbows should be at your side; you never want to look like you are training.
- The leash should be slack under the dog's chin, with the dog on your left.
- Now you're ready to turn left or right and pick up the pace in the other direction.
- Never yank or pull on their neck.
- You are hurrying in another direction to get them to pay attention and treat

them when they catch up.

Another concept is using Opposition Reflex to teach your dog to walk properly. Opposition Reflex is a trait that is innate in K9s where if you gently push them, they will lean *into* you instead of away from you. If your dog gets ahead, slowly pull forward *towards* the direction they are walking (gently, without force). This will make the dog go the opposite way. I'm not suggesting that you pull your dog hard, but just stopping and slightly leaning forward usually makes them go backwards. As soon as they stop pulling, continue taking them on their walk.

A trick to combat pulling (that I learned from John Rogerson) that I've been practicing for many years is to pretend to get tangled or even trip by using Opposition Reflex. In this instance, you lean forward or fall forward and act like you hurt your knee by limping. Dogs are sensitive…if you have a great relationship with your dog (and you're a good enough actor) they may react (if they could talk) by saying, "I'm sorry, Dude, I didn't mean to hurt you," and resume walking nicely again. If they pull ahead again, just stutter-step and they will probably slow down. This technique engages the Opposition Reflex response by getting the dog to walk in the direction you *want* them to go and also gets the dog to slow down (because they don't want to hurt you).

Teach a Dog "Choose to Heel" & "Drop it" (at the same time)

In an enclosed safe area, feed your dog a few tasty *dog bites* by your left side and then walk away and play hard to get. Next, you will drop a dirt rock on the ground. The dog will run over to see what it is thinking it is food. He may sniff or mouth it and then spit it out because he thought you dropped food. Now, run off in the other direction and play hard to get. When the dog comes back to you and finds your left side, he gets a bite of the good stuff. Soon he realizes that what's on the ground is not rewarding (the rock) and walking next to you on your left side is much more fun. What's on the ground isn't nearly as good as what you have! The dog will now "choose to heel". This also teaches the dog to "leave it" or "drop it" because when he runs over to the rock on the ground, you say "drop." This teaches your dog to associate the word "drop" with spitting something out of their mouth. Drop is also beneficial for a good game of retrieve or tug or if your dog tries to grab a chicken bone that fell on the ground.

Q: What about K9's that don't want to go for a walk?

If your dog locks up and refuses to take a walk, it could be because they may be scared, tired, or even sick. Here's how I rectify this problem once I determine they are healthy. If they lock up on me and don't want to walk, I go to the end of the leash and stop… I just stand there careful not to pull on the leash. I look straight ahead and don't turn around to look at them. Next, I kneel down and talk baby talk. Nine out of ten times, the dog will come up to your side. Once they do, you can reward, feed, pet, etc. and then resume your walk again. They may put on the breaks again – if they do, keep going to the end of the leash a few more times and repeat. Increase the value of the treats as they learn that being at your left side pays off.

If they are afraid to go out on a walk, try parking your car a couple houses down the street and once you get them that far, open the car door and take out an amazing treat. This will encourage her to want to walk down the street. We want to make walking to the corner worth their while. Eventually, you will be able to go around the block and even further on your daily walk. I've had to drive a dog that doesn't want to go for a walk to the end of the street. Once we get there they usually want to pull all the way back home.

DOG'S NAME

When you say your dog's name, it means they should look at you. You can teach a dog their name by first holding a treat behind your back or hidden somewhere on your body or in close proximity. If you feel lucky, say their name, and if they look at you click and say their name again to reinforce it. Get eye contact and connect for a second, then immediately give them the treat. Repeat several times. If you don't feel lucky, don't ask their name… wait until they look at you on their own. When they do look at you, bring your hand with the treat to your face for eye contact and label it by saying their name, pause for a second, take a deep breath, connect and immediately deliver the treat.

DON'T POTTY IN THE HOUSE

Don't potty in the house means do not potty anywhere inside! I find that if you don't allow a puppy or adult dog to make a mistake in the house for one or two months, they probably will never make a mistake in the house again unless they are sick or on medication. In my opinion, once a dog is eight or nine weeks old, there is no reason for them to ever practice going potty in the house again. Take those potty pads and bring them out to the yard and have the puppy go on the pad outside. Each day make the pad smaller, so that within two or three days, the pee pad has disappeared. Wake up in the early morning hours before your puppy wakes up and take your dog outside immediately. You want to beat them to the punch and start teaching them to practice going potty outside as soon as possible.

If you don't have a private outside area or yard, then a box with real sod, fake grass or pee pads might have to be an option. However, try to get your dog going on an outdoor surface as soon as possible. To potty train successfully, you can't let a puppy or a dog practice going potty inside. To do this you have to enforce strict management. I also find that teaching a puppy or dog to do a down/stay really helps the process because most dogs won't pee when they are laying down relaxing…it usually happens when they are off sniffing around somewhere and you're not watching.

To be successful in potty training, it also helps to confine your dog to a crate or small enclosed area for two or three hours at a time or when you can't watch them. They generally don't want to pee in their crate because they don't want to lay in it, but they might if the crate is too big. They might pee at one end and lay on the dry end. Some dogs will even pee on the bed because a bed will absorb the pee, so check for that.

After the dog awakes from a little nap in the crate, immediately take them outside on a leash to go potty in an appropriate area for approximately five minutes. It helps if you don't distract them. Try to get them to sniff and circle. Sometimes I take a tiny bit of dry kibble and crumble it up into little crumbs and sprinkle it in a circular pattern in the yard. That helps the dog to start sniffing and circling. Once they start to sniff and circle they are more likely to do their business. If they are not sniffing or relieving themselves after about five minutes or so, then put them back in the crate and try again in a few minutes. Make sure they only get off leash fun in the house *after* they learn to potty outside.

Keep in mind, if your dog eliminates in your backyard in a timely manner, rather than bringing him right in and ending their fun, reward them with a tasty dog bite, a walk, or a little play as a reward for doing their business. Once they have gone potty you can let them run around in the house. Do not leave your puppy or dog in a crate unsupervised all day long while you are away at work. They need an area to move about safely and freely. You can always hire a dog walker, get a neighbor to help, or come home from work at lunch to give the dog a potty break. Once your dog has not made a mistake for one to two months, you're probably in the clear and your dog will be potty trained. At this point you may not need the crate nearly as much or you may not need it at all.

Once a dog really knows the Dog-mandments solid as a rock, they are allowed to have much more freedom in the house because we can now call them back or stop them on a dime. Mistakes will happen, but you never want to punish your pooch. If you catch them in the act, try to get them immediately outside. Don't throw a fit, don't put their nose in it, and don't even let them see you clean it up. You can usually blame yourself for not keeping a better eye on them. Also, avoid ammonia-based cleaning products to clean up after your dog. Instead, use an odor neutralizer from a pet store or pet catalog.

Manage their food and water. This doesn't mean deprive them of food or water… it just means that you should pay attention to how much your dog is eating and drinking so you have a better idea of what their needs are. It helps to make a potty log (no pun intended). Have family members, dog walkers, etc. write down what the dog did and when the dog did it so you have a better idea of when your puppy really needs to go outside. Keep at it and they will be trained in no time! Remember, dogs want to go potty when they first wake up, after they play, drink water, when they are stimulated, when there are new people, new smells, and other doggies around.

I like to choose where and when my dog sniffs and urinates. While we're out on a walk I don't want my dog to sniff anywhere they choose because that may trigger them to pee in the wrong place. I don't want my dog to relieve himself in front of a restaurant or on the neighbor's new rose garden, either. I'd rather have my dogs walk without pulling for a few houses… then when I find a nice place for them to sniff and relieve themselves, I will ask for a "sit" first. I will let them sniff and pee as a reward. I want dogs to listen because they *want* to, not because they have to. You don't have to dominate, threaten, intimidate, or force your dog to get them to listen. I like to teach dogs to potty outdoors by rewarding them with a tasty dog bite and love and praise for going in the right spot!

HOW TO GET A DOG USED TO A CRATE

A crate should be big enough to stand up, turn around, lie down, and even place a small bowl of water. Plastic kennels are safer than metal ones. I have seen dogs get their paws and collars stuck in the bars of the metal crates and they don't have the same den feeling as the old-school plastic crates do. If a dog has separation anxiety, I don't recommend a crate until the anxiety is resolved. Keep in mind that too much crating can negatively affect a dog's mental state and cause all sorts of behavioral problems.

To get them used to a crate, place them inside the crate when they are tired after a walk with spa music or mellow classical music playing. It's been proven that classical music is a great way to calm your pet! It also helps to have the TV on in the other room on low so the dog hears voices and assumes you are still home.

Crate-Training Tips:

- Lavender, tangerine, or peppermint oil to scent the area with a calming smell. Lavender works best! Burn oils, use sprays, candles, or incense. Oils work best.
- Dog Appeasing Pheromones (DAP) are synthetic pheromones that mimic those released during lactation and give puppies a sense of well-being and reassurance. DAP helps to calm nervous puppies and dogs. You can get it as a spray or diffuser or you can get a DAP collar that the dog can wear for up to a month.
- White noise machines help calm your K9 in the crate
- Rescue Remedy calms a nervous nelly in the crate
- Never use a crate on a dog with severe separation anxiety, as it can be dangerous, and it's not fair to the dog. (Never let children (or adults) tease a dog in a crate).
- Leave the crate door open and place little treats inside periodically so when your dog walks by he just may find a jackpot in there and start to like going inside. The crate should be a safe place for your dog, like a den. Just as you like to going

to your room for a nap, dogs like to do the same thing. Make the crate a happy place.

o   Try putting an amazing tasty dog bite in the crate and close the door, but keep the dog on the outside. Put them on a leash and show them the goods. As the dog pulls toward the crate trying to get in, pop open the door and let him in for a bite. A little reverse psychology goes a long way!

o   Give your dog a toy stuffed with food, but remember, if you stuff a Kong™ toy and leave it with your dog when you leave the house, it may keep them busy for a while, but they may also get thirsty and have to go potty before you get home.

o   Don't put the crate in a noisy part of the house like the family room right next to the TV or where the kids play. Also, don't isolate your dog in a faraway basement or garage. You want the dog to feel like they are part of the family. You just don't want them to be able to see every move you make. Find a happy medium.

o   Moving the crate around to different rooms is fine too. It is actually good for the dog to be able to sleep comfortably in any room of the house.

o   Putting the crate next to the door that they use to go outside to go potty is a smart idea as well, so they don't have to run down the stairs and tinkle on the way out.

o   Crates help limit your dog's freedom until they know the rules solid as a rock. It's the same idea as a child having a crib, playpen, baby gate, nanny-cam or a swimming pool cover; children aren't free to do whatever they want until they learn the rules.

o   Just like preschoolers, children get nap time, recess, potty breaks, field trips, study time etc. The dog's crate is for nap time. I like to be the decision maker on what my dog is doing.

o   A crate isn't just for potty training. It's also a management tool, and the plastic ones, if secured properly, are safe for travel.

If your dog starts throwing a fit in the crate by barking and whining, you can't ignore it. If you're sure your dog doesn't have true separation anxiety and think they are just being a little attention seeking, keep a light towel on top of the crate and have it ready to flop over the front or over the side they're looking out of so they can't see out. Make sure the dog has plenty of air and don't cover the whole crate with a heavy blanket. If the dog's throwing a fit, I march into the room and don't talk, look at or give any attention to the dog. I just flip the towel down to cover the front of the crate and march out. If the dog is quiet for about five minutes, I calmly go back into the room, still not talking, looking at or giving the dog any attention and remove the towel from the front of the crate and walk out. If the dog starts to bark again, I just march back in and cover the crate again. Don't forget to uncover when they are calm. If you can't get your dog used to a crate or used to being in a room by themselves, check out more tips in this book, Verdine White: Separation Problems.

Thorndike's Law of Effect states that:
"Behavior changes because of its consequences."

BEHAVIOR MODIFICATION

Behavior Modification is changing (a dog's) feelings from something; say fear to joy.

Thorndike's Law – that behavior changes because of consequences, is important when it comes to *how* dogs learn… It's especially true if the consequence happens within seconds of the dog displaying a requested behavior. A consequence can be positive – like the dog getting a pet on the head, a treat, or a toy immediately after a Dog-mandment is performed. A consequence doesn't have to mean a correction; it can be immediately ignoring the dog. There are negative consequences that do not use force. For instance, if you ask your dog to sit before you throw his ball and he ignores you, a negative consequence can be immediately walking back into the house with the ball in your hand while displaying a disappointed look to the dog. Come out a few minutes later and ask your dog to sit… I bet this time he will!

In order to modify behavior, it helps to understand the ABCs of dog training commonly known as Antecedent, Behavior & Consequence.

A = Antecedent. An antecedent is an event that happens *before* a behavior is performed.

For example… my dog, Uni, runs to his bed whenever I open the fridge because he's pretty sure if he does, I will give him a tasty dog bite. I have actually trained him to perform the "Open the Refrigerator Door and Bring Me a Beverage" trick. When performed correctly, we both get a reward. He will get a delicious dog bite and I will get a refreshing beverage. My tying of the rope to the refrigerator door, which enables Uni to pull the door open, is the antecedent to Uni's performing the trick.

B = Behavior. A behavior is how a dog will act under a certain set of circumstances.

For instance, if I am running the garbage disposal and the dishwasher, the sounds of those machines might frighten my pup. So, if I want to succeed, I will think ahead and set myself up for success. I will put the pup in his crate or in another room before starting the dishwasher. Over time, I will work to get him used to the sounds. Your dog's health and mood will also affect their behavior.

C = Consequence. A Consequence is the result or the outcome of something that happened earlier.

Say you are at the door and you ask your dog to sit. The consequence to your dog sitting is they get a reward, like going for a walk and getting the rest of their meal on the walk. Let's say you have two dogs in the yard. You ask them both to come. One comes but the other does not. The consequence in this instance is that you reward the one that comes. The consequence for the dog that does *not* come is that they do not get a reward. How about when you are walking and your dog pulls on the leash? Here, the consequence is that you stop and do not move. A consequence does not have to be a correction.

Positive Reinforcement: a mathematical term used
to predict the anticipated frequency of behavior occurring.

POSITIVE REINFORCEMENT

Positive Reinforcement techniques developed by B.F. Skinner, a renowned researcher in behaviorism, include requesting and reinforcing a behavior, thereby increasing the likelihood that the behavior will be repeated. Skinner's research found that positive reinforcement creates lasting results, while punishment creates only temporary changes with negative effects. So this is why it's more effective and humane to practice positive reinforcement when living and working with dogs. Positive Reinforcement is anything given to the dog during or immediately following the desired behavior which will increase the likelihood of that behavior occurring again.

I recommend using training methods known as: Positive Reinforcement Training, Science-Based Training, Reward-Based Training, Clicker Training, and the like. There are dominance-style techniques (that I do not recommend or advocate) including: Compulsion Training, Traditional Training, Dominance Theory, and *Dog Whisperer*-style training. These techniques implement the use of forcing, kicking, choking, poking and even punching in the neck, pinning, and treating dogs as if they are wolves (which in fact, they are not).

> *Learning from wolves how to interact with pet dogs makes about as much sense as saying, 'I want to improve my parenting –*
> *Let's see how the chimps do it!'* **Dr. Ian Dunbar**

Trainers who implement harsh techniques believe dogs have a hierarchy (like wolves) where the 'alpha' or 'top dog' exhibits dominance over others. They then coach human clients on how to take on the role of the 'alpha' dog, forcefully if necessary, to keep they're dog in a submissive role. However, in my opinion, dominance techniques *as seen on TV* are dangerous to you and your dog and can destroy any trust you've built with your dog. Using dominance-type methods can work, but your dog will be listening out of fear. It will be because he has to; not because he wants to. You have to ask yourself, what's more important… a dog that listens out of fear and looks miserable doing it? Or a dog that listens while wagging their tail, because training is fun.

Abusive training methods can cause irreversible emotional damage.

Abusive methods can increase "bad" behavior because believe it or not, yelling, pushing, and jerking are still a form of attention for your dog. It may be a negative form of attention, but your dog may interpret it as attention nonetheless and seek to create more of it. More of a bad thing, I can assure you, is not the result you desire when it comes to training. Remember, if you use punishment, you may have to do it harder or more forcefully the next time to get a result because your dog can build a tolerance. If you use a shock collar, thinking that is all you need to create submission… beware. Fallout from using a shock collar can cause the dog to jump in the air in fear, scream, shake, cling to you, or bite you out of fear and confusion. They may also bolt further away from you over a fence or through a barrier. You may never be able to put a collar of any kind on your dog again because the dog associates pain and fear with a collar.

You would not put a pinch collar on a dolphin or a bear,
so why would you put it on your dog if zoo trainers don't use them?

The *American Veterinary Society of Behavior* (AVSB) considers Dominance Theory training to be abusive. Overwhelming science proves that these methods create negative results and are, in fact, less humane and effective than positive, reward-based training methods. So when it comes to training, I'd like you to at least be open to the idea of positive, Reward-Based Training as being the optimal method that is best for your dog.

My first training gig was working for a dog training facility (I didn't know better at the time) that taught me a method that makes me shudder to this day… I was instructed to use prong and shock collars and told that this was the *only way to train*. Popping the dog under the chin or pinning them on their back was the only way to show the dog whose boss. They were adamant about *never* using food to train dogs. They trained police dogs and had a slew of award-winning German Shepherds and even a Doberman Pincher that could walk down the street backward on two feet! This dog could literally walk up a flight of stairs on two feet! He would jump through a Hula-Hoop that was lit on fire! He even wore a saddle and walked with a real monkey on his back! I also witnessed this Doberman in a real-life scenario, where the dog pinned a robber after stealing a woman's purse up against a wall. Luckily, his trainer called the dog off within inches of biting the robber's neck! Mostly, I noticed that the dogs they trained became jumpy, distrusting, and even dogs that weren't aggressive before they came to training now became aggressive because of this type of training. I noticed that even though they would listen some of the time, they looked miserable doing it and were not having fun.

I believed those trainers the first few years of my career because, for the most part, they were very impressive with the results they achieved. The truth is I never felt good about it and was actively looking to find a better way to train. It wasn't easy, but I knew in my gut there was a better way…It wasn't until I decided I wanted to start my own company that I had a realization – dog owners would never be able to replicate and sustain the results that forceful methods garner. The fact is most people are not trained professionals with knowledge of body language and timing; either they will get hurt or the dogs will get hurt, and they will most likely lose their dog's trust.

The problem, and this is especially true with behavioral problems, is that by using forceful methods, you are only putting a Band-Aid on the problem. You're only getting a quick fix; you're not getting to the underlining issue and may never be able to get lasting results. There are other potential dangers in using forceful training. For instance, when your dog sees an approaching dog and you yank on a prong collar it will only make them more stressed and fearful of the approaching dog. A fearful dog is more apt to bite.

Once you change an emotion you can improve behavior. For instance, you can change a rescue dog's emotional state from fear to joy; or an aggressive dog's emotion from anxiety to enthusiasm. Let's say your dog has aggressive outbursts whenever he sees another dog on a walk. His aggression is most likely based on anxiety or fear. My goal in this instance is to change the dog's emotion from fear to joy. I want my dog to see another dog on a walk and learn to feel and believe that an approaching dog means that good things are about to happen rather than engaging in aggressive battles with every other dog it sees on a walk. If the two dogs don't have aggression problems, then letting the dogs have a quick, occasional butt sniff "hello" is fine. Dogs don't have to wrestle each other to the ground every time they meet. I just prefer that my dog finds me more interesting than the other dogs.

Behavior Modification sometimes takes longer than Compulsion Training to see results, but with behavior modification you can get to the underlining problem with lasting results and you will be more likely to fix problems then you will with compulsion training. You will feel more confident about yourself as a pet owner if you learn how to use rewards effectively.

Positive reward-based training means, if the desired behavior is performed, a reward is given. But if the behavior is not performed, the reward is withheld.

Ignoring bad behavior can be an effective way to train, but only if you are observant enough to catch your dog when she is doing something right and then marking what you like with "good dog", "yes" or a "click" sound, then rewarding with a reward off your real-life reward list the *second* you see the dog stop the undesired behavior. For example: if your dog is staring at a squirrel, then let him…but the second you see your dog look away, seem uninterested or yawn…that's the second you click and treat. Reward the dog for bringing their attention back to you! In order to implement Positive Reinforcement successfully, I use techniques including: Luring, Targeting, Shaping and Capturing.

Luring

Luring is holding a food treat (or a favorite toy) in your hand, enticing your dog to follow your hand into a desired position. It's okay to let the dog smell the food and sometimes even let them put their front teeth on it. The dog's nose should be stuck to the trainer's hand like a magnet. Your hand should be smooth and steady. You don't want to be teasing the dog with shaky hands or begging the dog to move. For safety, keep your fingers out of the way. For a grabby dog, it's safer if you hold the treat in a closed fist or even two closed fists touching each other and glued to your leg (the bigger the target, the less likely the dog is going to bite your finger!).

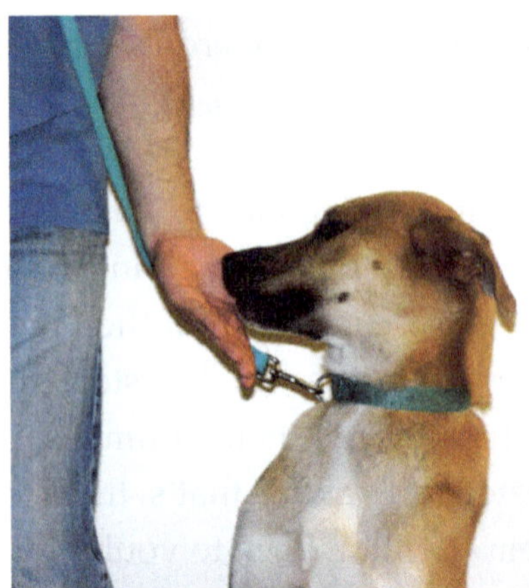

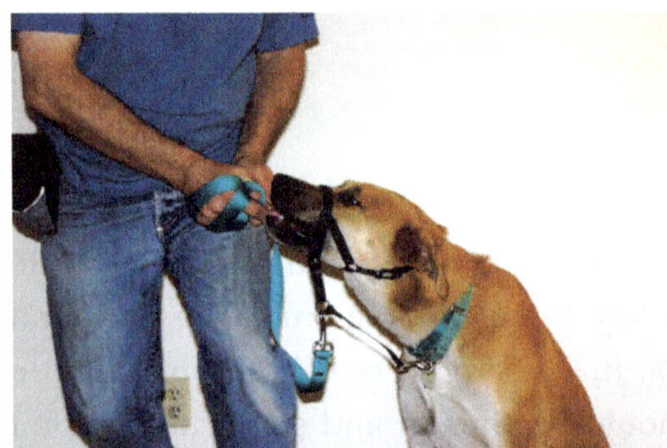

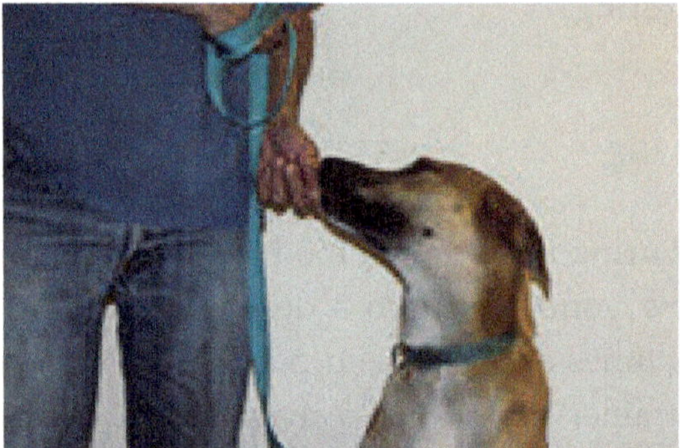

**Deliver treats with an open palm, or with one or two closed fists,
with fingers out of the way and glued to your body.**

I use lures when I first start training a new behavior, but my goal in training a dog is to put behaviors on cue. You want to teach your dog what it is that you *want* them to do. Luring is a way to teach your dog what it is that you want them to do without using force; targeting is another. When I first start luring a dog into a position, I don't mind using a lot of body language and energy on my part. My hand movements are big, not subtle, but as I fade out luring my movements become more and more subtle with less and less effort. When I first start teaching a dog to lay down, I don't mind bending, but I don't want to have to bend forever in order to get my dog to lie down. I always tell my clients to accept and be happy with any baby steps your dog offers you and be willing to lower your criteria if need be. It's also important to vary your rewards or the dog may get bored.

It is important to fade out your hand lures, usually after 10 good repetitions or by the end of your first session or once you feel your dog comprehends the training goal that you are trying to achieve. If not, you may end up with a dog that *only* listens if you have food in your hand. To start fading out the lure, you need to get the food out of your hand while using the same hand movements you did when you had food in your hand. I like to use slight-of-hand magic tricks. I don't want my dog to know what hand the food is in or where it's coming from. At this point, I'm ready to use just the verbal cue or behavior request to get the dog to do the desired behavior.

When luring, most people start by asking the dog to do the behavior with a verbal cue and then lure the dog into a desired position, mark the correct behavior, reward, etc. That's great if the dog has a concept of what you want – but if you find yourself repeating the word over and over again and if it feels like you are just cluttering up the dog's head with a bunch of jib-jab, then try not asking the behavior first and instead try adding the word or cue to the behavior *as its happening*. I work to label the behavior as it is happening until the dog is having fun with it. Labeling behaviors as they are happening as opposed to requesting the behavior up front works better with targeting, shaping, and clicker training than it does with luring. Once the dog has a concept of what I want, I start asking the behavior up front in a normal sequence.

Luring is not bribery; bribery puts the *dog* in control of the situation, not you. Bribery is *showing* the dog a treat before you ask him to do something. With luring, the reward is given *after* the requested action has been completed. Once your dog learns the basics, you will want to replace food lures with verbal requests and hand signals. Keep in mind that bribery is not a method you want to use when training and should only be used as a last resort in certain situations – like if you're trying to catch a stray dog you found on the street, or if you find yourself in a dangerous situation with an aggressive dog.

You don't want to have to be dependent on food to get your dog to listen for the rest of their life. Discipline yourself. It's up to you, not the dog, to start cutting the food back early on in training. This will help you dig deep within yourself to physically and verbally praise your dog like you mean it! Never under estimate the power of praise.

Capturing & Shaping

In order to capture a behavior you have to observe it and then mark and reward instantly. Marking a behavior you're trying to capture is usually done with a clicker or it can be done using a verbal click sound, or a verbal "yes, good boy or good girl". I've seen some amazing trainers adept at using a clicker to capture behavior without enticing the dog first (known as free shaping). I'm still learning, as we all are, and I've been incorporating free shaping more and more into my repertoire. The difference between free shaping and shaping is that with shaping, you are setting the dog up to do a behavior and then you capture it. With free shaping, the dog offers you all the behaviors on their own and you capture it. I like to mix these positive methods of clicker training, lure reward training, target training, capturing, shaping, free shaping and ignoring undesirable behavior while rewarding good behavior. I also work on managing my dogs well by using common sense, being proactive, achieving a solid training foundation, and using reward-based Behavior Modification techniques for problem behaviors.

Never use forceful methods – even if a trainer tells you that your dog is dominant or that a prong collar emulates the mother biting the dog's neck, or it's what a wolf would do – a little pinch won't hurt – or that your dog is in the "red zone" so he's a special case. Some trainers may tell you that because your dog is a certain breed (like a Pit Bull) she will need harsher methods to get results. But I promise you, the right trainer is out there and can help you with your dog in a humane and positive way!

Here are a few examples of Capturing to teach a Down:

- The trainer can tie or tether the dog (never unattended), ignore, and just wait until he lays down, then "click" and instantly give a reward. Then start adding the word "down" as the dog progresses and is having fun with it.
- Place a treat under a couch or chair…then when the dog attempts to reach for it to eat it, they usually lie down. Click or use the verbal request "down".
- The best time to teach a down is when they are tired. Exhausting your dog with a long run or walk is a good way to get out excess energy or anxiety and is also a great time for you to use Capturing by clicking when the dog lays down.

Shaping is marking a behavior and rewarding even the baby steps. I find that some of the hardest dogs to teach down to are short-haired, skinny, boney dogs like Italian Greyhounds, Dachshunds, Chihuahuas, and some Pit Bulls. Luring or targeting a dog's head down, guiding the nose to toes – rewarding the dog for moving even an inch at a time, can be a very effective method. In other words, if the dog lowers his head an inch, I will click and treat. In the next session I will try to get the dog to lower their head a little more and maybe in a few more sessions the dog will enjoy lying down all the way.

When a dog doesn't listen, rather than getting upset and forcing them,
know when it's time to lower your criteria and be happy accepting baby steps.

Both target training and luring are meant to guide your dog into certain positions without the use of force. The dog is rewarded by food, toys or other real-life rewards. You need to keep in mind that you will want to fade out physical prompts like lures and targets so that they don't become a permanent cue for that behavior.

COUNTER-CONDITIONING

Counter-conditioning is when we want to change or re-teach a reaction toward something that the dog fears or becomes aggressive around. The goal is to create a pleasant feeling by associating something good and more powerful than the scary thing. As soon as the dog sees that thing, I give him a delicious dog bite or other high-value real-life reward to create a positive reaction. Repeat this exercise several times a day by hunting for something that stimulates the dog and practice at a distance where you can be successful, gradually over time, getting closer.

Staying joyful and happy instead of tense and nervous and keeping a slack leash is preferred because K9's are great at reading our emotions. You want to replace bad or unpleasant emotional responses to a stimulus with a more pleasant reaction. At first, your dog may be too stressed to eat. Starting from a further distance will help. Try rewarding with treats that smell and taste delicious – preferably ones they have never tasted before! Your dog should learn to associate treats or other real-life rewards rather than fear of whatever they are afraid. The long-term goal would be, for example, that your dog sees another dog and before you can pop a treat in their mouth, they look at you. You become more interesting than the other dog!

DESENSITIZATION

Desensitization is eliminating or reducing an exaggerated, emotional reaction that a dog has to something – other dogs, the delivery person, noises, etc. The goal in using desensitization is to reduce anxiety to a given stimulus. To do this, a dog is exposed to something they fear, at such a low intensity, that it does not elicit an anxious or fearful response. In order to make a dog less sensitive to a stimulus, I expose them gradually to a less-intense version of the thing or event until a fearful or aggressive reaction dissipates.

Exercise: Desensitization - Overcoming Fear

1. Allow your dog to see the fearful item or object at a comfortable distance
2. Treat with small tasty *dog bites* as long as the object is in their sight, and as long as your dog will eat it… (if not, don't worry about it)
3. Move the fearful or distracting item out of sight, or turn and walk away the *second* your dog gives up on staring and looks away
4. Reward for giving up on the fearful object and for looking at you
5. Stop treating as soon as the fearful object is gone
6. Try to end each session with success – even if your dog is just a bit more relaxed, that is a win!

Q: What about using punishment to teach a dog?

Punishment is defined as "a penalty for a crime." When it comes to dog training, punishment simply does not work well. Why? Because when you punish a dog for an undesirable behavior, like chewing your brand new sunglasses, the dog has no idea why you are yelling, screaming, and crying at the fact that sunglasses aren't cheap and now you are hitting them with a newspaper. In fact, punishment will only cause the dog to be afraid of both you and the newspaper!

Let's say your dog digs a hole in your rose garden, shreds the couch, or pees on your bed. Unless you intervene at the exact *instant* the bad behavior is actually occurring, punishment after the fact is futile. Even if you intervene instantly, punishment has way more potential fallout then benefit. What you need to use instead is Negative Reinforcement; you need to ignore the bad behavior and replace it with a good behavior and then reward. When you use Negative Reinforcement rather than punishment, the offending dog stops the bad behavior and adopts a desired behavior. Now, in order to do that, the dog must know what behavior is better and must be rewarded and reinforced using Positive Reinforcement immediately.

Let me break it down for you:

1. Dog chews new pair of sunglasses
2. Owner requests dog to come
3. Owner rewards dog instantly for the desired behavior
4. Dog stops chewing sunglasses

Now, in the above instance, you still may be out the sunglasses but you get the idea. Ignore the negative behavior, replace it with a new behavior, and reward that new behavior. When training a dog you must be consistent and crystal clear so your dog can understand you. It's too easy to make excuses like, "my dog is stubborn" when the truth is, they just don't know what you want. Be clear with your words and use as few as possible so as not to clutter their head and remember to be distinct in your tone.

3

AGGRESSION & FEAR

If you have a food-aggressive dog... there are things you need to consider. When working with an aggressive dog, it's important to use a collar, like a martingale (or any collar that they can't slip out of) but never use a chain or prong collar. And, if you don't feel safe with the dog, don't be afraid or embarrassed to use a muzzle. First make sure they get accustomed to wearing it. Whenever I see someone walking their dog with a muzzle I think to myself, 'Now that's a responsible pet owner.' To get your dog accustomed to wearing a muzzle I recommend the YouTube video by Chirag Patel, "Teaching a Dog to Wear a Muzzle".

Managing food aggression is sometimes easier than trying to fix food aggression. Trying to fix food aggression without an experienced, positive reward-based trainer or Veterinary behaviorist can be dangerous and can even make the problem worse. When trying to modify a food-aggressive dog's behavior, teaching self-control is very important. A well-mannered dog should be able stay at the far end of the yard, away from a hot BBQ, and stay outside of the kitchen threshold while you're cooking.

It's not a good idea to feed dogs near or under the kitchen or dining table. You and your family may not mind the dog under the table because she's so cute when she begs... but trust me when I tell you that many of your friends probably feel very uncomfortable and just don't tell you. In fact, under the table seems to be where many dog fights occur due to jealousy and over resources like food, bones, or toys. When you're done eating, if you want to bring your dog a leftover dog bite, feed them for staying at a distance in a spot that you have chosen.

Double-Tie Tether

The most common places for a scuffle to break out is in close quarters where a dog doesn't have a way out – like when they are under a table, trapped between a coffee table and a couch, by a food or water bowl, in a hallway, on a bed, etc. If you ask an aggressive dog to stay and you don't feel comfortable putting them gently back in their spot, try using two leashes. I call this the Double-Tie Tether. One leash will be tied to a hook in the wall or a door and the other will be stretched out towards you in case you need to grab it for safety. You tie the dog and don't ask them anything, just ignore all their attempts to do anything but sit or lie down and relax. You're not asking them to do anything; you're just waiting for them to chill. If they get up out of the stay, then sit back down or walk away and use your facial expressions of disappointment or a worried look (not a look of anger).

If they sit or lay back down, then instantly relax your face, smile and bring them a reward. The reward can be a smile, a tasty dog bite, a pet, a massage, a bone or a safe chew toy. Eventually, your dog will figure out on their own that lying down and chilling is what works and getting up will get them ignored. The point of the Double-Tie Tether is that the second leash is there for you to pick up in case it's too dangerous for you to go back to the dog. By having that second leash stretched out, with easy access to grab it, you will have more confidence and control. By doing this method you never have to go back to confront the dog for getting up out of position. You simply praise the dog for relaxing.

I will also use the Double-Tie Tether method to practice behavior modification with a dog that's reactive towards house guests. Say the house guest stands up to leave the room. The standing may be a trigger for many aggressive dogs to charge and bite. With this method, the dog is tied just out of reach for safety, and you have the confidence that you can still get ahold of the leash and dog in a safe manner. Never tie a dog, especially an aggressive dog, if you have toddlers or young children present.

Be careful if you have a puppy that is inhaling their food (like a Labrador) and they eat faster when you approach. If you suspect they may turn into a food guarder, you can unintentionally turn them into a food guarder by making them wait too long for the food bowl. If a puppy is really excited or anxious around food, I recommend waiting to train them a "stay" until they are older or wait until you can get help from a Veterinary Behaviorist (ACVB Certified Professional Dog Trainer (CPDT), Certified Applied Animal Behaviorist (CAAB or ACAAB), a or an experienced Force-Free Trainer from the Pet Professional Guild. Exercise increases serotonin in the brain, which lowers aggression. I also suggest using carbohydrate treats rather than high-protein, as too much protein can contribute to territorial aggression. I have found that adding free-range turkey, eggs, flaxseed oil, wild fish (salmon, herring), free-range beef, or bananas to my Dog Bites Recipes can help reduce anxiety and calm dogs of all ages.

FOOD BOWL GUARDING

Food bowl guarding is the most common kind of resource guarding. I've seen dogs guard trash, personal items, beds, cars…all sorts of territories, but when a dog guards a treat pouch, food bowl, or a piece of food that has fallen on the ground…it can be pretty scary. Aggression is a combination of learned and innate behavior. Innate behavior is influenced by genetics and aggressive traits that get passed down from generation to generation. Resource guarding is innate in the sense that it's a primal instinct for a dog to react to what is considered a vital resource and attempt to keep it for themselves and away from predators. Learned behavior is where something is learned from their environment and, if the dog does a behavior and it works for them, they will keep doing it. I find that by modifying the learned behavior, it is easier to modify the innate behavior. Resource guarding is learned…if a dog learns that jumping up and biting or knocking your hand with his canine teeth in order for you to release the treat – and you drop the treat and they get to eat it, then that learned behavior will continue and escalate.

> ➤ If you are trying to feed or train a dog with food-guarding issues and you are unfamiliar with the dog, I advise you to use caution, especially if you are giving high-value tasty *dog bites* for the first time. Just because your dog lets you pick

him up, cut his nails, open his mouth, even brush his teeth – if it's the first time he tastes filet mignon, he may take a finger off trying to grab it out of your hand! I am a huge believer in using food to train and caution my clients that some dogs get pushy or aggressive over food…if they get a whiff or even just one bite they may get very pushy trying to take it away from you.

➢ If you get goose bumps or are afraid or leery of a dog, they can pick up on your fear… they can sense your emotions and may try to take full advantage of the situation. If you're ever uncomfortable with a dog you're working with, don't take a chance. Seek assistance from a Veterinary Behaviorist, Certified Applied Animal Behaviorist, (CAAB) a Certified Professional Dog Trainer (CPDT), or an experienced Force-Free Trainer from the PPG (Pet Professional Guild) before proceeding with training.

➢ I've seen some dogs wait until you turn away and then nail you when you let your guard down. Others might cooperate at first. For instance, they might lure toward your hand following the treat. But if you are waiving the treat in front of them, they may think you are teasing, so be careful because there are dogs out there that will bite your hand with intent to do harm to get you to release the treat.

➢ If a dog has a history of serious bite damage they should have strict management for life, be taught a solid set of manners in a positive way, and work with an experienced Force-Free Trainer as listed above. Even with behavior modification to reduce the dog's chance of aggression, if the dog's owner can't comply with strict management, sometimes dogs are better off finding a new home with full discloser of any bite history. There are instances where it may be best to euthanize the dog to ensure the safety of the community. I know it sounds cruel, but truly dangerous dogs do exist and the reality is that finding a skilled owner for that dog may not be available and sometimes the liability can be too great.

*Never reach for a bowl while an aggressive dog is eating
or you could lose a finger!*

Aggression will escalate depending on the value of food: table scraps, real bones, rawhide, etc. From my experience as a trainer, it is advisable to avoid the consequences of food-related aggression whenever possible by not giving rawhides or real bones to aggressive dogs as the high-quality food may result in aggressive, even dangerous consequences. They should only be allowed to have high-value treats in an environment where they are the only dog or while being fed separately – out of eye contact with any other dogs.

Keeping the dog away from environments and situations where he is likely to practice aggression is an absolute must. Keeping a leash on the dog if you give them a bone or using the Double-Tie Tether (as talked about above) is also a good idea. If you have to take the bone away in an emergency you can always toss another food treat, toy, etc. *away* from the dog to distract them. As they look towards the tossed item, you can quickly (and carefully) pick up the leash and walk the dog away from the bone or high-value guarded item. There's nothing like having a solid recall and having your dog so well trained that even if they are guarding high-value food, if you say "come" they come running!

Use caution: a dog is still an animal – pay attention to the warning signs! Pay attention to body language so you can avoid trouble before it happens. Some signs of imminent aggression to watch out for include:

- **Whale eyes: eyes get big and the whites are shiny, prevalent**
- **Full cheeks: you may see them slightly pucker their cheeks**
- **Freezing up**
- **Body may stiffen**
- **Ears may pin back or be extremely forward**
- **Tail may be tucked or extremely high**
- **Gobble down food quickly as you approach**
- **Growl to warn you or even worse…bite you for a tasty morsel**
- **Growl or bite just for walking past their food bowl**

If you observe any of these warning signs, abort the training session and try again later in a calmer environment. When you begin again, lower your criteria or use lower-value food. Other safety measures include a tether, gloves, or a muzzle. I find that the majority of dogs catch on pretty fast and learn to take food gently. Remember…more often than not, if you don't give a dog a reason to bite you, they won't bite you.

Puppies should learn that they do not have to compete for food and frequent feedings are ideal to reinforce this idea. If one puppy is given treats or bones, give a treat to all the puppies. No one puppy should be a bully and hog food and treats; sharing treats is best!

Puppies from large litters or K9's who didn't have enough resources may be more likely to become aggressive over food. John Rogerson, author of **THE DOG VINCI CODE** and, in my opinion, one of the top dog trainers in the world, conducted an experiment feeding six puppies out of nine bowls and found that food aggression subsides when there is more than enough food to go around. However, the study found that if a litter of pups feed out of just one bowl, "the puppies learn to gulp the food down as quickly as they can to get their fair share. They will push and shove to get at the available supply and the stronger puppies will push the weaker ones out of the way. When one of these puppies goes into its new home, it will not forget the lessons learned in the litter. The first thing that the new owner will notice is that when they approach their puppy when it is eating, it suddenly starts to eat faster. This is the first stage of food guarding."

By feeding with one-third *more* food bowls than puppies, Rogerson discovered that they tended to distribute themselves randomly around the many bowls available:

1. *"The feeding puppy is displaced by the approaching puppy but gets rewarded for leaving the food bowl by finding another food bowl of equal or greater quantity.*
2. *The approaching puppy, on seeing that this bowl is occupied, gets rewarded for walking away and finding an unoccupied bowl of equal or greater quantity.*
3. *The two puppies will happily share the food bowl with the knowledge that there are more available." John Rogerson*

In my experience, adding resources and enriching the environment doesn't always work because sometimes the dog's innate guarding instinct is still going to kick in and override any progress you've made. However, enriching the environment did work with my late soul mate, Sven the Love Dog. When I first rescued Sven, he would growl at anyone that would walk by his food bowl, raw hide, or even his bed. If you tried to reach to pick anything up, he would bite you. I once used a fake hand on a stick to test this theory and he put several punctures in the rubber hand! Sven used to growl at me if I would get near his favorite treat, a cow hoof. One day, I brought home a box of 100 cow hoofs and scattered them around the floor and just left them there for a few days. At first Sven seemed confused but slowly his aggressive displays subsided.

After successful training, Sven had such a good recall that even if he was guarding his favorite rawhide or food bowl, if I said "come" he would always come running. Sure he would object and vocalize a growl under his breath but he would at least come and spit out the rawhide when I would say "drop". Another way I got him to drop whatever was in his mouth was if I asked him to sit. Most dogs will drop what they are holding if you ask them to sit. I taught him such a solid sit, that even with a heavy bone in his mouth (it's hard for a dog to hold something heavy in their mouth in a sit position) if I said "sit", he would always sit and drop it.

Steve and Sven

While you always want to ensure a healthy diet for Fido, when practicing reducing resource guarding, you can do what I did with Sven. I lowered the quality of his food from gourmet, top-of-the-line dry kibble (with added goodies on top) and switched his food to a lower-quality kibble. Instead of sprucing it up with veggies, I cut the portion of kibble in half and added dry bran (a trick I learned from John Rogerson). I would feed Sven boring dry kibble mixed with dry bran and sit at a threshold where he was comfortable with me being there (about 15 feet away). As he was eating, I would toss an A-list yummy dog bite, something much better than what he was eating, toward his bowl. I would slowly walk closer and closer until he was eventually more comfortable with my getting closer to his food bowl.

My next step was to place several food bowls down. As he was eating out of one bowl, I would toss a better treat in an empty bowl. Eventually, I was able to bend down and pick up a bowl that he wasn't eating out of and place something better in it. Sven would still sometimes say one little *grrr-grgr-grgr* under his breath before he would gobble it down, but that was okay with me because a little growl is okay. You always want to respect the growl because it's a warning. If you try to correct the growl they might not growl anymore, they just might bite without warning instead!

The problem is when most dog owners try to "fix" food bowl guarding, they often choose to battle the dog over who is alpha. Believe me; attempting to battle the aggression out of the dog only makes the situation worse! The dog becomes less trusting.

While not always 100-percent fixable, sometimes food-bowl guarding is manageable to the point where the dog is okay with family members, but not with strangers. The dog may eventually let the dominant human in the household take food away, but not others. Always avoid putting your dog in situations where there may potentially be a battle over food. I suggest feeding a food-guarding dog in different rooms of the house where aggressive outbursts have *never happened* so they don't start guarding areas as well as a food bowl. Use a baby gate, a Double-Tie Tether, a closed door, or feed in the yard. Manage by locking all gates and doors so nobody walks in when the dog is eating until she is finished and the food bowl is removed. If you live with other kids or have frequent guests, I recommend putting a sign on the door "Do Not Enter". Let the dog eat in peace and don't let her out until she is calm for a few minutes. It's best to call the dog away from the bowl and put them somewhere else while you go back and remove the bowl until it is out of sight.

Who said that a dog has to eat out of a bowl anyway? Sometimes, to curb food-bowl aggression, it helps to take the bowl out of the equation. I want the dog to understand that I am not a threat; that my presence is a good thing. When I come close, I'm not trying to take something *away*; I'm usually delivering good things! Sometimes feeding in a kennel or crate is a safe management option, but only if the dog does not also have issues with guarding small spaces. For safety reasons, I may have to keep a leash on the dog while they are in the crate, with the end of the leash sticking out the door so that when I open the door, I have control of the dog and can walk him away, safely and slowly.

I don't know if it's ever just one thing that works... I think you have to look at it in a holistic way; the whole dog has to be addressed. A dog has to be healthy and we need to help build their confidence, reduce any anxieties they may have, give them a set of rules, and a job so they can work for a living. Dogs need to be taught a set of manners like retrieving (which is basically teaching the dog to share), self-control exercises like "stay", "leave it", and "take it." Also essential are "come", "go to your bed", and teaching a dog to take food or toys "gently" from the hand. The goal is we want the dog to realize that if they listen, good things happen! Fortunately, food-bowl guarding can be reduced with positive reward-based methods and modified with Behavior Modification training. Don't forget that managing well, being safe, and just letting your dog eat in peace is less likely to make the problem worse.

I also recommend checking out other resources and protocol for resource guarders. One is a book called **MINE** by Jean Donaldson; another is **THE DOG VINCI CODE** by John Rogerson; and a third is a protocol by Dr. Karen Overall.

TIPS: How to Prevent Guarding Issues

- Did you know that if a dog that has a food-guarding issue were to get spayed or neutered, the aggression is more likely to get *worse*? This is because the dog's appetite usually will increase after surgery.

- As long as you feel safe, feed a dog with food-guarding issues by hand during training sessions. It's a good way to build your relationship with your dog. If you don't feel safe don't take a chance! Get assistance from Veterinary Behaviorist (ACVB Certified Professional Dog Trainer (CPDT), Certified Applied Animal Behaviorist (CAAB or ACAAB), or an experienced Force-Free Trainer from the Pet Professional Guild.

- Controlling the space in the room, common sense, being proactive, and using strict management to prevent the dog from practicing unwanted behavior are vital for safety reasons. Thresholds are also very important to consider with a food-aggressive dog. Understanding the value of food as it pertains to each individual dog is essential. Some dogs don't care about certain foods, but that same dog might seriously hurt someone over another type.

- When it comes to dogs that are aggressive over food, the size of the food does matter. Yes, a small dog might be fine with getting kibble piece-by-piece, bite-by-bite, but for an aggressive Great Dane, I will feed handful-by-handful. Be careful not to frustrate an aggressive dog. Hand-feeding kibble-by-kibble to a serious food-bowl guarder could increase the food guarding and the frustration of being teased could be enough to push them over the edge and have an episode.

- Dogs that are free-fed, where you leave Fido's food bowl out all day for him to graze on, may be more likely to have food-bowl aggression.

- Don't ever put your hand in the bowl while a dog is eating just to prove that you are dominant!

- If you have a multiple-dog household, be careful of dogs fighting over high-quality foods. Remember, the higher the quality, the greater chance your dog will lose self-control.

- If you have a dog that inhales their food, wait until they are older to make them stay and wait to be fed. If you have a puppy that is inhaling their food (like a Labrador) and they eat faster when you approach or you suspect they may turn into a food guarder, you can unintentionally turn them into one by making them wait for the food bowl. If a puppy is really excited or anxious around food, wait to train them a "stay" until they are older, or until you get help from a Certified Professional Dog Trainer.

THE HAND THAT FEEDS: BITE INHIBITION

Playful biting is a natural and necessary behavior for developing puppies. It develops their jaw strength and teaches them how to interact with other dogs. However, you will need to teach your pup that biting human skin is a no-no!! If you do allow them to mouth your hand, they need to learn to do it gently. I hate to admit it, but I love the way it feels when my little 5.8 pound young puppy, Uni, play-bites on my hands. He does it so soft and gentle. I'm proud of the fact that he understands not to bite down hard and that it hurts me; if I say enough, he stops immediately.

If you start letting a pushy shepherd or chow mouth your hands as a game into adulthood then good luck with them not biting in the future! While many dogs do take food gently, there are some that have no idea or just don't care that your skin is soft… this can be dangerous. The key is to teach your dog that human skin is very fragile and not something they should be biting or chewing on. Bite inhibition means when your dog bites you without intending to break the skin (because they have learned that your skin is soft and that canine teeth hurt!).

When I have a dog that grabs food hard out of my hand, here's what I do… I keep the treat in a closed fist or even two closed fists touching each other and glued to my leg (the bigger the target, the less likely the dog is going to bite your finger). I don't deliver the treat until the dog backs off. The second he backs off even for just one second, I give him the treat to reward that behavior. Never just give the treat for grabby or aggressive behavior.

Think of it this way… If you give them a food treat and allow them to grab and bite, they will keep grabbing and biting. If you give them a food treat whenever they jump, they will keep jumping. If you give a dog food treat for begging, they will keep begging. If they are successful in their behavior, they will continue as long as you allow it to continue. Again, this is where food should be paired with self-control on the dogs' part. When luring your dog with a food treat, always keep your fingers out of the way…you never want to dangle a food treat between two fingers and tease a dog, because you might just get bitten.

Training begins… when a dog is just a pup. And when it comes to *puppy bites*, preparing and sharing human food with a puppy, you want to train them to take food from your hand "gently". If they take food too rough without any regard for your fingers, they probably learned that from their litter mates, or should I say, lack of litter mates.

When a young puppy bites a sibling in their litter, the sibling "squeaks" or "yaps" and the biter usually backs off. If a puppy is taken away from its litter at too early of an age, they don't learn bite inhibition; that human skin is soft. This usually means they did not get enough experience to learn that biting hurts from their mom or litter mates. If your dog grabs your hands with his teeth, you can act hurt by saying "ouch" in a high-pitched voice while giving a look of disappointment to teach your dog that biting can hurt. As soon as they stop the biting behavior and relax, pet the dog calmly. If a puppy is teething on your hands and you "squeak" like a hurt puppy, they may back off with an "I'm sorry" look. But other times, a squeak can escalate biting as the puppy thinks it's a game – screeching in feigned pain can sometimes get them more worked up! If you wave your arms around and squeal in surprise or pain, you sound and look like a human squeaky toy.

I do not advocate yelling or punishing the pup because they will not get *why* they are being punished. Scolding a dog verbally or physically usually creates a fearful, untrusting dog with a tendency to eventually cause harm. When your pup playfully bites your hand, try folding your arms, ignore the dog, or leave the room. She will wonder why her playmate left so abruptly. When you come back, if the pup offers you a few seconds of calm, then by all means give them an appropriate item to chew on – not your hands! Try keeping a leash on and gently stretch your arm away from your body so they can't practice nipping at you. Again, if you have any trepidation at all, seek help immediately from a Veterinary Behaviorist (ACVB Certified Professional Dog Trainer (CPDT), Certified Applied Animal Behaviorist (CAAB or ACAAB), or an experienced Force-Free Trainer from the Pet Professional Guild before proceeding with training.

Q: How do you curb on-leash aggressive outbursts?

When I see a group of dogs at a doggie daycare facility or dog park, I notice dogs that are overwhelmed, tired, want to be left alone or just need a private place to rest. When surrounded by a large group of dogs all day, they have a hard time reading each other's body language. Also, some daycares allow their staff to discipline your dog with squirt guns or correct with physical punishment. This can be very stressful. Daycares, dog parks, and even other dogs in your home may be the reason your dog is aggressive on a leash. I hear it over and over again, "My dog used to be able to play with other dogs, but now he's aggressive".

Most dogs don't mind a puppy's exuberance – like chasing, wrestling, or biting in excess, but once your puppy becomes a mature dog, other dogs aren't always so accepting of chasing and playing games the way they did when your dog was a young pup. Dogs that practice running up to every dog they see are likely to become aggressive when restricted by a leash. If your dog is allowed to practice fighting all day and is then restrained by a leash, the more you try to hold them back, the more aggressive they become.

Dogs need to spend quality time bonding with and being supervised by their humans and their humans should be influencing the *dogs* behavior; not the other way around. Dogs must to be taught to walk on a slack leash using positive, reward-based tactics. You may never be able to fix the problem if your dog can't walk on a slack leash or hasn't been taught that walking at your side is a good place to be. I suggest cutting back on your dog's off-leash playtime with other dogs for about a month and the on-leash aggression problem will usually subside.

You need to be proactive when out on a walk… When a fearful dog goes nuts at another mutt on a walk, having something that really matters like your dog's favorite toy or treat pouch full of his dinner or a surprise snack (if delivered at the right time) can be helpful. Once your dog knows how to walk properly on a leash without distractions, then it's time to be proactive by spotting the approaching dog *before* your dog has a chance to react. Learn about thresholds and be proactive.

A good starting threshold is when your dog sees another dog – but it's far enough away that you can get your dog's attention back when you say their name (for some dogs it's 10 feet; for others, 2 blocks). When you see a dog approaching, and if your dog will take it, immediately deliver a treat so they make a positive association with an oncoming dog. Say "Hey, it's a doggy!" and use Positive Reinforcement. Next do nothing until your dog stops behaving badly. Let them window shop, let them pull, let them bark and growl. *Do not react!* Let them work it out… the second they stop – even the smallest head turn away from the other dog is sufficient… that is when you turn and go for a walk the other way, deliver a treat and praise. A yawn or when the ears go from pinned back to relaxed, or the tail goes from erect or tucked into a natural middle position are also signs of appeasement.

The instant you see your dog display one of these appeasement behaviors is the second you mark it with a click or a "good dog," then turn, walk away, and deliver a treat. If the aggression towards other dogs on a walk is based on fear, which is usually the case, then just walking away from the threatening dog can be a great reward. The goal is that they will give up quicker the next time until they learn to ignore other dogs and be more interested in you. Save your dog's meals for walk time, then practice the above routine and try to slowly increase your dog's threshold until they can pass any dog without incident. *You* need to be more exciting to your dog than the other dog!

TABLE MANNERS: BEGGING AT THE TABLE

When it comes to begging at the table, one thing you want to do is to not let the dog sleep under the table. Don't let family members feed from the table and don't let guests feed or drop crumbs for your dog to pick up under the table or feed them for jumping up…all of which Marley does in the film, *Marley & Me*. It's all about consistency; if everyone's on the same page and feeding from the table is not allowed, the dog is going to catch on.

It's a good idea to teach your puppy to sit or lay down *away* from the dinner table. Avoid feeding a puppy from the table as this only encourages and reinforces begging behavior. K9's also need to be trained from an early age that even if something falls from the table, they are not a vacuum expected to clean up after you or your kids. If you do allow this, be forewarned, your dog will sit inches from your plate of food – waiting, begging, and giving you those "puppy eyes" to give them a treat from the table! While it may be cute at first, it is actually an undesirable behavior, so nip it in the bud early!

Dogs hanging out under a table can get aggressive and territorial. When they are under something like a table, they can feel trapped and may snap, beg, growl, etc. Until your dog has been taught a solid "down/stay", I suggest tying the dog with a leash in a corner of the kitchen (as long as they can't get tangled on a chair or eat your rug). This way, they can be with you and you can keep an eye on them. You need to remember to ignore them at first. Then, once they relax and sit or lay down, you can smile. Keep them away from the table in a "down/stay", and then reward them with a treat *after* you have eaten.

I have to admit that sometimes I feed my dogs before I eat, because if they are too hungry, the begging behaviors can get intense. If your dog is full before you eat, they are more apt to chill out and relax. There is no proof that feeding your dog first will make them think they are dominant over you, as some trainers believe. Most of the time, I eat first then I feed my dogs because I think it shows good manners and it teaches self-control, but I feel there should be no fixed rule; all dogs and all situations are different.

Dogs should also stay out of the kitchen while you cook. You can give them a small *dog bite* you are cooking as long as you ask for a "down/stay" at the far end of the kitchen. You want to get your cooking done without worrying about your dog getting under foot!

How to Calm Your Fearful or Aggressive Dog at the Vet

The best way to keep your dog calm when you take them to the Vet is to take them when they don't *have* to go. Put them in the car and drive to the clinic, sit in the parking lot, love on your dog, feed them some amazing tasty *dog bites*, and then drive home. The next day do the same thing, but this time, get out of the car and feed and love on your pooch. The third day, take them inside and give them a treat or meal. It's a good idea to drop some treats off with the receptionist ahead of time and then bring your dog inside. Have the staff feed your pooch A-list treats and give the dog some love. The goal is to get your dog to *like* going to the Vet. This way, when you do have to take them to the Vet, they will be acclimated and unafraid of the experience.

Another technique, inspired by John Rogerson, is the old "Ace Bandage on the leg trick". I used this on my dog, Sven and many other nervous and aggressive dogs while visiting the Vet with great success. I place an Ace Bandage on my dog's leg (even though they are not injured). Be sure not to put it on too tight. The Ace Bandage serves as a distraction; your dog will be concentrating on biting at the bandage rather than worrying about other dogs in the waiting room. You can also use a Calming Cap™. This filters a dog's vision as if they were looking through a filter or panty hose. Dogs can still see through it but it cuts out just enough vision and helps most dogs relax for a car ride, a visit to the Vet, or even a nail trim.

You can also try using a squeeze tube or piece of non-toxic hose (as I discussed earlier) filled with something sticky and tasty like peanut butter to reward and re-direct away from all the other distractions. If your dog is really hyper-anxious… call ahead before taking them to the Vet and ask to get your dog in a back room if possible, or wait in your car and have the receptionist call you when it's your turn.

Try these to calm your pup:

- Anxiety Wrap or Thunder Shirt: acupressure points helps dogs relax
- Calming Cap: cuts down the vision but they can still see
- Canine Appeasing Pheromones: relaxes puppies and adult dogs; Dog Appeasing Pheromones (DAP) are synthetic pheromones that mimic those released during lactation and give puppies a sense of well-being and reassurance.
- Lavender Oil: combined with massage; a sense of being calm; reduces anxiety
- Rescue Remedy: ingredients Rock Rose helps with panic and terror, and Cherry Plum, helps people and dogs with the feelings of losing control.
- Squeeze Tube or 3-4 inch non-toxic garden hose: fill tube with my homemade salmon paté, peanut butter, string cheese, hot dogs, etc.

K9 CUISINE

When it comes to your dog's health, knowing what foods are safe for canine consumption is vital. The time to start learning the difference between healthy foods and toxic foods is *before* you get a puppy or an adult dog. It's also good to select fresh ingredients, clean foods properly, trim fat, and thoroughly cook meat, seafood, poultry, and eggs to avoid foodborne illnesses. Now, some of you may want to stick to the basics like protein, carbs, and fats, which is perfectly fine. However, when it comes to preparing food to share with a pup, I like to include many diverse foods in the kitchen that are not only healthy but taste terrific in many delicious recipes!

DOG FOOD FACTS

While researching this book, I discovered that dog food was first sold in England in the 1860s. Before dog food was "invented" by James Spratt, dogs were fed a diet of hard biscuits and scraps of rotten food. Spratt created a dog biscuit – shaped like a bone – that contained beef blood to make it extra appealing and tasty. As the automobile became a means of transportation, horses were replaced by cars (and used to make dog food). By the 1940s, canned dog food comprised 90% of dog food sold in the United

States. A shortage of tin during WWII made canning too expensive and dry dog food has been outselling canned ever since.

It is also interesting that the use of dry kibble in the U.S. coincided with an increase in allergies to corn, wheat, and other fillers. Just because grains are non-toxic for canine consumption, it doesn't mean that they are necessarily safe. I attribute this increase in allergies and illness to the use of toxic chemicals and pesticides like Round-up which is why I recommend organic grains to my clients. Dogs may also have a harder time digesting certain foods. Good digestion is important when it comes to your dog's nutrition. As you will discover in this book, I recommend feeding your dog a varied diet of premium foods for health benefits, training purposes, and salivary satisfaction!

Q: How do I shop for the right dog food?

Read the label… When it comes to reading the list of ingredients on a label, the same rule applies to your food as it does to Fido's. By law, U.S. manufacturers must label food for canine consumption. This requires an accurate list and analysis of the food's percentages of protein, fat, fiber, and liquid, as well as nutritional value. Ingredients are listed by weight, from highest to lowest. However, be aware that many companies use lots of fillers containing flour (bran) or corn, making it look like there is less wheat and more meat! The quality and availability of USDA ingredients certified for human consumption is not the same as by-products used in most commercial dog foods. Remember, most dog foods are made up of ingredients left over from the production of food products for humans.

American Pet Products reports: "Americans will spend 60 billion on their pets in 2014, most going to healthier foods."

When a company sets out to make dog food, one of the "marketing targets" they want to hit is to manufacture a food that claims "100% complete and balanced nutrition". The words "complete and balanced" on the side of a bag might mean the contents will, along with water, "sustain life" but no single food can provide all the nutrients needed for good health. Optimum health is achieved by providing a variety of proteins, fats, carbohydrates, etc. from different food sources. I suggest feeding a diet made from high-quality ingredients to prevent nutritional deficiencies and food allergies. Buying dog food that provides your dog balanced nutrition is vital to their health. You need to consider: digestibility, calories, and cost. Pet food manufacturers spend millions researching and developing dog food and are held accountable by The Association of American Feed Control which regulates nutrients in food for canine consumption. Dog food you buy should be labeled "complete and balanced."

According to the AAFCO nutrient profiles, pet foods labeled "dinner" or "platter" are required to contain 25% chicken, beef, poultry, or fish, and foods labeled "Chicken Dog Food" are required to contain 95% chicken. The AFFCO "95% Rule" means at least 95% of the ingredients come from cows, lamb, poultry, or fish (excluding water for processing). So check the labels and work with your Vet to find the right mix for your breed. I suggest consulting the Animal Protection Institute (API) which recommends the following when purchasing dog food:

- **"AAFCO guarantee" should be on the label**
- **Meat should be the first ingredient listed**
- **Contains digestible grains (rice)**
- **Avoid corn more than once in the first five ingredients**
- **Smell the food; if it smells rancid, return it**
- **Pay attention to your dog's coat, eyes, and weight**
- **Your dog's stool should be firm with minimal odor**

Dog food should contain essential vital nutrients that provide energy, promote growth, and maintain bodily functions. Protein, carbs, fats, vitamins and minerals are all essential. "Complete" means that the food contains all the nutrients needed. "Balanced" means nutrients are in the right proportion. Now let's consider Digestibility, Calories and Cost.

Digestibility

Digestibility includes being able to tolerate a food without allergies, indigestion, and how well the nutrients are absorbed. My clients often observe the signs of indigestible dog food fairly quickly in the form of gas, diarrhea, vomiting, etc., which is why I suggest you read the label to ensure high-quality protein for your pup such as chicken, beef, poultry, and fish. The food that humans eat is usually much higher in fat than what dogs can handle. In fact, K9s have a harder time digesting certain foods than we do, and all of us are prone to food allergies.

A report by the Journal *Nature* (*LA TIMES* January 23, 2012) found that a dog's ability to "digest carbohydrates, from food scraps left behind by humans…a mix of roots, porridge, bread… and bone marrow, helped enable their domestication… A gene makes an enzyme for the next step in carb digestion: turning maltose into glucose. This gene is 12 times more active in dogs than wolves, and blood tests showed that maltose is processed into glucose twice as quickly in dogs." In the wild, the canine diet consists of mother's milk and prey. So it seems to me that "man's best friend" evolved by eating human food, thereby developing the ability to break down starch into sugar more efficiently than wolves.

Calories Count

Most owners know that puppies require more calories and nutrients, which is why many Vets suggest you buy puppy formula for the first two years, and when they are in their golden senior years; metabolism is 2-4 times slower than a puppy so try a senior formula. Look for the right balance of calories from protein, carbs, and fats. A moderately active 50-lb. dog requires about 1,200 calories per day. I suggest choosing a dog food that supports your dog's life stages.

Cost Is Key

Many people don't want to spend more than they have to on dog food, and I don't blame them. But think about it over the long term… First, you want to strive for high nutritional value, and what most people don't know is that many costlier foods can be fed in smaller servings for optimal health. Remember, "An ounce of prevention is worth a pound of cure" and this can mean lower Vet bills! So consider spending a little more early on and it may pay off as you and your pup stroll on many walks. There are pros and cons to dog foods from large companies, but they do more testing and if there is a recall, you may be more likely to hear about it. Before buying a new dry dog food, ask if they have a sample you can try. Many pet stores do because they know you want to try before you buy a large bag of kibble.

Dry VS. Canned VS. Raw

Dry dog foods contain grains, meat, poultry, fish, and vitamin and mineral supplements. They also can help prevent the buildup of tartar and plaque on canine teeth. The advantage of dry is cost; it is also lower in fat and higher in carbohydrates than canned food. If your dog tends to gain weight easily, a dry food may be the best choice. Commercial dog foods high in fiber and low in calorie density that meet your dog's specific needs are available at pet stores, or as prescriptive diets in Veterinary clinics.

Canned dog food, on the other hand, looks more like chopped meat or beef stew, and dogs certainly love to lap it up! Chemicals like BPA used as a preservative in canned food can contribute to diabetes and heart disease, so it is best to use in moderation. Canned and dry food can also stick to the teeth, creating plaque build-up, so in order to protect your dog's teeth; I suggest brushing your dog's teeth regularly to remove plaque and tartar.

You will want to avoid deli meats that are processed including ham, beef, and salami. Processed meats may contain growth hormones, antibiotics, and sodium nitrate (used as a preservative and antimicrobial). They also have a very high salt content and too much salt is not good for canines. So for these reasons, I recommend limiting the amount of processed meats you share with your dog. When cooking or grilling meats, avoid high temperatures or burning as this creates hazardous chemicals like Heterocyclic Amines (HCA's) linked to stomach and colon cancer.

Holistic Veterinarians may recommend feeding your dog raw meat…keep in mind that there are risks from bacterial contaminants. If you're going to feed your dog a raw diet, I suggest you follow safety standards and make sure the meat is frozen first for at least 72 hours to kill bacteria. Most meats can be refrozen one time safely, so once you prepare a meal, it can be put back in the freezer until thawed for feeding. Avoid thawing frozen food by running hot or warm water over it. Running cold water is fine or let it defrost in the fridge. You can also leave it out, but don't forget about it.

Homemade

This is what makes this book, *Dog Bites* unique. I advocate feeding your dog homemade cuisine in addition to her regular kibble, canned or raw dog food. When you prepare *dog bites*, make sure your dog is getting the best ingredients and highest nutritional value. Homemade diets are great for dogs with food allergies or are sensitive to artificial dyes and chemicals. If you do decide to switch to a more healthy food, do so gradually over a week or two by mixing the new food with the old until it is entirely replaced with the new. Studies show that K9's are discriminating eaters. They prefer beef to pork; pork to lamb; lamb to chicken… and they enjoy variety. There is a growing trend with dog owners toward making homemade foods… It's the best way to know exactly what your pet is consuming.

Corn has been used in foods for dogs since the beginning of time. It has a bad rap because of modern farming practices and the use of pesticides, so I recommend using organic corn if possible. Not all dogs are allergic to corn and if it's ground up it can be easily digested. If you are going to feed fresh corn (it might come out of the dog the same way it looked going in) they will have a hard time digesting it. Be sure to *never* give your dog the corn cob. When I was a Veterinary assistant I had to pull the cob out of a dog's mouth with needle-nose pliers!

Imagine if you had to eat the exact same food every day for the rest of your life…

Just the thought of it makes your taste buds run for the hills! You might lose weight, get depressed, salivate over your favorite long-lost cuisine, or find that the same monotonous food every day is simply unpalatable. Well, guess what? It's the same for your pet. Think about your dog's daily meal he eats day after day, year after year! Some people feed their dog just one food their entire life. I have heard clients say they feed their dogs the same food every day because "it won't upset their stomach" or "they are used to it" or "my friend recommended this dog food, so it must be good".

According to Stephen R. Lindsey in **THE HANDBOOK OF APPLIED DOG BEHAVIOR AND TRAINING: VOLUME 1:** "Food preference is a somewhat complicated matter involving broad factors including genetic preparedness to recognize a potential food item, past experience with the food item, pallet, ability of the food item to satisfy, and it's novelty." Lindsey cites a 1967 study where Chow puppies were taken from their mothers at birth and divided into three feeding groups:

- **Group 1: Fed exclusively a soy diet**
- **Group 2: Fed a fruit & vegetable diet**
- **Group 3: Fed a diet containing a variety of plant& animal ingredients**

The study resulted in each group developing a specific preference for the food which it was accustomed to:

- **Group 1: Pups refused all foods other than what they were fed**
- **Group 2: Pups (fed only fruit & vegetables) refused to eat meat when it was first introduced at six months of age**
- **Group 3: Pups would eat almost any food offered!**

The study concluded that dogs exposed to limited new foods tend to develop a preference for familiar foods. In my training facility, I find that dogs fed a variety of foods are easier to train, are not as finicky, and seem to outperform other dogs!

> *When a dog in the wild hunts and kills an animal like a deer,*
> *they eat the intestines filled with digested vegetables first.*

John Rogerson believes that "dogs can develop taste preferences in the same way that we can, so to deny a dog the opportunity to sample of varied diet would be the same as giving a child chicken and rice every day of its life…. There is no doubt that if a dog eats a varied diet, then, all things being equal, it will out-perform a dog fed the same food each day in exercises requiring discrimination and its sense of smell…. Taste and smell are linked, so it should make perfect sense to feed a puppy a very varied diet."

The truth is dogs are omnivores…they eat *both* meats and vegetables. So it makes sense that dogs are better off if they eat variety when they are puppies. They develop a taste for a variety of foods, and a variety of nutrients which reduces food intolerance and increases palatability. Even in the womb, puppies require different foods that provide nutrition for development, which can prevent food intolerances once they are born.

Q: Which foods are okay to feed your dog?

As a dog owner, you want to become accustomed to a variety of foods that are *doggone* delicious! The foods listed below should comprise no more than 10-20 percent of your dog's diet. It's best to try out new foods one at a time, until you're certain that they don't upset your dog's stomach. Many clients have asked me what they can and cannot feed their dogs. I always advise to first check with their Vet. In addition, I remind them that all dogs are different. Finally, I caution that many foods that are okay for human consumption are indeed toxic for K9 consumption. With this in mind, I wanted to provide you with a basic list of safe and unsafe foods; however this is not a complete list by any means. The safe foods are just some of the more common foods I use when cooking Dog Bites Recipes. This book is called *Dog Bites* for a reason….when feeding dogs *safe* human foods; feed only tiny bites, moderation is key.

Many foods, which are perfectly edible for human consumption, and even other animal species, can pose health hazards for dogs due to their metabolism. There are a host of foods that are *not recommended* for canine consumption; some cause stomach irritation, while others cause severe illness or are poisonous, toxic, or even fatal! The following list of foods contains Safe and Not-So-Safe foods; however, I caution that this list is not inclusive of all unsafe or toxic foods.

SAFE & NOT-SO-SAFE FOODS:

+ **Alcoholic Beverages.** Even a small amount of alcohol intoxication can cause coma or even death in canines. Symptoms include vomiting, diarrhea, loss of coordination, difficulty breathing, coma, and seizures. Not Safe

🔸 **Apples.** Sliced apples are tasty treats for K9's as long as you avoid core and seeds. The apple core and seeds contains cyanide, which is toxic. Kind of Safe

🔸 **Apple Cider Vinegar** treats arthritis, allergies, itchy skin, corrects pH levels, eliminates tear stains around the eyes, and fights fleas. It also aids metabolism and helps control blood pressure. Safe

🔸 **Asparagus** can be served plain as a healthy treat in moderation. Kind of Safe

🔸 **Avocado.** The leaves, seeds, fruit, and bark contain persin which can cause vomiting, and diarrhea or damage heart and lung as well as other tissues. Additionally, the high fat in avocados can upset a dog's stomach and cause vomiting and possibly pancreatitis. Symptoms are subtle and include breathing difficulties and a bloated abdomen. Not Safe

🔸 **Baby Food** may contain onion powder, which can be toxic to dogs (see "onion" below.) Not Safe

🔸 **Bacon.** High it salt and fat; a small bite provides protein. Kind of Safe

🔸 **Bananas** contain potassium, a vital mineral that helps normalize the heartbeat. If your dog has never eaten bananas before, give only small pieces at first to prevent digestive upset. Safe

🔸 **Beef (cooked)** is a great source of vitamins and protein; use lean cuts. Safe

🔸 **Beef (raw)** poses the threat of salmonella, bacteria, parasites, and bacterial organisms that can cause a variety of disease in canines. A certain species of tapeworm can also be found in raw meat and passed to a pet. If you're going to feed your dog a raw food diet, I recommend doing so with your Vet's approval and guidance. Safe & Not Safe

🔸 **Beef Jerky.** A-list treat for most dogs; jerky contains vitamins and protein.

(Avoid spices, excess sodium, etc.) Safe

- **Blueberries** are excellent anti-oxidants; a Superfood. They can improve cognitive function; great for skin and coat. Safe

- **Bones.** Dogs love to chew on beef bones. Chewing helps reduce tartar buildup on their teeth. (Never give your dog a cooked bone, as they are brittle). Fish, poultry, and rib bones can cause obstruction or laceration of the digestive system. Bones can cause: vomiting, diarrhea, constipation, intestinal obstructions, and internal bleeding. Opt for a safer alternative like American rawhide chew strips or a Nylabone. It's okay to give your dog large soup bones or a marrowbone dipped in boiling water or broth to kill bacteria (but do not cook them.) Some dogs are sensitive to bones; others are not. Safe & Not Safe

Got a Bone to Pick?

Ever wonder why dogs bury bones…? Well, the reason dogs bury bones has to do with a survival mechanism to prevent starvation. It's actually an innate, instinctive trait for canines in the wild to bury bones. When food is scarce, a dog may feel a need to horde his food and bury a bone after eating his fill to save it for later when there may not be enough food. The marrow in the bone contains vital nutrients. They also hide it from other dogs and burying bones in soil acts as a preservative to keep it fresh. Even though it may look dirty and awful, it looks rather tasty to your dog!

Bones are great for cleaning a dog's teeth and a good source of calcium. But if you have to pick a bone for your dog, pay careful attention to splinters which can cause intestinal perforations or digestive-tract obstruction. Never give your dog cooked ribs, poultry, or steak bones as they are more brittle could splinter, causing obstruction or colitis. Poultry bones should *never* be given to a dog as they are porous and splinter. I've seen dogs with a bone lodged in their throat or unable to pass, end up at the Vet with a case of colitis and worse.

I've seen dogs chew raw beef marrowbones, which have a tasty marrow center; as they are thicker they are less likely to shatter. However, I prefer giving large soup bones dipped in boiling water or broth to kill bacteria (do not cook them). When it comes to bones, rawhide, pig's ear, bully sticks, antlers, and chews… all dogs are different; some are very sensitive and some not so much. Your Vet will probably have their own opinion on which bone may or may not be right for your dog. The shape and size of the bone for each individual dog *does* matter; you want something large enough that they can't get the whole thing in their mouth at once. It's a good idea to take them away when the dog gets about half way finished. Natural, American-made raw hides and the like are recommended over ones from other countries (see more on bones under Chew Toys).

- **Bread** is a carbohydrate. It's all about moderation. A little plain white bread (baked) is fine to feed your dog. It's best to avoid some of the fancier breads and bagels on the market. Stay away from breads that contain poppy seeds and onions. Safe & Not safe

- **Yeast Dough (raw)** can expand and produce gas in the digestive system, causing pain and possible rupture of the stomach or intestines. Never give your dog uncooked dough! Not Safe

- **Broccoli** (cooked) and chopped is an excellent source of phosphorus, potassium, magnesium and vitamins B6, E, K, C & A as well as folate and fiber. Safe

- **Buffalo/Bison** is very lean which is good! It contains nutritious vitamins and protein. Safe

- **Carrots (raw or cooked)** are naturally sweet, crunchy, and nutritious and an exceptional source of vitamin A, C, and potassium. They also contain nutrients necessary for eye health and immune and digestive systems. Safe

- **Celery** (chopped small in moderation) is okay for Fido. Avoid giving to small dogs; celery is stringy and you don't want them to choke. Kind of Safe

- **Cereal** is a carbohydrate. (See cereal in Recipes). Kind of Safe

- **Cheese** is an excellent source of protein for dogs, but many are high in fat.

Cottage cheese is high in protein and calcium and can be a good way to add extra protein to your dog's diet. (Some dogs have dairy intolerance.) Safe

+ **Chamomile** has anti-inflammatory, pain relieving and antiseptic properties. It aids in digestive issues, such as gas and bloat. Can be given in the form of tea (let it cool first). It is also a mild sedative that is safe (even for puppies who may be suffering from poor digestion). I burn chamomile oil in a tea candle to calm anxiety in dogs as well as lavender, peppermint, and tangerine oils. Safe

+ **Cinnamon** can reduce blood sugar levels (only in moderation) and helps dogs with diabetes. Safe

+ **Coconut** is a healthy treat providing beneficial fats with numerous health benefits. Safe

  o **Coconut Milk** is classified as a functional food because it provides health benefits beyond its nutritional content. It is rich in vitamins, minerals, and a good source of fiber. (Use in moderation due to high fat content.) Safe

  o **Coconut Oil** is a saturated fat and is better to cook with than vegetable oil as it can be cooked at higher heats. Healthier oil that improves thyroid functions and add luster to a coat. Aids eczema, flea allergies, dermatitis, and itchy skin; regulates insulin, promotes healthy thyroid function, controls diabetes, reduces excess weight, increases energy and aids arthritis. Safe

+ **Cardamom** pods have a laxative effect on dogs and should be avoided. Not Safe

+ **Cat Food.** Not a good idea for K9s and is generally too high in protein and fat. Not Safe

+ **Chocolate.** Chocolate can be downright <u>deadly</u> to your dog! It contains theobromamine, a dangerous chemical that can cause a life-threatening rapid heart rate, respiratory problems, tremors, vomiting, and diarrhea in dogs. As little as three ounces of baking chocolate can kill a 25-pound dog! Not Safe

- **Citrus Oil** extracts can cause vomiting in dogs. Not Safe

- **Coffee.** Never use coffee in any dog recipes. Coffee contains theobromine (see chocolate above) which can cause vomiting and diarrhea and can be toxic to the heart and nervous systems. Not Safe

- **Corn** has a bad rap but actually has been in dog food forever. For some dogs, corn is a common allergen that causes dry, itchy skin and is difficult to digest. If it's ground up it usually fine. It's not toxic, but never give your dog the cob. When I was a Veterinarian assistant, I had to remove a corn cob out of a dog's throat not once, but twice! Kind of Safe

- **Cranberries.** Cranberry juice reduces urinary tract infections; provides vitamin C, manganese, K & E; fights bacteria like E. coli; prevents bad breath, plaque, and gum disease. Since Roman times, cranberries have been used to treat a variety of ailments from rheumatoid disorders, scurvy and fever, to skin wounds and eczema. Native Americans used cranberries as a blood tonic because of the iron content. It wasn't until the 1840's that German scientists began explaining the positive impact of cranberries on urinary tract health. Cranberries prevent and treat crystals and bladder stones in our K9 companions. In fact, the American Animal Hospital Association has suggested that people add an ounce of cranberry juice to their animals' food daily. Safe

- **Cucumbers** are a diuretic and can cause increased urine output, but in moderation they are fine. The potassium is good for teeth and bones. Peel the skin, especially if they are not organic. Safe

- **Currants** (like grapes) are toxic! Symptoms may include vomiting, diarrhea, lethargy, lack of appetite, abnormal drinking or urination, dehydration, and bad breath. Not Safe

- **Dandelion** contains more vitamin A than carrots. It is also a "friendly" bacterium in the gastrointestinal tract. It's good for the liver and heart. Okay in moderation; Consult a holistic Vet before using dandelion because dandelion is a diuretic and can increase urine output. Kind of Safe

- **Dates (pitted)** provide a good source of dietary fiber. Too many dates can cause diarrhea. If a dog ingests the pit, it can be fatal. Give just a small bite. Moderation is key. Kind of Safe

- **Eggs (cooked)** are a great source of protein and dogs love them! I suggest hard boiling cage-free organic eggs with Omega-3. Safe

- **Eggs (raw).** Never give your dog raw eggs as they can carry salmonella. Not Safe

- **Fat Trimmings** can cause canine pancreatitis. Not all fat is bad for dogs, but for the most part, the fat trimmings off your steak or pork chop are not advised. Not Safe

- **Fish (cooked)** provides protein and Omega-3's. Most fish if cooked is Safe

- **Fish (raw)** especially smelt, herring and catfish contain an enzyme that destroys the B-vitamin, thiamine. Fortunately, cooking destroys this enzyme. Raw salmon can be infected with a parasite and create salmon poisoning. Dogs are the only species susceptible to salmon poisoning and symptoms include vomiting, diarrhea, dehydration, etc. While you may love a dinner of sushi, skip any notions of serving your dog sushi. Not Safe

- **Fish (canned)** if fed exclusively or in high amounts can result in a thiamine (B vitamin) deficiency leading to loss of appetite, seizures, and in severe cases, death. Kind of Safe

- **Fish (farmed salmon)** is a high-risk cancer food often contaminated with carcinogenic chemicals, PCBs (polychAngelanated biphenyls), flame retardants, pesticides, and antibiotics. It also lacks vitamin D. Kind of Safe

- **Fruit Pits** (peaches, plums) can cause obstruction of the digestive tract. Peach and plum pits contain cyanide, which is poisonous to humans and canines. Not Safe

- **Grapes** can cause choking in canines. Grapes, raisins, and currants contain an unknown toxin which can damage the kidneys. Symptoms include: vomiting and/or diarrhea, loss of appetite, lethargy, abdominal pain, dehydration, passing only a small amount of urine, abnormal drinking and urination, Kidney (renal) failure and death. Not Safe

- **Figs (pitted)** provide a good source of dietary fiber. Too many figs can cause diarrhea. If a dog ingests the pit, it can be fatal. Give just a small bite. Moderation is key. Kind of Safe

- **Goat's Milk** is the most easily digested food on earth. In fact, goat's milk contains vitamins, minerals, electrolytes, trace elements, enzymes (over 30) needed for digestion (ideal for pets that are lactose intolerant), protein, probiotics and fatty acids. Raw goat's milk has so many nutrients that it has helped cure liver disease, kidney disease, diabetes, colitis, heart disease, malnutrition, etc. It can also be used to increase weight in underweight pets and is absorbed into a dog's body within 20 minutes after drinking! Goat's milk is readily available in most supermarkets and is used in cheeses, butter, yogurt, etc. When I bake with goat's milk, I use the same amounts in recipes that call for cow's milk. Safe

- **Goji Berries:** Nutrient-rich, high in protein, vitamins and minerals. They are considered to be a Superfood for humans. The polysaccharides in Goji berries are unique in that they work to support the immune system. They're even good for fighting cancer cells. Goji berries are a nightshade plant like eggplant and tomatoes, which I find most dogs don't do well on…but they have so many healing properties that in my experience, feeding a few Goji berries as treats have not posed a problem. Consult a holistic Vet before feeding your dog Goji berries. Kind of Safe

- **Hops.** An unknown compound in hops causes panting, increased heart rate, elevated temperature, seizures, and even death. Not Safe

- **Human Vitamin Supplements** containing iron and can damage the lining of the digestive system in dogs and be toxic to the liver and kidneys. Not Safe

- **Marijuana.** Certain types of marijuana with low amounts of THC are starting to be used with success by Veterinarians in treating K9's with cancer for pain and nausea. Marijuana is a drug, a medicine, and a food. Because it's becoming legal in many states, that means more and more dogs are getting into their owner's stash, especially the edible kind! I caution to *never* give your pet marijuana. It can be fatal! Signs of a dog that may have eaten cannabis include: dizzy, swaying back and forth, lethargic, dilated pupils, slow heart rate, urinary incontinence, vomiting and possibility of choking on their vomit (which can lead to death)! Not Safe

- **Milk.** An occasional splash of cow's milk may not be harmful, but I don't recommend ever giving your dog milk as some dogs lack the lactase enzyme needed to break down lactose and may suffer from diarrhea as a result. Avoid nut milk. Not So Safe

- **Moldy Food** is a definite no-no! They can make your dog very sick and can cause seizures and can even be fatal. Not Safe

- **Mushrooms** contain toxins and may cause shock or result in death. Some mushrooms are toxic and some are not; Shiitake mushrooms are known to have health benefits like lowering blood pressure, cholesterol and to help fight cancer. Unless you are giving your dog mushrooms under the guidance of your vet, I find it it's best to not even give your dog even a taste of mushrooms, just to be safe. Mostly Not Safe

- **Nutmeg** can contain toxins, which may affect organs in the body, cause shock, or result in death. Not Safe

- **Nuts.** Dogs should _never eat tree nuts_! Nuts are a "DO NOT EAT" item to add to Fido's list of toxic or harmful substances. Certain types of nuts can cause toxic poisoning, upset stomach, or obstruction in your dog's gastrointestinal tract, which can lead to illness. Keep your pet safe and make sure the nuts listed below are out of your dog's reach. If your dog has eaten dangerous or toxic nuts, contact your Veterinarian or the <u>Pet Poison Helpline</u>.

o **Almonds** are not necessarily toxic but they are fattening and can cause pancreatitis. They are hard to swallow and digest, especially for a little dog. I do not recommend feeding dogs almonds. Not So Safe

o **Hickory Nuts** contain the toxin, juglone, which can cause laminitis in horses. Eating hickory nuts can cause the same problems associated with black walnuts: gastric intestinal upset or an intestinal obstruction. Like walnuts, moldy hickory nuts can contain tremorgenic mycotoxins, which can cause seizures or neurological symptoms. Not Safe

o **Macadamia nuts and Pistachios** contain fat, which can give your dog an upset stomach and may lead to pancreatitis. They also contain a toxicity that may cause in canine neurological symptoms, weakness in the hind legs, vomiting, staggering, and seizures. Large amounts or if they ingest the shell (especially a small dog) can be fatal. Not Safe

o **Peanuts** are not nuts; they are legumes that grow in the ground. Some dogs can be allergic to peanuts. Peanuts are safe in moderation (if they are ground in to peanut butter). Peanut Butter is a good source of protein but is also high in fat. *Caution: if a family member is allergic to peanuts, <u>do not</u> have them handle a Kong toy stuffed with peanut butter; toys with just small traces can be deadly to people who are allergic, so wash toys after your dog is done dissecting. Peanut butter commonly contains mold which can fuel yeast growth. Your dog's ears may get red, stinky, and itchy or they may get hot spots from giving them just a small amount of peanut butter. Mostly Safe

o **Pecans**. Feeding dogs pecans can cause gastric intestinal upset or obstruction and pancreatitis. If a dog eats a large amount of pecans or if they swallow the whole shell, it can be fatal. Not Safe

o **Walnuts.** Some types of walnuts are fatal. Black walnuts contain the toxin, juglone, which can cause a vascular disease (laminitis) in horses. Eating black walnuts can cause gastric intestinal upset or an obstruction. Moldy black walnuts can contain tremorgenic mycotoxins (fungi toxins), which cause seizures or neurological symptoms. Because of their high phosphorous content, walnuts can cause canine bladder stones. According to VPI Pet Insurance, walnut poisoning is one of the most common claims for toxic ingestion. Not Safe

+ **Kelp Powder** speeds up metabolism and break down fats in the diet. Safe

+ **Lemon Juice** aids digestion, detoxifies and builds immunity; your dog may not like it. Dog's stomachs are sensitive to acidic juices, so we're not talking about giving your dog a full glass of juice; we're talking about a few drops mixed in a recipe is fine. Moderation is key. Kind of Safe

+ **Garlic** is a natural antibiotic, antioxidant, anti-allergen, antibacterial, anti-fungal, anti-viral, and anti-carcinogen. When garlic is ingested *in moderation and not every day* it is not harmful. It can also be used topically to treat specific ailments such as ear mite infestation. Garlic contains sulfur, a natural insect repellent! If fed in small amounts and not fed every day, garlic has health benefits. But in excess, it can damage a dog's red blood cells. Because I cook using a lot of garlic, and just to be safe, I opt. to skip garlic for my dogs. Mostly Not Safe.

+ **Ginger** capsules, fresh ginger, and ginger tea can help ease motion sickness. If you suspect your dog is prone to motion sickness, give ginger (check with a holistic Vet for dosage) 30 minutes before you travel to allow it to take effect. Fresh ginger is too spicy to give your dog. Kind of Safe

- **Gingerroot** (.5 to 35 mg. twice a day), helps prevent nausea. Do not give on an empty stomach and, if taking anticoagulants, it may enhance bleeding. Consult a holistic vet for proper dosages. Kind of Safe

- **Green Beans** (cooked, chopped) provide cardiovascular benefits and antioxidant support, and contain Vitamin C, A, Magnesium, and fiber to name a few. Safe

- **Licorice Root** can be used as a dry herb or dried concentrated extract or alcohol tincture. Principal uses are as a cough expectorant and anti-inflammatory. Consult a holistic Vet for proper dosages. Kind of Safe

- **Liver** is an excellent source of B vitamins (Thiamin, Riboflavin, Niacin, Pantothenic acid, and Folic acid), Vitamin A, Vitamin K, and iron. Too much liver can be toxic to dogs due to high vitamin A content. Therefore, it is best to limit the amount of liver fed to your dog to 1 g. of fresh liver/kg. body weight per day.) Use freeze-dried or bake your own liver treat (see Steve's Homemade Liver Treat recipe!) Kind of Safe

- **Meat.** Lean meat (chicken, beef, lamb, buffalo, etc.) with no visible fat provides protein and is an excellent balanced source of amino acids -- the building blocks of muscle in your dog's body. Meat is also a great source of B vitamins (Thiamin, Riboflavin, Niacin, Pantothenic acid, Pyridoxine, and Cobalamine) that give your dog energy and help metabolize the body. Safe

- **Meat (processed)** including deli beef, turkey; bacon, sausage and hot dogs, contain chemical preservatives that can cause cancer. Sodium nitrites have been linked to increasing the risk of colon and other forms of cancer, so be sure to choose only uncured meat products made without nitrates, preferably from grass-fed animals. Moderation is key. Not So Safe

- **Melon** (peeled, seeds removed. Most types of melons are healthy and a great treat (especially watermelon, honeydew, and cantaloupe). Safe

🞢 **Olives (pitted)** are a great source of healthy Omega-3's. Many are high in fat and too salty for dogs. Not So Safe

🞢 **Olive Oil** contains Omega-3 and creates to a healthy, shiny coat and has been shown to reduce triglyceride levels and play a significant role in preventing dangerous heart abnormalities and cognitive dysfunction. Good for treating ear mites. When cooking with olive oil, never cook on high heat. Safe

🞢 **Oregano** is an antioxidant rich in vitamins A, C, K, omega-3 fatty acids, minerals (calcium, iron, manganese), and fiber. It also has anti-bacterial properties. Safe

🞢 **Onions, Leeks & Shallots** (raw, cooked, or powder) can trigger diarrhea, vomiting, and fever in canines. In addition, onions contain large amounts of sulfur which can destroy red blood cells and cause severe anemic reactions. Pets affected by onion toxicity will develop hemolytic anemia where the red blood cells burst while circulating. Not Safe

🞢 **Parsley** (chopped small) aids digestion, prevents gas, and freshens "doggy breath". Parsley aids bladder and kidney infections, cleanses the blood, and improves stomach and liver functions. Parsley is a good source of calcium, potassium, and beta-carotene; rich in vitamins, potassium, and other minerals and can be added to your dog's meals once or twice a week. Anti-cancerous as it inhibits tumor growth. Safe

o **Parsley Oil** can be toxic for K9's, but fresh and dry parsley are safe and have many benefits. (See parsley above). Not Safe

o **Persimmons** seeds can cause intestinal inflammation, obstruction, and enteritis. The meat of the fruit is not dangerous in moderation. Not So Safe

🞢 **Peppermint.** Fresh peppermint leaves (chopped) in moderation aids digestion. Safe

- **Peaches** (pitted). Your dog can choke on the pit, which contains cyanide (toxic). A small bite of the fruit meat is fine, but too much can cause diarrhea. Peaches are often referred to as the 'Fruit of Calmness' in Hungary. Helps reduce anxiety and have been known to remove worms from the intestines in humans. Kind of Safe

- **Pears** (cored, seeded is a must!) Pears contain vitamin C, and antioxidants essential for helping prevent free-radical damage. Pears can help reduce the risk of cancer, but the pear pit also contains small doses of cyanide and can be fatal, especially to a small dog. The pit can also get lodged in the dog's throat or intestinal tract; more than a small bite or two may cause diarrhea. Not So Safe

- **Peas** are a good source of thiamin, phosphorous, and potassium. If using snow peas in the pod, remove the string to avoid choking in small dogs. Safe

- **Plums** (pitted) Contain vitamin C and antioxidants. A tiny bite of the fruit meat will probably cause no harm but for a dog especially a small dog if they ingest the pit it can be fatal. The pit contains cyanide and they can cause serious obstructions. Not So Safe

- **Popcorn** (air popped, stovetop; no butter or salt) is a great low-calorie treat for your dog. Contains potassium as well as bone-building minerals phosphorous, magnesium, and calcium. Un-salted popcorn is a great snack for most dogs, but a small dog may have trouble getting it stuck in their throat. Microwave bags are lined with chemicals linked to causing liver, testicular, and pancreatic cancer. The U.S. Environmental Protection Agency (EPA) says that perfluorooctanoic acid (PFOA) in microwave popcorn bag linings as "likely" carcinogenic. Some dogs have difficulty digesting corn. Mostly Safe

- **Microwaved Popcorn**: Not Safe

- **Potatoes** provide an excellent source of potassium, especially sweet potatoes. Avoid the potato eye (green sprouts contain solanine) which causes stomach upset, increased thirst, urination, and weakness. A large amount of white potatoes can cause a dog's blood sugar to rise quickly. Avoid giving dogs with diabetes white potatoes. If your dog doesn't have diabetes, then a small bite or two of white potato is okay. Avoid chives which are dangerous. Plain potatoes with a tiny touch of butter served in moderation are okay. Mostly Safe

- **Sweet Potatoes** are one of the healthiest foods you can feed a dog! Sweet potatoes don't have the same effect as white potatoes. Safe

- **Pomegranates** are high in Vitamin C, antioxidants, potassium, and fiber, but many dogs will have a hard time digesting the seeds. Although the juice is not toxic, I don't encourage feeding your dog pomegranates as the seeds cause GI irritation and central nervous system depression (according to ASPCA). Not So Safe

- **Pomegranate Extract** is an antioxidant that shows promise in prevention and treatment of canine cardiac disease. It also possesses significant antioxidants and cyto-protective activities in canine endothelial cells. I recommend consulting with a holistic Vet. Safe

- **Pumpkin** (cooked or canned; pure) I give a medium-size dog one tablespoon of pure canned to help alleviate constipation. Beware: if the can says "pumpkin spice," it contains Allspice and nutmeg which dogs should avoid. Safe

- **Pumpkin Seeds** (shelled, unsalted; whole or ground) can be used as a de-wormer for tapeworms. For a medium-size dog: 1 teaspoon twice a day until gone. Tapeworms look like long grains of rice. It's always a good idea to examine your dog's feces. Worms cannot always be seen by the naked eye, so when in doubt of parasites, always check with your Vet. Pumpkin seeds can also help with arthritis pain by reducing inflammation. For easier digestion it is best to grind or crush them first, especially for a small dog. Mostly Safe

- **Rice Flour** is a highly-digestible carbohydrate. Brown rice (higher in protein and a little lower in fat) is an easily digestible carbohydrate and good source of energy. Rice is also good when your dog has an upset tummy. Most commercial kibble and canned dog food contain feed rice (scraps of rice left over from rice products) which absorbs toxins during processing. Human-grade rice is Safe

- **Rosemary** (fresh and dry) contains oils that can cause stomach upset or depression of the nervous system if consumed in large amounts. Safe /Not Safe

- **Raisins.** Rid your dog's pantry of raisins! Raisins contain an unknown toxin, which can damage the kidneys causing (renal) failure and death. Symptoms include: loss of appetite, lethargy, and abdominal pain, dehydration, passing only a small amount of urine, abnormal drinking and urination. Not Safe

- **Raw Vegetables.** Dogs have shorter digestive tracts than humans and cannot digest most raw vegetables whole or in large chunks. It's best to put them through a food processor before giving them to your dog. Safe /Not Safe

- **Rhubarb** leaves contain oxalates which can affect the digestive, nervous, and urinary systems. Due to its tart flavor, rhubarb isn't something your dog may be attracted to, but it's still a good idea to keep it out of reach. The plant contains soluble calcium oxalates, which can cause renal (kidney) failure. Not Safe

- **Ribs.** Dogs can't have ribs! Like chicken bones, they can puncture intestines. Not Safe

- **Salt** (processed table salt). Excess salt intake can cause canine kidney problems, and, if consumed in large quantities, may lead to electrolyte imbalances. Salt regulates blood pressure, carries nutrients to blood cells, and allows the brain to communicate with muscles to move-on-demand via sodium-potassium ion exchange. Himalayan pink sea salt is the most concentrated and purest form of salt on the earth, mined from sea salt deposits from ancient sea beds. Moderation is key! Safe/Not Safe

- **Sugary Foods** are not very safe, especially for puppies. They lead to obesity, doggy dental problems, and diabetes. A small bite now and again and your dog should be fine. Not So Safe

+ **Tomatoes** contain tomantine and atropine, which can cause digestive issues in dogs. The stems and leaves are the biggest concern. Avoid any nightshade vegetables like eggplant (although a small amount of tomato with no stems, seeds, or leaves is usually okay). I avoid tomato sauce for my dogs as it may contain seeds, etc. In my experience, dogs don't do well with tomatoes, but if they do ingest a few bites they should be fine. Not So Safe

+ **Safflower Oil** contains essential omega-6 fatty acids. Safe

+ **Sage** (fresh leaves or dry seasoning) may help with repelling fleas. I don't recommend feeding your dog sage as a treat or in a meal, but if they ingest a little bite that was used as seasoning for one of your meals that is generally safe. Sage tea has been effective at fighting gingivitis. Sage as an essential oil mostly safe but not to ingest. Can cause skin irritation and should <u>not</u> be used orally. Mostly Safe

+ **Salmon** (cooked and boned) wild salmon contains omega-3 fatty acids which are good for a dog's coat and skin. (Avoid farmed Salmon). Never feed raw salmon to your dog. Safe

+ **Sardines.** The greatest nutritional value of sardines resides in their high concentration of omega-3 fatty acids which are good for a dog's coat and skin. Don't give a small puppy a large sardine. Moderation is key. Safe

+ **Shellfish** must be cooked and free of sauce. The shell can cause serious obstructions and are not safe for dogs, but when certain shells are ground up they can help with K9 Arthritis. If shellfish is given in excess, or cooked in fat, it can cause pancreatitis in dogs. I personally have never had a problem giving a small bite of cooked lobster, crab, shrimp, scallops or oysters to my dogs, but I only recommend sharing one small bite. Safe

- **Spinach** contains vitamins K, iron. In moderation it is Safe

- **Squash** can be added to bulk up a dog's stool and is a good source of beta carotene (vitamin A). Tip: remove the seeds (for little dogs). Safe

- **Strawberries** contain lots of vitamin C, are an antioxidant, and can strengthen a dog's immune system and even help whiten teeth. Safe

- **Sunflower Seeds** (shelled) contain Omega-6, good for healthy canine skin and coat as well as a visible sheen. For easier digestion, it is best to grind or crush them first, especially for a small dog. Safe

- **Thyme** (fresh and dry) contains vitamins C, A, K, iron, manganese and calcium. Thyme also contains antioxidants and is an anti-bacterial. Safe

- **Turkey** (organic) is an excellent source of lean protein for dogs; contains selenium, niacin, iron, zinc, phosphorus, potassium, and L-tryptophan, used in the body to produce the B-vitamin, niacin. Turkey is a precursor to serotonin and can calm aggression and mellow your dog out. Safe

- **Turmeric Root** has strong antioxidant and anti-inflammatory properties and is used as a cancer preventive. It also increases bile production and protects the stomach and liver. Safe

- **Xylitol (artificial sweetener)** found in gum, candy, and toothpaste, to name a few, can cause low blood sugar (hypoglycemia) which can result in vomiting, weakness and collapse. In high doses, it can cause liver failure. Not Safe

- **Yogurt (plain)** is an excellent source of protein; has less milk sugar, and is easily digested… even by lactose-intolerant animals. It contains beneficial bacteria that support the digestive and immune system and is also a great source of calcium. A tablespoon of low-fat plain yogurt with live active bacteria (the active bacteria works like probiotics) can restore some of the beneficial bacteria when your dog is on antibiotics. Safe

🍴 **Zucchini** contains foliate and potassium; the rinds are rich in beta-carotene. Safe

Disclaimer: While there are a vast array of delicious, nutritious foods that are safe for dogs, many human foods are not safe or recommended for canine consumption. This book only *suggests* that safe human food (in moderation) be used in addition to your dog's regular dog food. A list of unsafe foods is included in this book, but by no means is this list intended to be inclusive of all possible food hazards. Always check with your Vet before changing your dog's diet. If your dog gets sick from eating human food, immediately call **Animal Poison Control Center (ASPCA) 1-888-426-4435** or go to your nearest Veterinary Emergency Hospital.

Q: What about Toxic Plants?

Toxic Plants and Flowers: Aloe, Amaryllis, Autumn Crocus, Bird of Paradise, Caladium, Calla Lily, Daffodil, Day Lily, Dieffenbachia, Dumb Cane, Elephant Ears, English Ivy, Foxglove, Gladiolas, Holly, Hyacinth, Hydrangea, Iris, Kalanchoe, Lily of the Valley, Marijuana, Mistletoe, Morning Glory, Mother-in-Law, Narcissus, Nightshade, Oleander, Onion, Peace Lily, Poinsettia, Philodendron, Rhododendron, Sago Palm, Schefflera, Stargazer Lily, Tomato (green parts only), Tulip, Yew, to name a few…

Non-Toxic Plants: Acorn Summer Squash, African Violet, Air Plant, Baby Rubber Plant, Bamboo Palm, Banana Squash, Basil, Begonia, Bottlebrush, Cactus Camellia, Carob, Coriander, Crepe Myrtle, Dandelions, Dill, Forsythia, Marigold, Gardenia, Gerber Daisy, Hollyhock, Jacob's Ladder, Jasmine, Mint, Moss phlox, Orchid, Oregano, Peppermint, Petunia, Rose, Sage, Salvia, Snapdragon, Spearmint, Spider Plant…

(*This is not a complete list of every toxic or non-toxic plant. The ASPCA has a "Petoxins" App. Whenever I'm shopping for a plant, I consult Petoxins.)

Q: What about Grass?

Grass contains enzymes that aid digestion. For this reason, many dogs ingest outdoor grasses and vegetation. Pay close attention, however, as your dog may be trying to tell you that his stomach is bothering him. Avoid chemical-treated lawns and keep your dog away from all house plants, especially poinsettias as they can be poisonous. If you see your dog chewing on a houseplant, remove the plant or place it out of the dog's reach. If they have ingested the plant, consult your Veterinarian. (See more on Toxic Plants).

WATER & Your Dog's Health

Newborn Puppies: Water = 85% of body weight
Adult Dogs: Water = 50% of body weight

Your dog's health also depends on drinking adequate amounts of clean water. Water not only quenches thirst but also helps regulate body temperature which aids digestion, keeps tissues lubricated, and flushes toxins and waste from the body. If your dog's water bowl is dry, she cannot grab a water bottle from the refrigerator when she is thirsty. Even though I have trained dogs to grab a bottle of water out of the fridge for me (advanced trick), dogs depend on us to provide them with fresh, drinkable water. So whenever you reach for a glass of water, check the water level in your dog's bowl too! I like to put more than one water bowl out so it is always readily available. Dogs do fight over water bowls… so by having more than one if you have multiple dogs, they are less apt to fight over the bowl if you place several down, instead of just one. Also, by using a porcelain or ceramic bowl, the water will stay 10% to 20% cooler (plastic and aluminum tend to get very hot, which in turn, warms up the water.) Many dogs chew plastic bowls, so if you're not worried about the heat factor, I like to use stainless steel bowls.

Beware of Bloat

Just like I was told as a child, not to surf or swim after I ate and drank a lot...

I've talked to many Vets on the subject of bloat and no one really knows what causes it for sure. Usually bloat is most common in large barrel-shape chested dogs and most people think it's from eating and drinking too fast. That's why I recommend using a slow -feeder bowl and not allowing a dog prone to bloat to over eat, over drink, and then run and play. The same way you want your food to digest before you go swimming; it's the same for K9s. In fact, 25 percent of Great Danes will get bloat at some point in their lives. You have very little time to get your dog to the Vet. You have minutes to maybe a couple hours, and often, your only hope is surgery.

When I worked as a Vet tech, I was taught that when a dog is under anesthesia and they are laying on their side and it's time to turn them to the other side -- it should be done slowly with the paws and legs underneath, as opposed to paws and legs up over the top because their stomachs can twist. I've had Vets tell me that they have even seen 8-pound toy poodles get bloat, but generally, large dogs are more prone to bloat, probably due to large amounts of food being gobbled down too fast, or food paired with stress, etc....

Many people make pup-sicles (popsicles) for their pooches, but I don't recommend it. I used to put ice cubes in the dog's water bowl on a hot day, but not anymore. When a dog swallows ice it can cause cramps and muscle spasms and your dog can get bloat. If your dog is a breed that is prone to bloat, don't let them drink a large amount of water all at once, especially if they are overheated. You can slow a dog's overdrinking using a slow-feeder bowl if they drink excessively as it will take longer to drink. Whatever the reason is that dogs get bloat, I don't want it to be from a pup-sicle or ice cube -- I don't even want to take a chance, which is why I've taken them off my recipe list. I won't even give my dog water from the cool side of my water dispenser; room temperature water is just fine. You can always cool your dog off by putting a cool, wet towel on their inner thighs.

If you see the following signs and you think your dog may have bloat, get him to the Vet Emergency ASAP!

- Looking for a place to lie down and curl up
- Unable to get comfortable
- Constantly pacing or even just collapsing
- Heavy panting, breathing faster than normal
- Extreme drooling
- An extended abdomen

DOGGY DIET

Whether you choose to feed your dog commercial kibble for convenience, portion control, or balanced nutrition, you will want to be aware of nutritional requirements including protein, carbs & fats. I use homemade *dog bites* to supplement 10-20% of a dog's daily diet for training and (with your Vet's approval) I suggest you do the same. Some people choose to feed their dog homemade meals because it costs less, is healthier, they can control chemicals and GMO's (Genetically Modified Ingredients). An easy, balanced approach that I recommend (found in the Dog Bites Recipe section of this book) is to add cooked veggies or small bites of cooked meat to your dog's kibble.

You will find amazing human meals that you can share or modify and share with you dog, as well as dangerous foods you would never want to feed your dog. Serving guidelines are provided on most commercial dog food, so that is a good place to start when factoring in portion size. Remember…you need to feed your dog the right portions, preferably in two or more feedings per day. Keep in mind, most people feed an eight-week-old puppy three to four times a day; an adult twice a day. But I say you can feed a dog throughout the day as a means to train. (Try to do it around breakfast or dinner so you don't interfere with their potty training schedule). There is no reason you can't feed throughout the day, as dogs forage and hunt in the wild. I suggest using a measuring cup to feed your dog to ensure an accurate amount of food each day. Also, some breeds like Great Danes, even as adults are recommended to eat smaller meals three to four times a day to decrease the chance of bloat. All dogs are different…if you have any concerns I suggest you discuss your dog's weight and diet with your vet

According to many Vets I've spoken to on the subject, canines require 20%-30% from protein sources such as chicken, beef, poultry, lamb, eggs; 40%-60% from complex carbohydrates such as whole grains, potatoes, pasta; 20%-40% of their nutrients from raw- and lightly-cooked vegetables. Vitamin and mineral formulas with calcium, kelp powder, lecithin granules, etc. can also be supplemented. I also suggest adding Omega essential fatty acids to their diet by cooking with safflower oil, or sprinkling wheat germ or flaxseed oils on their food.

PROTEIN: A chain of amino acids used for tissue repair.

According to Veterinarian and nutrition experts I have spoken to, when it comes to protein for K9's, variety is critical to provide a full spectrum of amino acids, essential fatty acids, trace minerals, vitamins, and antioxidants necessary for Fido to stay fit and healthy. Protein is essential to the growth and maintenance of coat, skin, tendons, ligaments, and cartilage. Like humans, hormones and antibodies in the immune system also require protein. Since protein is vital for cell replacement (as cells and tissues wear out) it's essential that a dog's diet provide a regular supply of protein to replace these normal losses.

Feeding your dog a diet of primarily animal-based protein helps maintain muscle mass, reverse age-related skeletal and muscle loss in senior dogs, and enhances overall health. The quality of protein you give your dog matters… If the label says "crude protein" that means it may contain carcasses and other waste from slaughtered animals. Most Veterinarians and nutritionists I've talked to favor chicken as an ideal protein for dogs. Here are a few animal protein sources to feed your dog:

- Boneless chicken breast or thigh; chopped, ground, or minced
- Hard boiled eggs
- Lean beef, bison, lamb, or buffalo
- Turkey, duck, ostrich

- Salmon, trout (avoid raw salmon)
- Liver (in moderation)
- Rabbit, goat, pork (cooked)

VEGETARIAN PROTEIN: Here are just a few…

- Cottage cheese
- Tofu (firm)
- Soybeans (cooked)
- Lentils (cooked)
- Peanut butter (a legume, not a nut)

CARBOHYDRATES: Starches, sugars, and fibers from plants are used as a source of quick energy. All dry dog food contains carbohydrates.

Serve with Animal Proteins:
- Rice (cooked)
- Macaroni (cooked)
- Potato (cooked with skin) chopped or mashed
- Rolled oats (cooked)
- Yams or sweet potatoes (cooked)

Serve with Vegetarian Proteins:
- Cooked brown rice
- Cooked potato (with skin), chopped or mashed in moderation
- Cooked macaroni
- Cooked rice
- Cooked black-eyed peas
- Rolled oats, cooked (1-1/4 cup raw)
- Cooked kidney beans

FATS: A concentrated source of energy, necessary for vitamin transport.

Your Dog's body requires essential fatty acids (EFA's) to function and maintain healthy skin and a shiny coat. Itchy skin, fleas (fleas are less attracted to supple, unbroken skin), and joint issues can be improved with EFA supplements. Good sources of EFA's include salmon.

- Canola oil
- Rice bran
- Chicken fat
- Salmon oil
- Sunflower oil
- Safflower oil

MINERALS: inorganic elements that make up 4% of dog's body weight. Essential minerals regulate metabolic functions and sustain life by presenting tissue structure.

Q: How do you know if your dog is eating a well-balanced diet?

Check their eyes, coat, and breath. Are they bright-eyed? Do they have pleasant "doggy" breath and a shiny coat? Make sure they are fed foods made with the right balance of protein, vitamins and minerals to support growth and a healthy lifestyle. I suggest you train with their meals throughout the day. Like humans, all dogs are unique individuals, so when it comes to a healthy weight somewhere in the middle-weight range is actually ideal. Females are usually smaller than males and may weigh less as a result. Below is a list of some of the wonderful dog breeds that I train (does not include every breed). See if you can find your breed to determine an ideal weight?

SMALL/MEDIUM K9 BREEDS:

- Chihuahua: 4 lbs.
- Yorkie: 6 lbs.
- Affenpinscher: 6 -8 lbs.
- Brussels Griffin: 9 lbs.
- Italian Greyhound: 6-10 lbs.
- Fox Terrier: 7-11 lbs.
- Miniature Pinscher: 8-10 lbs.
- Silky Terrier: 8-10 lbs.
- Papillion: 8-10 lbs.
- Lhasa Apso: 10-11 lbs.
- Havanese: 7-13 lbs.
- Manchester Terrier: 10 lbs.
- Maltese: 5-9 lbs.
- Pekingese: 9 lbs.
- Shih Tzu: 9-16 lbs.
- Coton De Tulear: 10-12 lbs.
- Jack Russell Terrier: 13-17 lbs.
- Cairn Terrier: 14 lbs.
- Standard Dachshund: 5-9
- Bichon: 10-18 lbs.
- Mini Schnauzer: 15 lbs.
- Welsh Corgi Cardigan: 25-30 lbs.
- Welsh Corgi Pembroke: 30-38 lbs.
- Standard Schnauzer 35-45 lbs.
- Pug: 14-18 lbs.
- Pekingese: 9 lbs.
- Mini Schnauzer: 15 lbs.
- Boston Terrier: 19 lbs.
- Beagle: 30 lbs.

- o Pembroke Welsh Corgi: 30 lbs.
- o Brittany: 35 lbs.
- o Siberian Husky: 50 lbs.
- o Standard Poodle: 50 lbs.

LARGE K9 BREEDS:

- o German Shepard: 75-90 lbs.
- o Golden Retriever: 70 lbs.
- o Old English Sheep dog: 95 lbs.
- o Great Pyrenees: 115 lbs.
- o Cane Corso: 90-125 lbs.
- o Doberman Pinscher: 70-110 lbs.
- o Mastiff: 175-220 lbs.
- o Neapolitan Mastiff: 110-150 lbs.
- o Great Dane: 130 lbs.
- o Newfoundland: 140 lbs.
- o Bernese Mountain: 80-110 lbs.
- o Akita: 85-130 lbs.
- o Alaskan Malamute: 75-85 lbs.
- o American Bulldog: 70-100 lbs.
- o Saint Bernard: 120-180 lbs.
- o Rhodesian Ridgeback: 85 lbs.
- o Rottweiler: 95-130 lbs.

K9 WEIGHT	DAILY CALORIC REQUIREMENT
10 lbs.	400-500
20 lbs.	700-800
40 lbs.	1,100-1,400
75 lbs.	1,750-2,000

As a general rule of thumb, you want to feel your dog's ribs but not see them visibly. Ideal-weight dogs have an hourglass figure and a visible waistline. You don't want a dog with a table back you could rest a beer on! If this is the case, then they are in need of a diet and exercise plan to ensure they live a long, healthy life as a member of your family!

Underweight:
- Ribs are easily visible; little or no fat
- Waistline visible

Ideal Weight:
- Thin layer of fat covers the ribs; you can feel ribs easily, but they are not obviously visible
- Defined "cut" muscles in the loin area

Overweight:
- You cannot see ribs, spine or hips at all due to layer of fat
- Waist may be visible, but not prominent

Obese:
- Excess, thick layer of fat cover ribs, spine & hips
- No visible waistline

Q: What Causes Obesity in Dogs?

So, you are probably thinking... "How do I tell if my dog is overweight? I am blinded by love and food is love!" If they weigh 20-25% above the ideal weight for their age, gender and breed, they are overweight. If your pooch weighs 30% or more above the ideal weight, they are obese. Too much food and too little exercise can lead to diabetes, heart disease, arthritis, and lethargy, to name a few.

The reality is that humans contribute to obesity in their pets so be mindful when it comes to feeding and giving treats. Yes, treats count! Dogs can't diet; they need your help to keep them healthy. Try keeping a food journal for a week to determine who is feeding Fido. To avoid overfeeding, post a note that says, "Fido has been fed," so other family members don't feed him again. Trust me; many dogs will act like they have not eaten a morsel all day! As many as 1 in 2 dogs in the United States are overweight or obese, so you don't want your pup to become one of them. Contributing factors to canine obesity often overlooked:

- Hypothyroidism (or other ailments)
- Lack of physical activity
- Over-feeding; pay attention to what neighbors or dog walkers are feeding
- Not knowing what family member has fed the dog?
- Kids dropping food from the table
- Feeding dogs table scraps in the kitchen
- Free-feeding: dog's bowl is full of kibble all day so you don't know how much they are eating
- Nervous eating: dogs will often adopt the behaviors of their owners

- Treats, rawhides, and bones add extra calories to a dog's diet – it's like eating fast food!

Obese dogs are harder to train and would prefer to nap rather than take a long walk or fetch a ball, so walking is great for both of you! The number-one health issue for older dogs is obesity, so practice portion control rather than feeding on demand – even though your dog looks at you with those hard-to-resist puppy eyes. Over feeding a senior dog can cause a myriad of health issues and may even shorten her life. Avoid killing your canine with kindness. According to Arden Moore, "Excess weight can reduce the length of a dog's life by as much as 20%... Calorie wise, one burger with all the trimmings fed to a 40-pound dog is the equivalent of a 150-pound person eating six burgers."

Excess weight can reduce a dog's lifespan by 20%.

Check the Canine Weight Guidelines (in this book) or ask your Veterinarian to give your dog a complete check-up which will include assessing weight. If indeed your dog is overweight or obese, and after ruling out hypothyroidism or other disease that can cause weight gain, you want to cut back calories gradually and increase exercise slowly to avoid nutritional deficiencies and injuries.

If your dog has put on a few pounds… and, since a dog can't go on a diet by themselves, try adding more fiber to their diet. Fiber is a necessary carbohydrate that pulls water from the colon to aid digestion and stimulate intestinal movement. Fiber not only helps Fido feel full, it also aids digestion and helps prevents constipation. Try adding canned pumpkin, carrots, or cooked oatmeal to their meal (see Dog Bites Recipes). Measure meal portions and try treating with metabolism-boosting carrots, apple slices, zucchini, etc. Kelp powder is also an excellent way to speed up metabolism and break down fats in the diet. Sprinkle a teaspoon of kelp powder on their food or add a teaspoonful of apple cider vinegar to their water bowl.

How do you help a K9 lose excess pounds? Vets say dogs should lose no more weight than: 1-2% total body weight per week. Your dog may have trained you too well to over-feed them! Try to limit calories while meeting nutritional needs daily. Use every opportunity to play and exercise with your dog!

Senior Dogs & Nutrition

Senior dogs require more protein than you may think. According to **THE WHOLE DOG JOURNAL:** *Diet and the Older Dog*, senior dogs have difficulty metabolizing protein, and therefore, require 18% protein in their daily diet. For most pet food companies, chicken seems to be the protein of choice. Other proteins like beef, duck, lamb, goat, trout, turkey, ostrich eggs, and dairy are good; but eggs and dairy shouldn't be the sole protein in your dog's diet.

A concern many of my older dogs experience is muscle wasting. If a senior dog doesn't get enough protein, muscle wasting can occur because the body needs protein for many functions, and if the body can't get it in the diet, it breaks down existing muscle tissue. Now, you may be concerned that feeding more protein would result in higher calories and weight gain; keep in mind that protein and carbohydrates provide *equal* calories.

Consuming too many carbs can increase inflammation and contribute to arthritis pain and immobility in senior dogs, so pay attention to fats and carbs. You may also want to consider adding a dog vitamin supplement to ensure your dog is getting all the nutrients required. Always ask your Vet before changing your dog's diet in the event they have a medical condition where too much protein is contraindicated. Keep in mind that dogs in their "golden years" burn one-half as many calories as young dogs, so check with your Veterinarian on how much to either scale back or increase your dog's daily serving amounts. Remember to measure portions to avoid overfeeding. Have fun with your senior dog…make a trail of small meatballs around the yard and have an older dog hunt and forage for the treat. This is great exercise and also stimulates their brain.

Tell-Tail signs of senior or geriatric dogs:

- ❖ arthritis
- ❖ obesity
- ❖ deterioration of skin and coat
- ❖ loss of muscle mass
- ❖ more frequent intestinal problems
- ❖ dental problems
- ❖ decreased ability to fight off infection

*Teaching an older dog to do new tricks or
going on a walk in a new place can generate new brain cells.*

I get calls from clients all the time asking, "What can I feed my dog?" "Do I need to take him to the Vet if he ate something he shouldn't have?" With my own dogs it's the same; I want to know when I'm cooking for myself what is safe and what is not safe because I like to share bites of my food with my dog for about 10-20 percent of his diet. I love to share my passion for cooking human meals to teach you how to share with your family; your dog is part of your family. I hope I can enlighten you with some amazing human meals that I enjoy and teach you how to train your dog at the same time. As a Certified Professional Dog Trainer, I've worked (and lived) in animal hospitals and have been successfully training dogs for over two decades. And let me tell you, I've worked with senior dogs with liver disease, diabetes, Cushing's, cancer, arthritis, etc., so it's a good idea to have your senior dog's diet individually tailored by your Vet especially if they have an underlining medical condition.

Fast-Food Fido

If you are on the road with your traveling companion – whether a day trip or a trek across country – you may want to think ahead and bring some of my homemade Granola Bark, Salmon Rice Cakes, Yam, Apple, or Banana Chips, organic carrot snacks or other healthy *Dog Bite* Recipes found in this book. If you forgot to bring healthy snacks and end up at a fast food joint while on the road with Fido, here are some tips on how to share safe fast food bites with your dog! If your dog has not eaten a variety of different foods, it's a good idea to start with small bites. I'm not suggesting feeding your dog fast food in place of their entire meal, but rather, just sharing just a few bites. When in doubt on whether a food item is safe don't take the chance! It's always best to check with your Veterinarian first.

The best part is… you and your hounds can order off the drive-thru menu and pick it up within minutes without ever leaving the car! **McDonalds, Arby's, Wendy's, Jack In The Box, In n' Out, Carl's Jr., Subway, El Polo Loco** and even **Der Weinershcnitzel** all have dog-friendly menu options. Give one bite for a small dog; two for medium; three for a large breed. Order a plain, sauce-free burger with bread, cheese and meat only. If your dog loves chicken, order a plain grilled chicken sandwich, "Hold the sauce." Avoid pickles, lettuce, and tomato (non-toxic but may not agree with Fido). Always avoid onions which *are* toxic. Breakfast items like a bite of an Egg McMuffin are fine! A bite of oatmeal is great as long as you avoid toppings like nuts and raisins that can be toxic to K9's. Jack in the Box has a tasty turkey-bacon-cheddar grilled sandwich and a dog bite or two is fine for most dogs. The same applies to Arby's – a bite or two of a plain roast beef or turkey sandwich and a bite of cheese or bacon (no sauce) is okay to share. What about French fries? One or two fries are usually okay, but avoid ordering your dog their own super-sized serving.

You can even share a non-seasoned chicken or turkey sandwich from Subway with egg, cheese, a bite of bacon, and cucumber if your dog likes it and a tiny bite of tuna from your tuna sandwich. Subway drenches their tuna in mayo which is not good for K9's (but a little bite shouldn't hurt). If you're in the mood for El Pollo Loco, order chicken breast (remove skin, bones, and fat) with steamed vegetables and sweet potato fries. Carl's Jr. has tasty sweet potato fries and delicious turkey. At Der Wienerschnitzel, a plain hot dog (turkey or beef) with a touch of cheese will make Fido pleased!

RECIPES

Eat like a king and love to cook!

I've lived with dogs so long I think I might be part Labrador! I'm a food hound for sure…I get great satisfaction out of cooking delicious meals for friends and relatives when they come over for a BBQ or Holiday feast. Over the past 20 years, many of my Steve Brooks K9U clients have gotten to taste my delicious *dog bites*, so I thought I would share some of my favorite recipes with you and your family. You will discover as you cook that your four-legged family member wants to have a taste too! So make sure to pay close attention to using ingredients that are *safe* when cooking Dog Bites Recipes!

My recipes include healthy Southern California inspirations intended to be shared (in small bites) with your dog because food is fun and a great way to train and bond. I'm a Dog Trainer, not a Veterinarian or nutritionist, so I want to emphasize that these recipes are not meant to replace a balanced diet for your K9. Keep in mind that any change in diet may take a few days for a dog's digestive system to adjust and be sure to refer to the section on non-toxic and toxic foods in this book. While most of these delicious foods can be shared with Fido… the key when feeding K9's human foods is moderation.

STEVE BROOKS' DOG BITES COOKING TIPS:

- Always choose fresh ingredients; it makes a big difference in nutrients and how delicious food tastes!

- Thoroughly cook meats, seafood, poultry, and eggs; dogs can get salmonella just like humans.

- Wash your hands and clean all food products thoroughly making sure to wash vegetables in cold water to remove pesticides, dirt, and insects.

- Avoid foods that contain chemicals, byproducts or additives that are difficult to digest.

- Many foods are heavily treated with pesticides, so I recommend buying organic whenever possible. When cooking with root vegetables like spinach, kale, collard greens, summer squash, or potatoes, I always choose organic. I'm a little less picky if it's something like a banana or a coconut.

> Vegetables are easier for K9s to digest and retain nutrients if they are cooked. I suggest chopping and steaming veggies for K9's consumption. Let the veggies cool until they are just warm to the touch.

> Provide plenty of fresh, clean drinking water for your dog. Change the bowl several times a day – and wash your dog's water bowl once in a while for crying out loud!

DOG BITE RULE: Serve one tiny dog bite to a tiny dog; one small dog bite for a small dog; two for a medium dog; and three for a large breed. Daily K9 diet consists of 90% Vet-recommended foods supplemented with 10% *dog bites*. All recipes should be given in moderation. *Please read all K9 Notes before sharing bites with your dog!

Dog Bite: Portion of fish for small K9

***K9 NOTE:** Be sure to read the K9 note for each recipe before sharing bites with your dog. While many recipes are completely *dog friendly*, others are only dog friendly if modified. I've added a few recipes that you may not love, but your dog sure will! I will also show you how to make a completely separate doggie version of human meals to please both you and your pup! Look for the added bonus section with a few recipes that dogs should *never* eat, so please read the K9 notes before sharing bites with your dog! When in doubt if a certain food is safe for your dog, or if your dog has underlining health issues, never take a chance - always check with your veterinarian first!

APPETIZER, SALAD, SIDE & SAUCE BITES

APPLESAUCE

- 5 lbs. baking apples (Spartan or Macintosh)
- ¼ tsp. cinnamon
- 1 cinnamon stick (optional)
- ½ tsp. fresh finely grated ginger or 1/8 tsp. ground ginger
- Juice of 1 small lemon
- 1 cup water
- 3 tbsp. honey

<u>DIRECTIONS</u>: If using organic apples, wash and cut off any blemishes. Don't remove all the skin. Don't cut too close to the core. Discard all cores, stems, and seeds. Chop apples into 1-inch pieces. Place chopped apples into a pot with a tight-fitting lid. Add 1 cup of water, lemon juice, ginger, cinnamon stick, and/or ground cinnamon. Turn the heat to high for one minute only; then reduce heat to low and simmer the apples for 30 - 45 minutes, depending on the amount or until they're tender enough to mash. Turn off the stove. Gently mix in the honey and let cool a bit. Remove and discard the cinnamon stick and blend a small amount at a time in a blender or food processor; pulse until smooth.

K9 NOTE: *Minimal Modification.* The apple core and seeds are toxic to dogs. If you are using store-bought applesauce, you never know how much core and seeds are in the jar, probably not enough to cause a problem, but I still prefer homemade.

BAKED SQUASH

DOG BITE: Portion for Med-Large K9

- 1 butternut squash, cubed
- 1 fennel (bulb), chopped
- Green beans, chopped
- Blueberries
- 1 ½ tbsp. rosemary, minced
- Salt & pepper
- Olive oil

<u>DIRECTIONS</u>: Preheat oven to 450 degrees.

Peel and cut butternut squash into 1-inch cubes. Cut the bulb off the fennel and chop fine. Wash and string the green beans, then chop fairly small (so dogs won't choke on them). Mix the squash, fennel, beans, and blueberries in a bowl and season with rosemary, salt, pepper and olive oil. Coat the bottom of a Pyrex baking dish with canola oil spray. Add mixture and bake for 20 minutes until golden brown.

K9 NOTE: *Minimal Modification.* Cut everything small if you're sharing this dish with your dog; keep salt and pepper to a minimum.

BARBECUED SARDINES

- Sardines, fresh
- Lightly salted or unsalted saltine crackers
- Salt
- Lemon, sliced
- Parsley (garnish)

DIRECTIONS: Put fresh sardines on a fish rack; season with salt. Grill on the barbecue for 3 minutes on each side. Place on flat bread or cracker, garnish with parsley and lemon slices. For larger sardines you will need to clean and gut the fish and cook two extra minutes on each side. You can also make and share a canned sardine sandwich with your dog's using white bread and plain canned sardines (for humans, add mayo, tomato, and raw white or red onion).

K9 NOTE: *Minimal Modification.* For dogs, never feed onions, and skip the tomato, and lemon peel, but a couple drops of lemon juice is fine. Don't season your dog's sardine bite with salt. Too much salt is not good for your K9, so I wouldn't give your dog more than 1 or 2 saltine crackers. Sardines are rich in omega-3 fatty acids, which are good for a dog's coat and skin. Don't give a small puppy a large sardine. Moderation and common sense are key.

BEET ROOT SALAD WITH GOAT CHEESE

- Mixed greens
- Beet root
- Asparagus
- Goat cheese (Greek)
- 1 tbsp. pine nuts (avoid for K9)
- Chives, chopped (*humans only)
- Vinaigrette dressing

DIRECTIONS: Cut beet root into small cubes. Wash, peel and chop asparagus tips. Sauté asparagus in a pan, add salt and pepper, cook until al dente. In the same pan, toast pine nuts for a minute or two to warm up. Wash and dry chives and mixed greens and place in large salad bowl. Add goat cheese, asparagus (for humans, add pine nuts).

K9 VERSION: For Fido, create bites of asparagus, goat cheese, and beet root with a few drops of apple cider vinegar and olive oil.

K9 NOTE: *Minimal Modification.* Avoid giving pine nuts to your dog, but if they ingest a few by accident they should most likely be fine. Instead of the vinaigrette dressing, substitute with apple cider vinegar. Never give K9s onions or chives! Most dogs won't eat mixed greens. (See notes on nuts; some nuts are toxic.)

BABY POTATOES

Wash, poke with a fork, douse with olive oil, season with salt, pepper, Italian seasoning, fresh garlic, fresh thyme and rosemary. Place in Pyrex and bake at 350 for 45 min. until tender and golden. Serve with Whole Roast Chicken and Veggies.

K9 NOTE: *Minimal Modification.* Avoid giving dogs garlic. It's healthier to steam or boil a plain potato for Fido. Although non-toxic, dogs don't need the salt or butter. Moderation is key! (See notes on potatoes.)

BEST BAKED POTATO

- Russet potatoes (1 per person)
- Kosher salt
- Olive oil
- A touch of butter

DIRECTIONS: Pre-heat oven to 375 degrees.

Wash potatoes thoroughly with a paper towel and olive oil, (not water). Poke several holes in potatoes with a fork on both sides before or after you wash it with oil. Rub olive oil all over (the oil will keep the skin crispy and delicious). Sprinkle generously with kosher or Himalayan sea salt. You can always rub off a little bit of salt before you eat it. Set in hot oven with tongs directly on oven rack and bake for 1 hour. Serve with butter, salt and pepper.

K9 NOTE: *Minimal Modification.* It's healthier to steam or boil a plain potato for Fido. Although non-toxic, dogs don't need salt or butter. Only share a small bite of potato. Moderation is key!

BRUSSELS SPROUTS

- Brussels sprouts
- Olive oil
- Italian seasoning
- Salt optional
- Bacon

DIRECTIONS: Wash Brussels sprouts, then slice off the knobby bottoms and peel off any out of shape leaves. Slice in half, drizzle with olive oil, sprinkle with Italian seasoning, salt and toss to coat. Rub some oil onto a fry pan with a paper towel to coat the pan. Cut bacon strips into 2 – 3" pieces and place in fry pan on medium heat. About 1 - 2 minutes after bacon starts cooking, add Brussels sprouts in with the bacon to the pan. Flip/stir once or twice with a wooden spoon and cook for about 15 min. If the bacon starts to burn, turn down heat or take the bacon out and add back in at the end.

K9 NOTE: *Minimal Modification.* For Fido: serve 1 Brussels sprout cut small for a small dog; 2 for a large dog, with a few crumbs of bacon. For your K9, skip the salt or only use a dash.

CAULIFLOWER MASH

- 1 large or two small cauliflowers
- 1 tbsp. goat's or plain rice milk
- 2 tsp. of unsalted butter
- ¾ tsp. salt
- Dash white or black pepper (optional)

DIRECTIONS: Cut cauliflower into quarters and place into a pot of boiling water with an added pinch of salt. Boil for one min. then turn down heat to med-low and cover. Cook for about 4 more min., then turn down to simmer for about 8 - 10 min. until tender. Drain cauliflower; place back in the pot. Mash with a potato masher. Add milk, butter, salt, and pepper and mash until fluffy. Add a bit more milk if needed.

K9 NOTE: *Minimal Modification.* Use salt and pepper sparingly or skip it and season yours separately if sharing with your dog.

CAULIFLOWER WITH SAGE BACON

- 1 large or two small cauliflowers, cut into florets
- A touch of olive oil
- 1 tbsp. fresh sage leaves, chopped
- Bacon

DIRECTIONS: Lightly rub fry pan with olive oil using a paper towel. Cook two slices of bacon on med-low heat and remove when done. Then cook cauliflower flowerets in the bacon fat. Add a touch more olive oil if you need to on med-heat. About two min. later, add the sage cook about ten min. until tender. Add chopped bacon and serve.

K9 NOTE: *Minimal Modification.* The sage in this dish is too strong for Fido, so I make a separate plate for my dog consisting of a few bites of steamed cauliflower and a few crumbs of bacon.

GURDU YOGURT RICE

- ½ cup rice, rinsed, soaked
- Rice milk
- 16 oz. non-fat Greek yogurt
- 1/2 cup Yogurt Water and 16 oz. goat's milk
- Butter
- Sugar
- Cinnamon, ground

This recipe was handed down from my wife, Yasmine's grandmother and is a traditional Assyrian recipe. You can find yogurt drink already made in most Middle Eastern stores.

DIRECTIONS: Rinse and soak rice for at least one hour. Drain rice. Place yogurt in a mixing bowl. Using a mixer or Cuisinart, blend in water until smooth. Or use the pre-made drink or option above. Place rice and yogurt in a sauce pan on the stove and cook on low for about 30 minutes. Stir frequently with a wooden spoon, making sure it does not curdle. Add a touch more water only if you need to. Once it is soft and creamy, remove from heat. Add butter, cinnamon, sugar, and rice milk (if desired). Another option is to mix together and cook the rice in 16 oz. non-fat Greek yogurt and 16 oz. of goat's milk.

K9 NOTE: *Minimal Modification.* Great for dogs with diarrhea or as a treat or a Kong™ toy stuffing! Only give a bite of butter and cinnamon; skip the sugar.

HONEY CARROTS

- 3 – 4 carrots sliced
- 1 tbsp. honey
- 1 tbsp. butter
- 2 tbsp. Parmesan cheese, grated

DIRECTIONS: Wash and cut carrots as desired. Steam or boil carrots. While hot, add butter and honey and mix to coat. Add grated cheese on top.

K9 NOTE: *Minimal Modification.* Surprise your pup for good behavior! Moderation is key!

HONEYDEW CRAB ROLLS

- Crab meat, cooked and chilled
- 1-2 tbsp. Safflower or vegan Mayo
- 1/4 tsp. Vanilla extract
- 1 large Honeydew melon (ripe)
- Honey Vinaigrette dressing
- Salt
- Lemon
- Mixed greens

DIRECTIONS: To select a ripe melon, try playing it like a drum and listen for a hallow sound! Peel melon, cut into quarters, and remove seeds. Carefully use a mandolin slicer and thinly slice large rectangle shapes about the size of a piece of nori as if you were going to make a sushi hand roll. In a bowl: mix a couple of tablespoons of safflower or vegan Mayo with one ¼ of a lemon juiced, ½ capful of vanilla extract and a touch of salt.

Add 4-5 tablespoons of cooked and cooled crabmeat. Mix together. Place a teaspoon of crab mixture onto a thin slice of melon and roll up. For humans: top with baby lettuce greens and a bit of honey vinaigrette.

DRESSING: Mix olive oil, sherry vinegar, and honey.

K9 NOTE: *Minimal Modification.* A bit of melon, 1 or 2 small bites of cooked and cooled crab, a touch of mayo mixture, 1-2 drops of honey on top is fine for K9s. Crab can be too salty for dogs so just share a bite or two depending on the size of your dog. Skip lettuce and dressing for Fido as he probably won't eat it. Moderation is key.

BBQ OYSTERS

- 1 – 2 doz. oysters, fresh
- Butter, unsalted
- Pinch kosher salt
- Black pepper, freshly ground
- Touch of garlic, minced (not for Fido)
- Parmigianino cheese, grated
- Italian parsley, minced
- Lemon juice, squeezed

DIRECTIONS: Keep fresh oysters cold but do not store in water as oysters are alive and need to breathe. Never seal them tightly in a plastic bag. Place a layer of live oysters, deep-side-down (to retain their juices) between two layers of ice. Wash whole un-shucked oysters in cold water and dry.

RAW: Shuck oysters (up to an hour or two in advance). The colder the oyster, the easier it is to shuck. Keep oysters cold; partly for safety and to enhance flavor and texture.

GRILL: Place oysters in the shell (big-side-down) on the BBQ and grill 5 minutes depending on size. Use grilling gloves or long tongs to place and remove oysters from the grill. I like oysters grilled with just a dash of hot sauce, lemon, or Worcestershire.

SKILLET (humans only): Melt unsalted butter with a pinch of Kosher salt, freshly ground black pepper, a touch of minced garlic, Parmigianino cheese, minced Italian parsley, and a squeeze of lemon juice. Whisk together all ingredients to pour on top of oysters.

K9 NOTE: *Minimal Modification.* If your dog has never had oysters, test a bite first. Serve 1 plain cooked oyster (cooled and removed from shell) topped with Parmigiano-Reggiano and a diced leaf of parsley.

SALMON PATÉ

- 6 oz. fresh wild salmon (boneless, skinless)
- 1tbsp. celery, finely chopped
- 2 tbsp. Parsley, finely chopped
- 1 tbsp. butter (room temperature)
- 2 tbsp. plain cream cheese (room temperature)
- 1 lemon, cut in half
- 4 shakes dry Italian seasoning
- 1/2 tsp. Dijon mustard
- 2 tbsp. olive oil
- Sea salt to taste 9about ¼ tsp. total)

Season the salmon with a touch of salt. Poach or place salmon fillet in pan with enough cold water to just cover. Add another pinch of salt to the water. Bring to a boil, then reduce heat and simmer for 5 minutes. Remove from pan and cool completely on a plate. If you're in a hurry you can put it in the freezer for 5 minutes to cool.

In a glass bowl: mix in celery, parsley, butter, cream cheese, and squeeze half of the lemon.

In another smaller bowl: mix in the other half of the lemon juice, mustard, a pinch of salt, dry Italian seasoning. Whisk in the olive oil. Whisk well.

Combine bowls and add the salmon. Mash everything together with a potato masher, stir. Serve immediately while warm or cover and put in the fridge and serve later. I like pate served between two pieces of white bread or as a dip with carrots and celery.

K9 NOTE: *Minimal Modification.* Dog Friendly. Stuff pate in a squeeze tube, Kong™ toy, or marrowbone and feed on a walk during training. This dish makes enough for one to two human size sandwiches, and a few bites for the dog.

POULTRY BBQ SAUCE

- 1 egg
- 1 cup vegetable oil
- 1 pint cider vinegar
- 1 tbsp. salt
- 1 tbsp. poultry seasoning

<u>DIRECTIONS</u>: Beat egg. Add oil, beat again. Add vinegar, salt, and seasoning, stir. Brush sauce on chicken while grilling.

K9 NOTE: *Minimal Modification.* A bite of cooked sauce and chicken breast is great for Fido!

PARMESAN CHEESE GRITS

- 14-oz. organic, low-sodium chicken broth
- 1 1/2 cups coconut or goat's milk
- 3/4 cup uncooked quick-cooking grits
- 1 tsp. of butter
- 1/4 tsp. salt
- 3/4 cup Parmigiano-Reggiano, freshly grated
- 1 tsp. freshly ground pepper

<u>DIRECTIONS:</u> Bring chicken broth and 1 1/2 cups coconut milk to a quick boil in a large saucepan. Slowly stir in grits and 1/2 tsp. salt. Start whisking immediately then cover and reduce heat to medium-low. Cook, stirring occasionally (6 - 7 minutes) or until mixture is thickened. Add Parmesan and butter, stirring until cheese is melted. Add pepper and a bit more salt on yours if you like.

K9 NOTE: *Minimal Modification.* Grits are made from corn, so unless your dog is allergic to corn, a small bite is okay for Fido. For a corn-free alternative, try making it the same way with rinsed amaranth instead of corn grits. Amaranth is controversial when it comes to feeding dogs, but is found in many foods and treats and considered non-toxic. Most people find the benefits outweigh the risks, but I advise you do your own research.

SWEET *PUP*-TATO CHIPS

Oven Baked or Dehydrated

Dehydrated Prep Time: 10 minutes
Cook Time: 12 hours
Oven baked Prep Time: 10 minutes
Cook Time: 3 - 5 hours (or longer)

- 2 sweet potatoes, cut very thinly
- 1 tsp. melted coconut oil (per sweet potato)
- Sea salt (to taste) *for dogs, only a touch of salt or none at all

DIRECTIONS: Peel and slice sweet potatoes as thinly as possible (I use a mandolin for this). Place in a bowl and soak in water for 1 hour, changing the water at the half-hour point. Place on a towel to dry a bit… Drizzle a drop or two of coconut oil; stir and coat evenly. Season sweet potatoes with a touch of sea salt.

Place sweet potatoes onto a cake cooking rack so that it gets proper ventilation on all sides. Place the sweet potatoes into an oven, turn on lowest setting and leave the door slightly a-jar. Cook 3 to 5 hours or until desired crispness. You can also try Kale Chips - Throw some kale in a bowl, season and bake or dehydrate… and you have dog friendly kale chips too! If using a dehydrator dehydrate at 145-155 F for about 12 hours. Check your potatoes periodically to get your desired crispness.

K9 NOTE: Dog friendly. Limit amount of salt as well as the amount of coconut oil.

SWEET *PUP-TATO* FRIES

- 4 sweet potatoes, peeled and cut into fries
- Sunflower oil
- 1 tbsp. coconut or olive oil
- 1 3/4 lbs. sweet potatoes, cut lengthwise into 8 wedges
- 1/2 tsp. paprika (skip for K9s)
- Herbs of Provence
- Salt (Himalayan or sea salt)
- Pepper
- 1/4 tsp. salt 1/4 tsp. ground red pepper

<u>DIRECTIONS</u>: Pre-heat oven to 425 degrees.
Brush a large shallow pan with 1 tsp. oil. Place pan in oven. Combine 2 tsp. oil and remaining ingredients in a large bowl; toss well. Carefully remove pan from oven; place potatoes on hot pan. Bake at 425° for 35 minutes or until crisp, stirring occasionally.

K9 NOTE: *Minimal Modification.* Small amounts of paprika should not pose a risk, but if you're uncomfortable with giving your dog paprika, leave it out or try Herbs of Provence or Italian seasoning. And skip the peppers and salt.

TURKEY BACON GREEN BEAN ROLL

- Green beans
- Greek goat's milk feta
- Turkey Bacon: 94 % fat –free, uncured (antibiotic-free, no nitrates)

DIRECTIONS: Wash beans thoroughly, cut off ends, and the stringy part. You can cook the green beans in the same pan as you cook the turkey bacon in, but the bacon may cook a little faster than the green beans due to the turkey bacon having very little fat. If you don't like your beans al dente, boil the beans 7 -10 minutes first, using a covered pot of boiling water. Cook the turkey bacon separately in a non-stick skillet or use a regular skillet and rub the pan with olive or coconut oil. Drain bacon on paper towels. Wrap beans and feta up in a slice of bacon when cool.

K9 NOTE: *Minimal Modification.* Surprise your pup for good behavior!

WATERMELON APPETIZER

- 1 small watermelon, cut into cubes
- Mint leaves
- Greek goat's milk Feta cheese
- Extra-Virgin Olive oil

DIRECTIONS: Cut watermelon into cubes and arrange on a platter. Place a mint leaf on each cube of watermelon. Top with Feta and drizzle olive oil on top.

K9 NOTE: *Minimal Modification.* Chop the mint small for your dog.

YAM MASH

- 2-3 yams
- Salt to taste
- 1 tbsp. Butter
- 3 to 4 tbsp. Goat's milk

BAKE: One of the easiest and healthiest ways to prepare yams. Place into the oven whole and bake at 375 degrees for one hour. Then let cool for about ½ hour, peel and mash with butter and goat's milk until creamy. Salt to taste and add fresh herbs (optional).

BOIL: Peel the yams and cut them into long pieces. Add to boiling, salted water and boil until fork tender. Drain water and mash with butter or goat's milk until creamy.

GRILL: Slice yams into one-inch pieces, brush with olive oil, and place them directly on the grill until tender.

BROIL: Slice the yams into thin pieces for faster cooking. Coat in olive oil and arrange on a tray. Broil on high for 5-10 minutes, then flip over and broil for an additional 5 minutes until cooked through.

K9 NOTE: *Minimal Modification.* You can share a bite of Yam Mash with your dog. Keep the butter, salt and goat's milk to a minimum, or skip it completely for your dog's portion and just feed plain yam.

YOGURT & COOKED BEETS

Serves: 4

- 2 large beets, cooked & peeled or 1- 16 oz. can beets, drained
- 1 cup plain yogurt
- 1 tbsp. fresh mint, chopped or ½ tsp. dried mint

<u>DIRECTIONS:</u> If using fresh beets, remove skins (you can also buy cooked beets from Trader Joe's.) Cut beets into ¾ inch cubes. Steam for 45 minutes; drain and cool. In a serving bowl: add yogurt and beets. Mix well. Garnish with mint and serve immediately. This tastes great, but it may turn pink and look like Pepto-Bismol if you mush it together or if you don't eat it right away. You can just place the beets and mint onto the yogurt without mixing.

K9 NOTE: *Minimal Modification.* Great for dogs! Beets cleanse the liver.

LUNCH & DINNER BITES

BUFFALO BURGERS

- 1-2 lbs. Buffalo or beef (I prefer a mixture of both), ground
- Hamburger buns
- 1 tsp. egg per burger, uncooked (optional)
- American or cheddar cheese, sliced
- Onions, diced and sautéed (*not for K9s)
- Canned or fresh Ortega or Pablano chili, whole
- 1 - 2 anchovies (optional)
- Salt & pepper (if using anchovies, skip the salt)
- Garlic, crushed, or garlic powder (to taste) (*not for K9)
- Few drops Worcestershire sauce (per burger)
- Lettuce, tomato, pickles, mustard, ketchup (optional)

DIRECTIONS: Place the raw meat in a bowl. Mush the anchovy into a paste with mortar and pestle and mix into ground meat. Add one tbsp. of finely-chopped onion to the meat and sauté the rest of the onion in a cast-iron skillet on low. If you use too much egg, and too much onion, your meat will be too watery. Add ½ - 1 raw scrambled egg and a few drops of Worcestershire sauce. Add salt, pepper, and a touch of garlic to taste. Mix well. Rub a drop of safflower oil onto the palm of your hands. Form mixture into hamburger patties. Don't over-work the meat!

Grill burgers on a hot barbecue, careful not to flip over until seared on one side. Avoid pressing down with a spatula as juices will run out and your burger will be dry. Keep one side of your BBQ charcoal free so you can move the patty away from the heat if you need to. Add a slice of cheese the last two minutes of cooking so it melts perfectly over the sides of the patty.

Take a fresh whole Ortega chili: If using canned, put on the grill the last minute to enhance the heat; if using fresh, cook for about 5 min. then peel off the thin layer of skin before adding it to the burger. Toast the buns on the grill for about 30 seconds, then flip, using caution not to burn. Serve burgers on buns and add garnishes as desired.

K9 VERSION: For Fido - unseasoned, grilled cooked meat patties with a touch of anchovy or dash salt (optional) and a slice of cheese served on an open-faced bun.

K9 NOTE: *Modification Required.* Do not feed K9s onions, peppers, or garlic (see notes on garlic and onions). Let cool, then place bites into a Kong toy™, in their food bowl, or use for training on a walk when you pass another dog, to redirect your dog from a big distraction, or for a trick!

BBQ HERB CHICKEN BREAST

- Boneless chicken breast, organic, free-range (1 per person)
- Safflower mayonnaise
- Dry Italian Seasoning or Herbs of Provence
- Salt & pepper (to taste)
- Cellophane wrap (for pounding chicken)

DIRECTIONS: Wash and dry chicken thoroughly and place on a large piece of cellophane wrap. Season with Italian seasoning (Herbs of Provence); salt and pepper on both sides. Wrap chicken in the cellophane. Using a mallet or rolling pin, pound the chicken flat to pound in herbs, enhancing the flavor. Remove chicken from cellophane and place on a plate. Rub a touch of safflower mayo all over, careful not to rub off spices.

Grill chicken on the barbecue (BBQ preferred) until done. Optional cooking method: sear chicken in a hot cast-iron skillet, then place hot skillet into a hot oven on broil and cook for about 4 minutes. Before the top of the chicken starts to burn, turn the oven from broil to bake and bake at 350 about 15 - 20 more minutes.

K9 NOTE: *Minimal Modification.* A small bite or two of a bone-free, lightly-seasoned piece of BBQ chicken breast is great for K9s! For more frequent chicken *dog bites*, the best way to prepare chicken for dogs is to boil it.

POACHED CHICKEN WITH HERB DRESSING

- 6 - 7 oz. chicken breast (boneless, skinless), diced
- 1 bunch asparagus (10 oz. tips)
- 1 tbsp. olive oil
- 1 tbsp. apple cider vinegar
- 1 pinch sea salt & black pepper
- 1 pinch brown sugar
- 1 tsp. fresh rosemary
- 1 tsp. fresh thyme

DIRECTIONS: In a large saucepan, boil the asparagus tips for two minutes. When poaching, barely cover with water. Drain. Chop using tips and middle. Reserve the liquid. In the same pot you cooked the asparagus, barely cover the chicken with liquid and let the liquid bubble for about 5 minutes or until cooked thoroughly. In a large mixing bowl, combine: oil, vinegar, salt, pepper, sugar, rosemary, and thyme. Add the asparagus and diced chicken and toss to coat evenly and serve.

K9 NOTE: *Minimal Modification.* Just a little sugar and salt if sharing with your furry friend. Catch your dog doing something right! Share this dish as a great reward for good behavior.

CHICKEN PARMESAN

- 1 lb. chicken breast cutlets
- Tomatoes, cut in half
- Olive oil
- Sea salt
- Black pepper, freshly ground
- Rosemary leaves
- Thyme leaves
- Dry Italian seasoning or Herbs of Provence
- Bread crumbs or flaxseed sprinkles (or a combination) to coat chicken
- 2 tbsp. fresh parsley, chopped
- Parmesan cheese, grated
- 1 stick butter, melted

DIRECTIONS: Preheat oven to 200 degrees.

Cut tomatoes in half and place (cut-side-up) on baking tray. Drizzle with olive oil, sprinkle with salt, pepper, rosemary, thyme, and dry Italian seasoning or Herbs of Provence. Bake for about 45 min and remove from oven. Cover tomatoes with tin foil to keep warm. Increase oven to 300 degrees.

In a bowl: mix breadcrumbs, Parmesan, flaxseed, dry Italian seasoning or Herbs of Provence, and parsley; lightly season with salt and pepper. Melt butter. Dip chicken pieces into melted butter and roll in the crumb mixture. Place crumbed chicken in a baking dish and bake for 40 to 45 minutes.

Just before the chicken is done cooking, place grated parmesan cheese on top of the tomatoes and put them back into the oven (uncovered) for two minutes to melt cheese. I like Parmigiano-Reggiano or a slice of Munster cheese. Serve with a salad and asparagus. This dish also goes well with my Sardinian Pasta recipe!

K9 NOTE: *Minimal Modification.* Tomatoes aren't toxic except for the stem, leaves, and plant (see notes on tomatoes). In my experience, dogs don't do well on tomatoes, so I would skip the tomatoes for Fido.

CHICKEN *PUP* PIE

DOG BITE: Chicken Pup-Pie K9 Portion

Yield: 4 servings

- 1 lb. chicken breasts (skinless, boneless) organic free range, chopped
- Sunflower, canola, vegetable, safflower, or olive oil
- ¼ - ½ tsp. salt
- 3 cups chicken broth, fat-free or low-sodium
- 10 oz. baby new potatoes, sliced or chopped
- 1/2 cups celery, diced small
- 1 small zucchini (about 7 oz.), chopped or sliced
- 2/3 cup frozen green peas & diced carrot blend
- 1 tbsp. all-purpose flour
- 1 tbsp. fresh thyme, chopped
- 1 tbsp. fresh sage, chopped (see notes on sage)

- 2 tbsp. parsley, chopped fine
- 1 tsp. dry poultry seasoning, Herbs of Provence, or Italian seasoning
- A couple shakes of black pepper
- 2 - 3 sheets buttered puffed pastry rounds
- 1 organic free-range egg

<u>DIRECTIONS</u>: Preheat oven to 400. Take the puffed pastry out of the freezer; bring to room temperature. Lay out all of your ingredients. Chop, slice or dice all veggies and herbs. Chop chicken into bite-sized pieces. Season the chicken with salt, pepper and a little dry poultry seasoning. Brown the chicken in a large pan with a touch of oil and sauté over med-high heat. After 1 to two minutes, add ½ the fresh herbs, and a few more shakes of the dry herbs, Continue sautéing about 2 to 3 more minutes until almost done; 5 - 6 min. total (don't overcook). At the same time you start browning the chicken, in another big pan sauté the potatoes, zucchini, and celery. Season with the fresh and dry herbs the same way you are cooking the chicken. Then mix the two pans together and continue sautéing about 5 more min. You can even slightly undercook because all of this is going to cook in the oven for about ½ hour more.

Next, pour in the chicken broth; boil and stir. Keep cooking over medium-high heat about 5 minutes. Stir in peas and carrots. Add more salt, pepper and seasoning if needed. Reduce to thicken the broth and stir fairly constantly. After about 5 min. of boiling and stirring, turn down heat to low and slowly stir in flour with one hand as you whisk with a hand whisker with the other hand. Use enough flour to whisk into a creamy consistency like gravy.

Take your ramekins/Pyrex dish and lay in the sheet of puffed pastry over the sides a bit and mold into the dish. Then brush with egg wash but don't brush the edges. Pour in the chicken and veggie mix, then cover with another sheet of puffed pastry and brush egg wash on top (don't brush edges). Then slash a few lines with a knife and put in a pre-heated oven at 400 for about ½ hr. or until crisp and brown. Let cool and serve.

Save enough filling to make a small pie for your pooch. I like to make one large pie and serve family style. If you don't have enough puffed pastry left for Fido's pie, take a strip from the middle of the bottom layer of your big pie and use that to cover the top of your dog's pie. You don't even need a bottom layer for your dog's pie; trust me, they won't mind! You can also buy an extra bit of puffed pastry and you will have some left over. If you would like to add pearl onions and mushrooms (to your pie only!) and if you are sure your dog won't be eating the one for humans, cook them in a separate pan and pour them directly into your pie only.

K9 NOTE: *Minimal Modification.* For a healthier K9 version, boil instead of cooking with oil—even though a little oil is not bad—it's actually good for their coat in moderation. Make sure the crust is cooked. Never feed K9s uncooked dough. Never feed onions or mushrooms to your dog (see notes on mushrooms and onions).

CHICKEN SANDWICH

- Sourdough bread, toasted
- Chicken breast (organic, boneless, skinless), to be pounded
- Ham, organic (1 to 2 slices per sandwich)
- 1 squash or zucchini, sliced
- Cheese (optional)
- Mixed greens
- Pickles, sliced
- ½ tsp. Herbs of Provence
- Salt & pepper (to taste)

- Garlic, fresh or powdered (as desired) *not for Fido
- Paprika (as desired) *minimal or none for Fido
- 1 tbsp. parsley, chopped
- ½ tbsp. thyme & sage, fresh (*see note on sage)
- Vegan Mayo
- Dijon mustard

DIRECTIONS: Coat chicken with canola or safflower oil and season with dash of salt, pepper, and the other dry spices as desired. Wrap in cellophane and pound with a mallet or rolling pin. Slice zucchini, drizzle with olive oil, and season lightly with salt, pepper and Italian seasoning. Sauté zucchini in olive oil on medium heat, until golden. Add fresh thyme, sage, and parsley at last minute to avoid burning. Remove zucchini and herbs from pan and place in a dish to keep warm. Using the oil in the pan, sauté chicken, 3 - 4 minutes per side, until done. If chicken is thick, you can finish in a preheated oven at 350 for the last 5 minutes. Sauté ham for 1 minute to heat. Prepare a sandwich with all ingredients as desired.

K9 NOTE: *Minimal Modification.* For Fido, skip the mayo and mustard, and avoid the paprika, sage, and garlic. They probably won't eat the pickle or mixed greens. Everything else is okay in moderation. For even healthier chicken, boil it; the same goes for yellow squash. Make Fido's appetizer size!

COUNTRY-STYLE CHICKEN SOUP

Human Version:

- 1 chicken, whole
- 3 - 16 oz. boxes low-salt chicken broth
  (or 2 chicken; one vegetable broth)
- 1 can butter beans
- 2 large carrots, sliced
- 3 stalks celery, sliced

- 1 onion, chopped
- ¾ pack fresh poultry seasonings
- Dry poultry seasoning, Italian seasoning, or Herbs of Provence
- Za'atar to taste (optional)
- Salt
- Pepper
- Paprika
- Garlic powder
- Dash cayenne
- 1 tbsp. cooking oil

DIRECTIONS: Wash, dry, and salt chicken. Remove liver and giblets from cavity, wash and brown in oil for a minute or two. Heat oil in a big soup pot and sear chicken on all sides in a bit of oil. As chicken is searing, add onions, celery, and carrots. Add back browned liver and giblets. After chicken is browned, add broth, then spices. Stir and boil for about 10 min., then turn down heat to medium and cover for about 10 - 15 minutes. Scoop off the top layer of foam that floats to the top. Turn to low and keep covered for 25 – 30 min. Add the butter beans the last 20 minutes. Garnish with parsley. As chicken is cooking, during final 25 minutes, discard any skin and bones.

TIP: You can use bone-in breast, thighs, or even a pre-cooked chicken. If you use a pre-cooked chicken, you don't have to sear it first and it won't take as long to cook. It's country style! (Please see K9 version below.)

CHICKEN SOUP FOR K9's

DOG BITE: K9 Portion

CHICKEN SOUP FOR DOGS

K9 VERSION:

- 1 chicken breast (organic), diced
- 1/2 box low-sodium chicken broth
- 1 cup of water

- 1 tbsp. butter beans, slightly mushed
- 1 medium carrot, sliced
- 1 celery stalk, diced fine
- 1 tsp. parsley, chopped fine (garnish)
- Touch dry poultry seasoning (to taste)
- Pasta or rice (optional)

DIRECTIONS: Put everything into a pot of boiling, low-sodium chicken broth or 8 oz. chicken broth; and 8 oz. water. Add rice (optional) and boil for 5 minutes. Simmer (covered) for ½ hour. Let cool.

K9 NOTE: *Modification Required.* Feed small amounts over kibble and beware of too much salt for Fido.

YASMINE'S INDIAN CHICKEN

Human Version (See K9 recipe below)

Human Version: My wife, Yasmine, is an excellent cook!

- Chicken breast or thighs
- 1 medium yellow onion, chopped
- 4 - 5 cloves fresh garlic, chopped
- 1 -2 tbsp. fresh ginger, chopped
- ¼ tsp. cinnamon
- ¼ tsp. cardamom
- ¼ tsp. clove
- 1/8 tsp. turmeric
- 1 can coconut milk
- Pinch cayenne
- Pepper
- Potatoes
- Peas
- Cilantro and cucumber (garnish)

DIRECTIONS: Sauté onion, garlic, and ginger on medium heat with a little butter and touch of oil; sauté until opaque. Add two to three breasts (cut into cubes) or several thighs and legs, adding a bit more butter and oil (optional). Add ¼ teaspoon cinnamon, ¼ teaspoon cardamom and ¼ teaspoon clove. Continue to cook on medium for 2 to 3 minutes. Once chicken is no longer pink, add one can of coconut milk. Add 1/8 teaspoon turmeric, a pinch of cayenne, and pepper. Let cook on medium for ½ hr. (covered). Add potatoes. A few minutes later, add peas. Mix and turn down heat (cover with lid) and cook ½ hour. Serve with chopped cilantro and salted Persian cucumbers.

RICE
- 1 cup Basmati rice
- 2 cups water
- 1 tsp. butter
- Oil
- Salt

DIRECTIONS: Wash rice first. Boil water in pot and add a teaspoon of butter and a little oil and salt. Then cover and add rice and bring to a boil again. Turn down to a simmer. When water reduces 10 to 15 minutes, turn off and put in oven for about 5 minutes at 250 to 300 degrees. Serve with cilantro, cucumber garnish over rice.

K9 NOTE: Not Dog Friendly. *Modification Required.* (See K9 Version below.) When we make this dish I always buy an extra breast to boil for my pooch. I cook some rice and add a touch of cinnamon, turmeric, and even a small touch of ginger, a few slices of carrot, and 1-2 slices of chopped cucumber and add it to my dog's kibble!

WILD ARTIC CHAR WITH TANGERINE & FENNEL

DOG BITE: This is my 6-lb. puppy's portion!

- Wild arctic char or salmon - ½ lb. per person
- 1cup olive oil
- 1 tbsp. butter
- 2 small fennel bulbs, chopped
- 1 oz. Pernod (optional) *see K9 note below
- 1 star of anise
- 1 cinnamon stick
- Sea salt
- Black pepper

- 1 pkg. frozen peas
- 1 pkg. pancetta
- 2 cups tangerine juice, fresh
- 1 heaping tbsp. wild sturgeon caviar (*not for Fido)
- Parsley or dill (garnish)

DIRECTIONS: Pre-heat oven to 250 degrees.

For the sauce: cut an inch off the bottom of the fennel bulb, also cut an inch just above the bulb before the bulb turns into the stalk. Then peel away a couple outside layers like you would an onion and wash. Slice and chop fennel bulb and place in a sauce pan on the stove. Add tangerine juice, Pernod, the star of anise, and the cinnamon stick. Bring it to a simmer and cook the fennel until tender. (Start this step before you put the fish in the oven.) When the tangerine fennel sauce is done (about 20 min.), reserve cooking liquid for later and take the fennel, the star of anise and the cinnamon stick out.

For the fish: pour olive oil (about 1 cup) in a Pyrex or oven-proof dish but don't put the fish in the oil yet. Warm the oil in the low-temp. oven for a few minutes while you wash and dry the fish and season with salt and pepper. Make sure the fish is room temperature before setting the fish into the warm oven into the olive oil. Cook 250 degrees until it's medium-rare (about 10 minutes). Remove fish from oil to stop the cooking.

Next: make a pea puree. Bring one cup of water to a boil with a pinch of salt. Add frozen peas and cook for 1 min. Strain and refresh under cold water. Puree the peas in a Cuisinart or blender with a teaspoon of butter and dash of salt.

Put the reserved fennel cooking liquid in a pan and simmer until reduced by half. Then add the other teaspoon of butter. In another frying pan, heat a touch of olive oil and cook up some pancetta until crispy. Heat the pea puree and spoon on top of each plate. As soon as you take the fish out of the oven, take it out of the oil, and put it right on top of the pea puree, and then spoon sauce around it. Sprinkle with crispy pancetta and arrange fennel on plate. Garnish with caviar, dill, or parsley.

Alternate Cooking Method: Make the same tangerine sauce and use it by taking a fillet of salmon, halibut, cod, or fish of your choice. Season fish with salt and pepper and wrap it securely in wax paper. Place it on a baking sheet in a preheated oven at 250 degrees and steam fish in the oven on Bake for about 8 minutes or until done, depending on thickness. This version is a healthier way to cook fish!

K9 NOTE: *Minimal Modification.* Never give K9s caviar or raw fish. If you plan on giving your dog more than a bite or two, I recommend cooking their portion of fish separately (boil or steam). Pernod (alcohol) burns off during cooking. Never give your dog uncooked sauce. If in doubt, skip the Pernod if you will be sharing it with your dog.

BBQ WHOLE FISH WITH TANGERINE & TARRAGON

Red Snapper, Orata, Branzino, or Trout

- 1 whole Red Snapper, Orata, Branzino, or Trout; scaled, gutted, fins removed
- 1 tangerine, segmented
- Tarragon or marjoram
- Salt & pepper (to taste)

DIRECTIONS: Scale and gut fish; remove fins. Wash and dry fish then place skin-side-up on a cutting board. Using the tip of a sharp knife, make several shallow slashes in the skin about 1-inch apart. Turn the fish 90 degrees and make several more slashes to form a crisscross pattern. Season inside and out with salt and pepper. Stuff fish with tangerine segments and fresh tarragon. Rub a dash of oil on the outside of fish, add a little more salt and set on a medium-high BBQ. Let it sear thoroughly and flip minimally without burning. For smaller fish like trout, I recommend using a fish rack.

K9 NOTE: *Modification Required.* Thoroughly check for and remove bones for the dog's bite. I usually share only one bite with my dog for good behavior! This is not a dog friendly dish, but it can be a dog friendly bite. Nothing is dangerous except the bones.

SVEN'S CATFISH

When I was in Nashville and found my rescue dog, Sven, who inspired me to become a professional dog trainer, I remember being a starving musician living off catfish I caught in Tennessee. Me and my dog, Sven, and even my band, lived in our rehearsal studio and cooked on a hot plate. I would cook catfish and scrambled eggs. Sven loved this dish!

- Catfish, Trout fillet, or Rock Cod, 1/2 lb. per person
- Salt & pepper to taste
- Garlic (not for K9s, see notes on garlic)
- A touch of butter
- 1 tsp. oil
- Cayenne (*not for K9s)
- Eggs, scrambled (two per person)
- Parsley, chopped (garnish)

<u>DIRECTIONS</u>: Wash and dry fish, lightly brush with a touch of olive oil and season fileted fish with spices. (Add cayenne if you like a little heat.) Sauté catfish in a skillet in a touch of butter and olive oil. Remove the fish and scramble eggs in the same pan to retain the flavors. Add a touch of chopped parsley to garnish.

K9 NOTE: Check for bones before feeding fish to your dog. Steam, boil, bake, or use a non-stick skillet to cook fish for Fido. Add a touch of scrambled egg and garnish with a bit of parsley. K9's can have one or two small bites of fish, scrambled egg, and a bit of rice. Avoid garlic and cayenne, although in moderation it would be fine and thoroughly check for bones.

BBQ HALIBUT

HUMAN VERSION:

- Halibut, fresh (½ lb. per person)
- 1/3 cup olive oil
- 2 tbsp. lime juice
- 3 tbsp. red wine vinegar
- 1 tbsp. fennel or dill, fresh, chopped
- 4 cloves garlic, crushed
- 2 tbsp. Pernod (*See K9 note)
- 3 red bell peppers, chopped
- 12 basil leaves, torn
- Salt & pepper

DIRECTIONS: Wash and dry fish; season with salt and pepper. Mix in all marinade / finishing / basting sauce ingredients slowly, whisking in the olive oil last. Marinate fish for about 10 to 15 minutes while the BBQ is getting hot, but save some sauce for basting. BBQ the fish on the grill about 2 to 3 min. per side. Try not to flip too often. On the last flip just before you take fish off the grill; baste the fish with a touch of sauce. Let the sauce cook enough that the alcohol burns off if you plan on sharing a bite with your pooch Top with salsa. Serve halibut with Best Baked Potato (see recipe) and steamed carrots with broccoli. Goes well with a glass of Sauvignon Blanc!

K9 VERSION: Using the above BBQ Halibut recipe: cut off 1-3 bite-size pieces of halibut for your pooch (depending on their size). Before you cook the fish, make sure all bones are removed. Cook Fido's piece with a couple of bite-sized pieces of chopped fennel. Cook by steaming, barbequing, or using a non-stick skillet. Serve fish and fennel plain without seasoning or sauce. Side of plain steamed carrots and plain chopped broccoli.

K9 NOTE: Pernod (alcohol) burns off during cooking. Never give your dog uncooked sauce. If Fido does have a bite of your fish, the amount of alcohol in the sauce is minimal and it cooks off. If in doubt, skip the Pernod if you will be sharing it with your dog.

STEVE'S SALSA FRESCO FOR HALIBUT

HUMAN'S ONLY!

- 3 red bell peppers, chopped
- 2 cloves garlic
- 12 basil leaves, torn
- 1 tbsp. red wine vinegar
- Salt & pepper (to taste)

<u>Directions:</u> Wash peppers, remove seeds and chop. Grill bell peppers on the barbeque or in the oven on broil; let cool and chop. Add garlic, basil, red wine vinegar and salt and pepper. Mix well. You can use this marinade/basting sauce on a plethora of different fish – sturgeon, halibut, red snapper. I personally like sturgeon and swordfish with this dish as well as halibut! (see recipe).

K9 NOTE: Do not serve salsa to dogs. Avoid peppers and large amounts of garlic.

FILLET MINON

- Filet Minon steak (6-8 oz. per person)
- Kosher or sea salt
- Black pepper

- Paprika
- Garlic, chopped
- Safflower oil
- Fresh rosemary

DIRECTIONS: Grilling is always my first choice when it comes to steak. I recommend cooking this on an old-fashioned Weber charcoal grill. Fifteen minutes before grilling, gently rub your hands with a drop or two of oil and gently pat your hands on the fillet. You only need a very small amount. Season evenly with spices and wedge fresh crushed garlic between crevasses (no garlic for your dog's bite).

Cook on the grill on med-high. Drop fresh rosemary into the fire underneath the steak throughout the cooking process so the smoke of the rosemary will add flavor to the steak. Get a nice sear on each side before flipping. Flip minimally and never squish the meat into the grill. I recommend medium-rare for this cut of meat. The steak should be reddish-pink inside with visible juices. Let rest 5 minutes before slicing.

Alternate cooking method: cook steak on the stove top with a touch of Canola or safflower oil in a hot iron skillet. You can add a touch of butter on top just before you take it out of the pan. If you're cooking a thick cut of fillet, you can start by searing the steak in a hot cast iron skillet on the stove and then transfer the hot skillet into a hot oven on Broil for a few minutes. Watch it carefully as it will burn fast. You can crack open the oven door a few inches to help keep it from burning or put in on Bake for a couple minutes until done. Let rest 5 minutes before slicing. (For humans only: goes well with sautéed onions and mushrooms.)

K9 NOTE: *Minimal Modification.* Do not season your dog's piece of meat but cook it with yours. This way, you can test for doneness by checking the "doggie" piece by cutting into it so the juices won't run out of your piece. Fillet Minon is one of the leanest pieces of meat which is better for both you and Fido. Don't feed your dog a whole steak! This book is called *Dog Bites* for a reason. One fillet can last several days; feed one little dog bite at a time for good behavior! Don't feed your dog onions and mushrooms.

BBQ WHOLE LOBSTER

- 2 fresh, live lobsters
- Butter
- Salt
- Basting sauce
- 2 tbsp. tarragon or parsley, chopped

<u>DIRECTIONS</u>: Fill a large pot with 3-4 inches of water. Heat to boiling. Add lobster to steamer and steam covered, for about 4-5 minutes. Remove lobster from steamer and put in a bowl of ice to stop cooking. Flip upside down and cut the tail vertically. Crack claws with a crab cracker (one crack) then slice other side of tail.

Place on hot BBQ. Half-way thru cooking, baste with sauce and flip a few times. Remove from grill. Remove tail and claws and serve with melted butter, tarragon, and parsley. Add a squeeze of lemon (optional).

You can also grill just the tails by cutting them down the back of the shell just enough to crack and slice about one inch deep down the back. Slightly slice the other side. Place on hot BBQ basting as you grill until lobster becomes orange and hot all the way through (8 min.) and curls up a bit. When it cools a bit the shell should peel off easily. Save some sauce for dipping.

K9 NOTE: *Minimal Modification.* A little cooked lobster is not toxic but only feed Fido a small bite of lobster meat because it's rich and has a lot of cholesterol. Keep your dog away from the shell and claws, and only share a small bite, not a whole lobster!

TANGERINE BUTTER SAUCE

- 1/2 cup butter
- 1/4 cup tangerine juice
- 1 tbsp. white wine (optional)
- 2 tbsp. tarragon or parsley, finely chopped
- A touch of salt & pepper
- Dash paprika (optional, not for K9's)
- Salt and pepper (to taste)

DIRECTIONS: Slowly melt butter and wine on simmer in a small pot. Discard any foam that rises to the top. Add all other ingredients and simmer for one more min. without burning the butter. Set aside and use to baste fresh lobster while it's cooking on the grill.

K9 NOTE: This sauce is *not* recommended for K9's as uncooked sauce containing wine is dangerous for K9's. It you cook the alcohol out of the sauce and only give your dog a few bites of the protein with a few drops of cooked sauce, you should be okay. Paprika should be skipped or only a little and butter in minimal amounts.

MARVELOUS MUTT MEATLOAF

K9s ONLY! This one is for dogs only. I personally don't like to eat this dish, but my dogs go nuts for this dish.

- 1 lb. Buffalo or Bison , ground
- 2 tbsp. tomato sauce (optional)
- 1 anchovy, crushed (plus anchovy oil from the jar or can)
- 1/4 cup oats (quick or old fashioned) uncooked
- 1 organic free-range egg, lightly beaten
- 1 small apple, chopped
- 1/1/2 carrots chopped and steamed / cooked
- Pinch Italian seasoning
- 1/16 tsp. salt (optional)
- 1 tsp. flaxseed sprinkles or flax meal
- 1 tsp. fresh parsley finely chopped
- A small amount of grated parmesan cheese
- 1 tbsp. cooked mac & cheese (optional)
- 2 strips of sodium-free turkey bacon

DIRECTIONS: Pre-heat oven to 350°.

In a large bowl: combine all ingredients except the bacon, mixing lightly but thoroughly. Spray small loaf pan with cooking oil spray and place the bacon on the bottom or on each side of the pan. Press meat mixture into a small loaf pan. Bake 50 min. (350°F) until it's not pink in center and juices run clear about 165 internal degrees. Let stand 5 minutes; drain off any juices before slicing.

K9 NOTE: *Minimal Modification.* This one is for dogs only! Cool meatloaf before you feed to Fido. The apple pieces stay hot for a while. The small amount of tomato should be of no risk, but in general, I try to avoid giving dogs tomatoes. The meat of the tomato is not toxic but the plant, stems, and leaves are. I just find that dogs generally don't do well with tomatoes. Only serve your dog a few small bites. This can last 4 to 5 days in the fridge if stored properly.

SARDINIA PASTA

HUMAN VERSION: (see K9 Pasta below)

- Angel hair pasta
- Parsley or basil, torn
- 2 tbsp. anchovies
- 4 tbsp. olive oil
- Salt
- 1 tsp. red pepper flakes
- Parsley, chopped (garnish)

DIRECTIONS: In a large pot of boiling water, add a generous amount of salt and a tbsp. of olive oil. Add pasta. Stir with a wooden spoon so it doesn't stick. Sauté 4 cloves garlic in 4 tbsp. olive oil in a sauté pan for 3-4 min. Add parsley or basil and 1 tsp. dried red pepper flakes.

Ahead of time: smash anchovies with mortar and pestle so it's ready to go and take out any big bones, then add the anchovies to the pan the last minute and cook for a couple of minutes. Time it so when the pasta is done, you drain the pasta and place in the pan with the sauce. Add 1 tbsp. of pasta water to the pan and cook for 1-2 more min. Top with fresh chopped parsley.

K9 VERSION: A healthier version of pasta for dogs is gluten-free pasta with my Organic Turkey Meatballs. Serve with chopped parsley, peas, carrots, broccoli, or cauliflower and a touch of the leftover anchovy oil. Chop pasta the size of mac and cheese before serving to your pooch.

K9 NOTE: *Minimal Modification.* Dogs can have a bite of this dish without the pepper flakes. Give one bite to a little dog; two bites to a medium size dog; and three bites to a big dog. Surprise your dog for good behavior!

PORK ROAST WITH APPLE SAUCE

- 1½ lb. pork tenderloin roast
- 1-2 tbsp. safflower oil
- Kosher salt
- Pepper
- Paprika
- Garlic, chopped
- Garlic, powdered
- Orange marmalade (for glaze)

<u>DIRECTIONS</u>: Pre-heat oven to 450 degrees.
Take 1-2 tbsp. safflower oil and rub all over roast with hands. Season with salt, pepper, paprika. Push freshly-chopped garlic into nooks and crannies in the meat. Cook to sear 5 minutes per side in a cast-iron skillet on medium-high heat. Transfer to a hot roasting pan and roast in oven on medium rack for 20 minutes. Last 5 minutes: glaze with orange marmalade (careful not to let it burn). Serve with green beans and a side of Applesauce.

K9 NOTE: *Minimal Modification.* Fido can definitely have a bite of applesauce and plain green beans. I might even share a small bite of the middle of the pork, making sure it doesn't have garlic paprika or salt and it's cooked all the way through.

PORK CHOP WITH APPLE, FIG, & SWEET POTATO

Pork Chop with Apples, Figs, and Sweet Potato

Serves 2 humans and 1 medium-size dog!
- 2- 12 to 14 oz. pork chops, lean, bone-in
  or one boneless pork loin (approx. 16 - 24 oz.)
- Salt & pepper
- Cinnamon, ground
- 1 medium sweet potato, sliced thin
- 4-6 figs, chopped
- 1 apple, sliced
- Cooking oil spray

DIRECTIONS: Season meat with salt, pepper, and cinnamon. Slice the sweet potato thinly. Quarter, core, and slice the apple into eight pieces. Slice or chop figs. Spray a large piece of aluminum foil with cooking oil spray. On each pork chop, layer sweet potato slices, apple slices, and figs. Wrap well with foil and bake for 35 to 40 minutes.

Dog Bite: My little dog's portion of Cauliflower Mash & Pork

K9 NOTE: *Modification Required.* Figs can cause an allergic reaction in some dogs, and may cause diarrhea and vomiting if given in large amounts. Figs are not poisonous but when feeding Fido figs, feed only a small bite without the pit. Never let them ingest the pit and never let your dog get a hold of the bone (see notes on bones).

STEVE'S STIR FRY

HUMAN VERSION: (see K9 Version below)
- 1 ¼ chicken cutlets or beef, scallops, shrimp, fish
- Sesame oil
- Chili oil
- Olive oil
- 3 tbsp. ginger, chopped
- 3 cloves garlic, chopped
- 1-2 yellow squash, chopped
- 1 zucchini, chopped
- ½ bunch Asian broccoli, chopped
- ¾ of a bag bean sprouts
- 3 - 4 green onions, chopped
- ¼ cup snow peas
- ¾ of 1 can water chestnuts
- ¾ of 1 can bamboo shoots

<u>DIRECTIONS:</u> Slice chicken into 3" strips along the grain. Put into a shallow bowl and season with a touch of salt and pepper. Pour 3 tbsp. sesame oil and ½ tsp. of chili oil over chicken. Add a tsp. of fresh garlic and ginger mixture and mix in over chicken. Let sit for 10 minutes.

Beef: Slice against the grain into strips. If using beef or carne asada, make a marinade of 50% soy sauce / 50% white Miso liquid. Add fresh chopped ginger and garlic. Add 2 tbsp. honey, or 1 tsp. sugar and 1 tbsp. sake or white wine (optional), 1 tsp. rice vinegar, and 1 tsp. Mirin. Mix and marinate for about ½ hour.

Wash vegetables. Cut the broccoli into medium pieces and slice the squash. Cut off the white end of the green onion and slice into 2" pieces. Cut edges off snow peas and remove the stringy part. Put vegetables in another bowl and season with touch of salt and pepper and add 3 tbsp. sesame oil and ½ tsp. chili oil and mix with hands. Rub olive oil with paper towel onto a frying pan. Heat frying pan with 2 tbsp. olive oil and lay chicken flat to allow searing. Once it's seared, flip and cook the other side. You want to get it crisp with a crust on it and then turn it down after about 3 or 4 minutes.

Heat the wok and throw in vegetables along with garlic and ginger mixture (but add the bean sprouts last when the chicken is just about done). Mix the chicken into the Wok. Add the bean sprouts on top of the chicken and dribble a little more sesame oil on top. Stir-fry for another two minutes and serve.

Scallops: Use only fresh large-sized. Wash, dry, and season with salt and pepper. Make chili oil by chopping up just a pinch of Habanero, Serrano, or red chili peppers or a combo of all, and add some chopped ginger and garlic to a sauté pan. Sauté in olive oil. We are just seasoning the oil for the scallops to be cooked in. You can scoop out the pepper, garlic, and ginger mixture with a slotted spoon if the peppers start to burn. Cook scallops, flipping a few times in the flavored chili oil, for about four to five minutes.

Use a wok to stir fry veggies. Rub wok with paper towel and oil then heat on high. Pour a bit more sesame oil over the veggies then stir fry on high while mixing. Then add the scallops into the wok and finish cooking the last minute together - save the bean sprouts to add the last 2 or 3 min. put them in right before you transfer the protein in. I like my veggies al dente.

K9 VERSION:
- 1 squirt salmon oil (from a pet store or catalog)
- ¼ lb. chicken or beef, plain, unseasoned
- 2 tbsp. broccoli, chopped small
- ½ yellow squash, chopped small
- 1/4 bag frozen peas
- 1 small carrot, chopped

<u>DIRECTIONS</u>: Steam, boil, or use a non-stick pan with just a touch of Canola oil or olive oil to cook everything. Dogs can have a touch of plain boiled chicken or meat with steamed bean sprouts, broccoli, peas, squash, and zucchini. Add a little salmon oil for the sauce after it's cooked. A side of rice for Fido would be nice!

K9 NOTE: This K9 version can be used as a dog bite for good behavior!

ORGANIC TURKEY MEATBALLS

- 1 & 1/4 lb. organic turkey breast, ground
- Fennel, finely chopped
- Apple, cored, seeded, finely chopped

- Celery, diced, finely chopped
- 1 tbsp. pine nuts (optional) (*not for K9s; see note below)
- 1 - organic free-range egg
- 1/2 tsp. fresh sage, finely chopped (optional) (*see K9 note)
- 1 tsp. rosemary, finely chopped
- A few shakes of dry Italian seasoning
- A touch paprika (to taste, optional) (*see K9 note)
- Dash salt & pepper
- 1/8 cup flaxseed sprinkles or ground flaxseed meal
- All-purpose flour
- Cooking oil spray
- 1 tbsp. olive oil
- ¼ cup Italian parsley, finely chopped
- 1 tbsp. parsley butter or plain butter

Make parsley butter ahead of time by placing a blend of parsley, sweet butter, and a squeeze of lemon in a food processor or blender. Blend until smooth. Transfer to a bowl, cover and store in refrigerator up to one week. You can also roll the butter into a long cylinder shape and wrap in plastic and then freeze up to one month. Sometimes I blend in a few anchovies and use it for basting fish, but don't add anchovies to this meatball dish.

<u>DIRECTIONS</u>: Organize all ingredients. Place ground turkey in a large bowl and add ingredients. Mix thoroughly by hand (don't over mix). Add seasonings, egg, and everything listed above except the cooking oil, cooking oil spray, parsley butter and flour. Wash hands or use rubber gloves: form quarter- or half-dollar size meatballs and place on a piece of wax paper.

TIP: Lightly wet your hands with water and your meatballs will be easier to roll and form and less likely to stick to your hands. Now roll each meatball lightly in flour. Place a few dabs of parsley butter into an oven-safe fry pan and cook on stovetop at a med-high heat and sear meatballs. Don't flip or roll them around until you get a nice sear on one side, then sear all sides of the meatball before you give them a shake.

Once evenly seared, place the whole pan in a pre-heated hot oven at 350 degrees for another 5 to 10 minutes or until they are thoroughly cooked. Cooking time will depend on how big the meatballs are and how hot your oven is. I usually do about 5 min. on stovetop and 10 to 12 min. in oven. Serve as an appetizer or add to small bowl of hot chicken broth and sprinkle finely-chopped parsley and Parmesan cheese on top!

K9 NOTE: ***Minimal Modification.*** If sharing with your dog be sure you use minimal amounts of butter, sage, paprika. It's best to skip the pine nuts in your dog's meatballs. If your dog ingests a few little pine nuts it shouldn't pose a problem (see notes on nuts). A few bites of sage are fine but avoid giving dog's large amounts of sage (see note on sage).

DOG BITES THANKSGIVING FEAST

STEVE'S ROAST TURKEY

- 1 – 8-9 lb. free-range turkey
- 3 stalks celery, chopped
- 1 large apple, chopped (no core)
- 1 large orange, chopped
- Root veggies (optional)* No onion
- 1 pkg. fresh poultry seasoning
- Herbs of Provence (dry)
- Kosher salt
- Pepper
- Paprika
- Olive oil
- Butter
- 1 cup white wine

DIRECTIONS: Wash and dry the turkey. Stuff the fresh poultry seasoning carefully tucked under skin and inside both sides. Rub oil or butter (or both) salt, pepper and seasonings all over the turkey. Stuff with apples, oranges, celery, fresh poultry herbs and spices. Place cut root veggies at the bottom of the pan: turnips, rutabaga, celery, and carrots, as well as more orange and apple and white wine (Sauvignon Blanc).

Put in oven and roast (based on pounds per hour). Start basting after the first hour of cooking using the drippings that have dripped into the bottom of the pan and have blended with the root veggies and wine. When you baste, take out of oven fast and close oven door right away, baste and put right back in oven to avoid losing heat. Also you may need to lightly cover the bird with a sheet of tin foil the last ½ hour of cooking in order not to burn the top of the bird. Let cool before slicing.

K9 NOTE: *Minimal Modification.* Give your dog a small bite of white meat with no skin, fat, or sauces. Alcohol burns off during cooking and you are only feeding Fido a bite, but if in doubt, use apple juice instead of wine if you will be sharing it with your dog.

Roasting Times for Stuffed Turkey	
Turkey Weight	**Hours**
6 to 8 pounds	3 to 3-1/2 hours
8 to 12 pounds	3-1/2 to 4-1/2 hours
12 to 16 pounds	4-1/2 to 5-1/2 hours
16 to 20 pounds	5-1/2 to 6 hours
20 to 24 pounds	6 to 6-1/2 hours
Roasting Times for Unstuffed Turkey	
Turkey Weight	**Hours**
6 to 8 pounds	2-1/2 to 3 hours
8 to 12 pounds	3 to 4 hours
12 to 16 pounds	4 to 5 hours
16 to 20 pounds	5 to 5-1/2 hours
20 to 24 pounds	5-1/2 to 6 hours

STUFFING

HUMAN VERSION: (see K9 Version below)
- 1 - 32 oz. box low-sodium, organic chicken broth
- Turkey liver, lightly browned, chopped
- Chicken livers, chopped and browned (optional)
- French, challah, matzah, sourdough, or French rolls, torn
- Yellow onion, chopped
- 1 box mushrooms, sliced
- 3-4 stalks celery, chopped
- 1 tsp. dry poultry seasoning
- ½ to ¾ pack fresh poultry seasoning
- Salt (to taste)
- Pepper (to taste)
- Paprika (to taste)
- 1-2 tsp. garlic, fresh, minced or chopped

DIRECTIONS: Pre-heat oven to 350. On the stovetop: brown the livers, onion, chopped celery, and mushrooms. Let cool slightly, then mix everything together gently by hand in a large bowl (including season). Spray large Pyrex with cooking oil or rub lightly with oil and lay stuffing in the Pyrex. Season more on top with a generous amount of paprika and poultry seasoning. Place in oven and bake at 350 for 35 – 60 min. depending on how much you make. You may have to cover with tin foil the last 25 min. of cooking in order not to burn the top.

K9 VERSION: Make a separate batch of stuffing for Rover without mushrooms and spices. Use a modest amount of liver, and the celery should be diced very small. You can also add carrots, peas, and little bits of diced apples and cooked turkey breast. A few tbsp. of low-sodium chicken broth and a small bite of bread are okay.

K9 NOTE: *Modification Required.* Dogs cannot have several ingredients in Stuffing, so be sure to modify using the K9 Version. Remember, we are only feeding little bites to dogs; don't over feed Rover.

SWEET CRANBERRY SAUCE

- ½ lb. cranberries (fresh or frozen)
- 1 cup water
- ½ cup honey or maple syrup (or less to taste)

<u>DIRECTIONS</u>: Wash the cranberries (if fresh) and put them in a pan with the water. Cover and simmer over low heat for 12- 20 minutes or until berries break down. When the cooking is done and the sauce is still hot, add the sweetening to taste. Chill thoroughly before serving. For a finer sauce, blend or strain the sauce. This is also delicious on cake and ice cream.

K9 NOTE: *Minimal Modification.* Dog friendly (in moderation) due to sugar. Fido's Thanksgiving dinner includes: a small side of dog friendly stuffing, one small bite of plain turkey breast (no fat, bones), a tiny bite of Cranberry Sauce, a small bite of Steamed Baby potatoes, Cauliflower Mash, Baked Squash or Honey Carrots and you have a great Holiday meal for your pooch!

WHOLE ROAST CHICKEN

- 1 free-range, antibiotic-free organic chicken
- Herbs of Provence or dry Italian seasoning
- 1 pack fresh poultry blend
- Salt, Pepper (inside and out)
- 1 orange or tangerine, segmented
- 1 or 2 apples
- Safflower oil
- Butter

DIRECTIONS: Wash and dry the chicken. (Save the chicken livers and set aside to make Steve's Chicken Liver Doggie Treats below.) Rub oil or butter (or both) salt, pepper and dry seasonings all over the chicken - enough to cover the bird inside and out (as shown in the picture). Stuff the fresh poultry seasoning carefully tucked under skin and inside. Stuff with apples and oranges, fresh and dry poultry herbs and spices.
Optional: Place root veggies at the bottom of the pan: turnips, rutabaga, celery, and carrots, as well as more orange and apple.

Put in oven and roast based on pounds per hour (see chart above under Turkey). The average chicken takes about 60 to 75 minutes to cook if you do it on bake at 350. Start basting the last 20 minutes of cooking using the drippings that have dripped into the bottom of the pan and have blended with the root veggies if you used any. When you baste, take out of oven fast and close oven door right away, baste and put right back in oven to avoid losing heat. Also, you may need to lightly cover the bird with a sheet of tin foil the last few minutes of cooking in order not to burn the top of the bird. Let cool before slicing.

K9 NOTE: *Minimal Modification.* Give your dog a small bite of white meat (with no skin, fat, or sauces) and a bite of apple.

STEVE'S HOMEMADE CHICKEN LIVER DOG TREATS

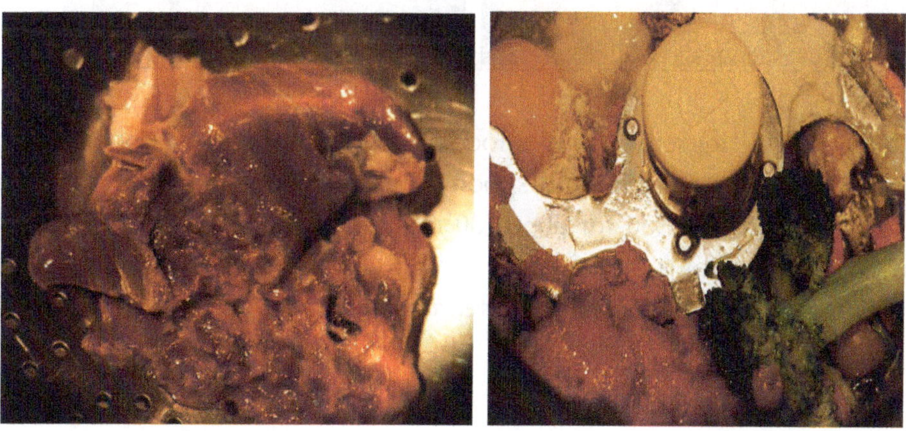

Recommended for K9's only!

- Chicken livers (from your bird)
- 2 pieces steamed broccoli
- 1 or 2 steamed carrots
- 1 or 2 baby steamed potatoes
- 1 raw egg
- ½ cup of flower
- A touch of salt
- ½ tsp. of honey or maple syrup (optional)
- 1 tsp. butter (optional)
- 1 large tbsp. old fashioned rolled oats (optional)
- 1/4 tsp. aluminum-free baking soda (optional)
- 1/8 tsp. aluminum-free baking powder (optional)
- Cooking oil spray or butter

DIRECTIONS: Put all ingredients in a food processor except the cooking spray and blend. Then grease the muffin tin and spoon the mix into the muffin tin and place in a preheated oven on bake at 350 for about 30 minutes. Let cool before serving. This K9 snack can be stuffed into a Kong™ toy for good behavior or served a plethora of different ways (like picture below) with steamed carrots, broccoli, and one small baby potato.

VEAL SCALOPPINI

*Certified Humanely Raised Veal

- Veal, ½ lb. per person (*Certified Humanely Raised Veal)
- A touch olive oil
- A touch of butter
- A few sage leaves, chopped (*see K9 note below)
- A few tbsp. parsley, chopped
- Salt & pepper
- Herbs of Provence or Italian seasoning
- Italian Pancetta bacon

<u>DIRECTIONS</u>: Season Veal with salt, pepper and Herbs of Provence. Sauté veal in butter and oil. Add pancetta, sage, and parsley. Cook on med-high for 5 minutes. This dish goes great with my Sardinian Pasta!

DOG BITE: Medium-size K9 Portion of Veal Scaloppini

K9 NOTE: *Minimal Modification.* One serving of Veal Scaloppini as shown above for a medium-size dog! Don't feed your dog more than a crumb-size bite or two of sage, if any. Less is more, and moderation is key!

SWEET TREAT DOG BITES

APPLE-CINNAMON OATMEAL COOKIES

Yield: 2 dozen cookies

- 2 tbsp. honey
- 1 cup coconut flour
- 1 cup uncooked oatmeal
- 2 apples peeled, cored & chopped
- 3/4 tsp. cinnamon
- ¼ cup applesauce (Steve's Homemade)
- 3/4 cup apple juice
- 3 tbsp. water

DIRECTIONS: Pre-heat oven to 350.
Grease a cookie sheet. Peel, core, and chop apples into small pieces. Add all ingredients into a big bowl and gently mix with a wooden spoon. In two to three small batches, scoop into a food processor on the dough setting (or blender) and mix into a thick paste until all the mix is blended together. Add more apple juice if needed. Spoon onto cookie sheet in the shape of cookies. You can flatten just a little. Bake for 30 minutes. Turn oven off and let them cook for an additional 20 to 30 minutes.

K9 NOTE: *Minimal Modification.* Moderation is key! These are a great dog treat to use for training. This is an A-list treat for dogs and a C-list treat for humans but not bad.

APPLESAUCE BREAD

- 1 ¼ cup homemade applesauce (Steve's Homemade Applesauce)
- 1 tsp. baking powder, aluminum-free
- 1 tsp. baking soda, aluminum-free
- ¼ tsp. kosher salt
- 1 tsp. ground cinnamon
- 1 cup all-purpose flour
- ½ cup brown rice flour
- ½ cup amaranth flour
- 1 small hand full of dried cranberries
- 1 pinch or two of plain whole dried oats (optional)
- Cooking oil spray or butter
- 1 room-temp. large egg
- ¼ cup maple syrup
- ¼ cup sunflower, canola or lite olive oil
  (Use melted and cooled butter instead or a mixture of oil and butter)
- ½ cup plain low-fat yogurt
- ½ tsp. vanilla extract

DIRECTIONS: Pre-heat oven to 350. Use loaf pan coated with cooking oil spray or butter.

In Dry bowl: mix all-purpose flour, brown rice flour, Amaranth flour (2 cups total). Whisk flours with aluminum-free baking powder, aluminum-free baking soda, ¼ tsp. kosher salt, ground cinnamon

Wet Bowl: 1 room-temp. large egg; beaten. Add homemade applesauce. Then add sunflower oil, canola, veg, or lite olive oil. You can use a bit of melted and cooled butter instead or a mixture of oil and butter. Add plain low-fat yogurt, maple syrup, and vanilla extract. Mix together.

Combine wet to dry bowls and mix using a plastic spatula. Add a handful of cranberries (optional). Then smooth into a greased baking loaf pan and top with dried rolled oats. Cook 45-55 minutes until golden brown. Use toothpick to check for doneness. Let cool before serving.

K9 NOTE: *Minimal Modification.* Feed tiny bites only. Moderation is key!

BANANA BREAD

- 3 large bananas, mashed
- 1 large egg, room-temp.
- ½ cup fat-free plain yogurt
- ¼ cup sunflower, canola, or lite olive oil
- ¼ cup unsalted butter, melted and cooled
- 1 tsp. vanilla extract
- ¼ cup Turbinado sugar or light Broun sugar
- 1 cup: all-purpose flour

- ¼ cup Brown Rice flour
- ¼ cup Amaranth flour
- 1 tsp. baking powder (aluminum free)
- 1 tsp. baking soda, (aluminum free
- 3/4 tsp. salt
- ½ tsp. cinnamon, ground
- ¼ cup flax seed sprinkles or flaxseed meal
- Cooking oil spray

DIRECTIONS: Pre-heat oven to 350. Using a loaf pan, spray with oil or lightly butter to coat pan.

Glass Bowl #1: 3 large ripe bananas, mash. Add ½ cup low fat plain yogurt, raw room temp egg and mix with fork, sugar, sunflower oil, Melted and cooled butter, and vanilla. Hand whisk.

Glass Bowl #2: 1 cup all-purpose flour, ¼ cup Brown Rice flour, ¼ cup Amaranth flour, ¼ cup flax seed sprinkles or flaxseed meal, 1 tsp. baking powder, 1 tsp. baking soda Aluminum free, ¾ tsp. salt, ½ tsp. cinnamon, ground.

Mix bowl # 1 & #2 ingredients together and whisk until blended together, but don't overdo it. Then immediately pour into a sprayed or greased loaf pan and bake in a preheated oven of a temp of 350 for 50 - 55 minutes. Test with toothpick for doneness. Use spatula or knife to run along edge of pan then flip, cool, and eat.

K9 NOTE: *Minimal Modification.* I personally don't like it too sweet, so this is perfect for me and perfect to share a small bite with my dog. If you're not going to be sharing with your pooch, and if you like it sweet, you can double the sugar. Moderation is key! Only share small bites with your pooch!

BANANA CHIPS

- Bananas, sliced
- Coconut oil
- Pineapple juice
- Olive oil

DIRECTIONS: Slice bananas as thinly as possible and place in a bowl of pineapple juice. Ladle the banana slices out and on to a paper towel to blot excess water. Arrange bananas on parchment paper on a cookie sheet. Drizzle with coconut oil. Bake on low (200 degrees) for about 3 hours. After 3 hours, turn the bananas over so the underside can get crispy. Cook 1 more hour or until desired crispness.

Alternate Cooking Method: You can also do the same method using a dehydrator. Slice bananas thin and fry in coconut oil. Another snack recipe is use root veggies like yams, sweet potatoes, or beets and slice thin, then coat evenly with a little olive oil, (salt yours but not Fido's). Arrange slices on a cookie sheet and bake at 400 degrees for about 30 minutes. Check every so often to avoid burning. Let cool.

K9 NOTE: *Minimal Modification.* Great for a road trip!

BANANA & YOGURT PARFAIT

- Banana
- plain yogurt
- Honey or date syrup

DIRECTIONS: Slice bananas and place on top of plain yogurt. Drizzle with honey or date syrup. Serve as a simple breakfast, snack or desert.

K9 NOTE: Share a small bit with your furry friend.

BLUEBERRY COFFEE CAKE

- 1 1/2 cups flour
  (I use a 50-50 mixture of all-purpose flour and either gluten-free or whole wheat)
- 1tsp. aluminum-free baking powder
- ¼ tsp. aluminum-free baking soda
- ¼ tsp. salt
- 1/4 cup (minus 1 tbsp.) Turbinado sugar, sugar-in-the-raw, or brown sugar
  (for cake)
- 1 tbsp. Turbinado sugar, sugar-in-the-raw, or brown sugar (to sprinkle on top)
- 6 tbsp. melted butter
- 1 tsp. vanilla extract
- 1 large organic egg (room temp.)
- 1 large egg white
- 1 1/3 cups goat's milk or low-fat buttermilk, plain rice or coconut milk
- Cooking oil spray
- 2 cups fresh organic blueberries

DIRECTIONS: Preheat oven to 350.

In bowl #1: combine flour, baking powder, baking soda, half the sugar and salt. Stir with a wire whisk. In bowl two: add the other half of the sugar except for one tsp. and butter;

beat with an electric mixer on medium until blended. Then add vanilla, egg and egg white to bowl #2. Beat and mix. Start and end with the flour mixture, but alternate flour and the goat's milk to the sugar/butter mixture. Mix it all together.

Spoon half of the batter into a nine-inch round baking pan that's been sprayed with cooking oil spray or rubbed with butter. Then drop ½ the blueberries on top and sprinkle with a bit more sugar over the berries. Pour the rest of the batter and rest of the berries and a bit more sugar on top. Bake at 350. Cool on wire rack.

K9 NOTE: There is no coffee in this recipe, so it is okay for dogs in moderation. Feed tiny bites as dogs shouldn't have too much sugar. Suggestions: Cut back on the sugar a bit or try using maple syrup, or molasses instead, but still not too much.

CHARGRILLED NECTARINES

- 4 Nectarines, halved and pitted
- 1 tbsp. honey

<u>DIRECTIONS</u>: Cut nectarines in half. Brush cut sides of nectarine halves with honey. BBQ, cut-side-down, over medium-low coals for 5 minutes until lightly charred but still firm. Or try broiling, cut-side-up for 5 minutes. Drizzle with honey.

K9 NOTE: Never give young puppies honey, and the nectarine pits are, of course, dangerous for dogs. Keep pits away from your K9. Feed only a few bites of the meat of the fruit; moderation is key!

PUP-KIN PIE

CRUST

- 2 tbsp. butter, melted
- 1 tsp. date sugar (or 1 teaspoon honey or molasses)
- 1/4 cup sunflower seeds, crushed

- 3 or 4 dates, seedless
- 1 tiny pinch salt
- 1/8 tsp. cinnamon, ground

DIRECTIONS: Grind dates and sunflower seeds in a food processor. Mix in warm butter with crust ingredients: Add honey, sugar, or molasses to both the crust and the filling. Add salt and cinnamon until it is a doughy consistency. Then roll out and press in a deep-dish pie pan, pressing up against the edges.

In a pre-heated oven at 350: heat crust for 5 min. until browned; let cool. Turn oven up to 425. In a glass bowl: add filling ingredients and mix with a hand mixer or fork. Pour into pie crust. Place back in oven at 425 for about 15 min. Reduce heat to 350 and continue to bake for an additional 50-55 min. Place toothpick in center; if it comes out dry, it is done. Chill before serving.

PUMPKIN PIE FILLING

- 1 - 15 oz. can pure pumpkin (sugar-free, organic)
  (do not use pie filling as it contains nutmeg)
- 1/8 tsp. cinnamon, ground
- 3/4 cups coconut milk
- 1/2 cup goat's milk or rice milk
- 1 tbsp. date sugar or 1 tsp. honey or molasses)
- 4 eggs

DIRECTIONS: Mix all ingredients together in a bowl. Pour into pie crust ½ in. from top.

K9 NOTE: *Minimal Modification.* Read the label: if you buy "pumpkin spice" instead of pure pumpkin it will contain nutmeg, which is toxic. Cinnamon is good for the heart and for K9 diabetes (in moderation). Avoid date pits as they are dangerous. Give your dog only minimal amounts of crust as too many dates can upset their stomach.

TOFU WHIP CREAM

- 1   6 - 8 oz. package soft, plain tofu
- 4 tbsp. maple syrup
- 1 & 1/ 2 tbsp. vanilla flavoring
- 1 - 2 dashes of cinnamon
- Blueberries (optional)

<u>DIRECTIONS</u>: Rinse the tofu (avoid processed, flavored varieties) in cold water and press between several layers of paper towels to squeeze out all water possible. Break the tofu into small pieces or chunks and put it in a blender or food processor. Add the remaining ingredients and blend to taste. Chill and serve.

K9 NOTE: *Minimal Modification.* Less is more; feed in moderation.

ZUCCHINI BREAD

- 1 cup all-purpose flour
- ½ cup brown rice flour
- 2 large zucchini, grated
- 3/4 tsp. baking soda

- 1/2 tsp. baking powder
- ¼ sea salt or kosher salt
- ½ tsp. cinnamon, ground
- ½ cup sunflower oil (or canola, safflower, or lite olive oil)
- ½ - ¾ cup (about 5 oz.) Tubinado sugar
- 2 large eggs, room temp.
- 1 tsp. vanilla extract
- ½ cup apple, grated
- 1 tbsp. coconut, grated

DIRECTIONS: Pre-heat oven to 350. Spray loaf pan with oil or butter to coat. Wash zucchini, cut off ends (keep skin on) and grate.
Medium mixing bowl #1: mix all of the dry ingredients together and hand whisk.
Large mixing bowl # 2: add wet and fresh ingredients together and blend with your hands. Then add the dry and wet bowls together and mix with a hand whisker. Pour into loaf pan. Sprinkle grated coconut on top. Bake 60 - 65 min. Test with a toothpick; let cool. Use spatula or knife to run along edge of pan, then flip, slice and eat!

K9 NOTE: *Minimal Modification.* Serve one tiny dog bite to a tiny dog; one small dog bite for a small dog; two for a medium dog; and three for a large breed. Daily K9 diet consists of 90% Vet recommended foods supplemented with 10% *dog bites*. Surprise your dog for good behavior! Moderation is key (mainly because of the sugar).

BREAKFAST BITES

BLUEBERRY-RICOTTA *PUP*-CAKES

Feeds 2 humans and 1 small to medium-size K9!

- 1 cup wheat-free, gluten-free or multi-grain pancake mix
- Dash of oats (optional)
- 1 tbsp. safflower or vegetable oil
- 1 tsp. honey
- 1 organic free-range egg
- 1 tbsp. Ricotta cheese or yogurt
- ¼ cup plain rice milk or goat's milk
- Blueberries
- Maple syrup

<u>DIRECTIONS</u>: If using oats, cover and soak the oats with a couple tbsp. of milk for about 15 - 20 minutes. Mix all ingredients (except blueberries and maple syrup) in a blender or mix by hand. If it's done by hand, make a well in the flour, then beat in the egg, honey, oil or melted cooled butter, ricotta, and a dash of oats. Transfer to a pitcher for easy pouring. (It helps to let the batter rest about ten minutes before pouring.) The batter should be thick with little tiny bubbles on the surface.

Heat a cast-iron fry pan or non-stick griddle or heavy frying pan over medium heat until a drop of water sizzles when splashed on the pan. Add oil or butter or a bit of both; then pour in one pancake and immediately add a few blueberries on top. Flip once or twice until golden brown. Serve with a touch of maple syrup.

K9 NOTE: *Minimal Modification.* One medium pancake can be shared with your dog with a bit of honey or salmon oil in small bites for good behavior.

CEREAL

Cereals like plain rice puffs or Cheerios, cream of rice, cream of wheat, or oatmeal with a dash of cinnamon, bananas, blueberries and plain rice or goat's milk are okay for dogs.

K9 NOTE: *Minimal Modification.* However, most cereals are not good for dogs due to sugars, artificial sweeteners, and nuts. Dogs can be lactose intolerant just like humans, can so pay close attention -- if you have never given them dairy products before and they are lactose intolerant, they will display the same symptoms including diarrhea, and gas. Some rice milks are high in sugar and salt so it's best to use plain unsweetened, or use only a minimal amount. Goat's milk is very healthy for dogs in moderation. If your dog is sensitive to wheat then of course avoid.

EGG-IN-A-HOLE

- French or sourdough bread, sliced
- Eggs, 1 per slice of bread
- Smoked salmon or lox (optional for humans; K9's - too salty)
- Turkey or ham, sliced (optional)

- Olive oil
- Touch of butter (or Earth Balance for Vegans)
- Spinach, sautéed (optional)
- Parsley, finely chopped
- Vegan hollandaise sauce (optional)

DIRECTIONS: Cut out the middle of each slice of bread (the size for an egg to fit). For a perfect hole, use a cookie cutter or small glass. Put a dab of butter and a few drops of olive oil into a medium-hot frying pan. Put the bread into the pan. Then put the egg in the hole in the bread (try not to break the yolk; some people like to break the yolk but then you have nothing to ooze out). Wait until the egg is nearly cooked, then flip once (careful not to break yolk). I like to make a stack with a slice of turkey or ham topped with a slice of tomato. You can also finish with Vegan Hollandaise sauce (recipe below).

K9 VERSION: A healthier version of an egg bite for Fido would be to hard boil a free-range organic egg. Cool, peel, and chop. Mix in a squirt of salmon oil and sprinkle with a dash of finely-chopped parsley and place on ½ slice white bread.

K9 NOTE: *Minimal Modification.* A bite or two of plain egg-in-a-hole with a bite of low-sodium turkey is fine with a touch of homemade Vegan Hollandaise (as most are made with raw eggs). Be sure your dog's egg is fully cooked and avoid smoked salmon or lox due to salt content. Although tomato isn't toxic, the stems and leaves can be and, in my experience, dogs just don't do well with tomatoes.

VEGAN HOLLANDAISE SAUCE

- 2 tbsp. all-purpose flour or tapioca flour
- Pinch (about 1/8 to ¼ tsp.) turmeric
- 11 oz. coconut milk
- 2 tbsp. nutritional yeast
- Juice of half a lemon
- 1 tbsp. Veganaise or safflower mayo

- 2 tbsp. Earth Balance
- Salt and pepper (to taste)
- A tiny pinch of cyanine pepper (optional)

DIRECTIONS: Heat a small saucepan over medium-low heat. Add Earth Balance and heat until sizzling. Whisk in the flour to make a paste and continue to whisk constantly for one minute. Add a pinch of turmeric for color and mix well. Slowly whisk in coconut milk. Bring sauce to a boil, whisking frequently. Boil for 2 - 3 minutes; remove from heat. Whisk in the cayenne and nutritional yeast. Add the lemon juice and mix well. Season to taste with salt and a bit of black pepper. Add Veganaise. Keep the sauce warm by covering it with a lid or put it oven on low heat.

K9 NOTE: *Minimal Modification.* Only feed ¼ tsp. to 1 tbsp., depending on the size of your dog. Surprise your dog for doing something good!

FRENCH TOAST

Serves: 2

- 3 eggs
- 2 egg whites
- Challah, French, or sourdough bread, sliced
- Butter
- Olive oil
- Vanilla (a few drops)
- 1-2 tsp. goats milk, or plain rice milk
- Maple syrup
- Blueberries

DIRECTIONS: Mix the eggs, milk, and vanilla together. Dip the bread into the mixture, turning to coat both sides with a soak; 30 seconds per side, gently turning once or twice. Add a dab of butter and a few drops of olive oil to a medium-hot frying pan and put the bread into the pan and cook until brown on each side. Add toppings.

K9 NOTE: *Minimal Modification.* Use honey or Salmon oil instead of syrup. Share a small bite for good behavior.

GRANOLA *BARK!*

Yield: 12 bars
- 8 oz. shelled, unsalted sunflower seeds
- 5 oz. shelled, unsalted pumpkin (pepitas) seeds
- 2.5 cups rolled oats
- 1/8 - ¼ cup dried coconut flakes
- 1/8 - ¼ cup dried cranberries
- 1/8 cup carob chips
- 2 tbsp. honey
- 2 tbsp. maple syrup
- 1 tsp. molasses
- 1 tsp. vanilla
- A touch of salt

<u>DIRECTIONS</u>: Pulse the sunflower and pumpkin seeds in a food processor. Then add oats and pulse a second more (don't overdo it). You don't want a powder and want it a bit crunchy. Pour mixture into a large ungreased Pyrex and place in a pre-heated oven at 350 for about 5 min. Remove from oven; mix and put back for another 5 min. Take out of oven and pour into a large bowl and let cool about 5 min.

In a small sauce pan, melt butter, honey, maple syrup, and molasses. Stir with a wooden spoon until blended together and hot. Then pour into the big bowl and mix everything together. Rub a little olive oil on a paper towel and rub on a large Pyrex dish and push in and flatten the mixture. Press hard into the Pyrex. Cover and refrigerate for two hours. Take out of fridge and cut into bars.

K9 NOTE: Only crumb size bites for your dog. It is too sweet to give large amounts.
Some dogs have trouble digesting the seeds, so you may want to crush your dog's bite before serving.

MATZAH BREI WITH APPLESAUCE

Serves 2 people & 1 dog!
- 5-6 Matzah crackers (for Fido use salt-free or low-salt)
- 4 organic free-range eggs
- Salt (to taste)
- Olive, or Vegetable oil
- Butter

DIRECTIONS: Run cold water over matzah on a plate or in a strainer until soft, but not quite mushy. Drain the matzah with a strainer. Mix the eggs in a bowl, then poor the eggs and matzah at the same time into a medium-hot frying pan. Add a dash of salt and fry, gently flipping with a spatula. Cook until the eggs are cooked and the matzah is hot all the way through. This goes great with my homemade Applesauce and sausage.

K9 NOTE: *Minimal Modification.* Use salt in moderation, especially for K9's.

RICE CAKES WITH FRESH WILD SALMON

- 1 lb. fresh wild salmon
- 1 tbsp. olive oil
- Salt (to taste)
- 2 cups medium-grain Cal rose or sushi rice, cooked
- 3 ¾ cups water
- 1 tsp. butter (optional)
- 1 tbsp. dill, chopped
- 1 tbsp. parsley, finely chopped
- ¼ cup. plain yogurt
- 1 egg (optional to serve on top)
- 1/2 of a large lemon or juice of 1 small lemon

<u>DIRECTIONS</u>: Rinse rice for about two minutes and cook rice per package instructions. Add butter (optional). I like 2 cup of rice and 3 & 3/4 cup water. Bring to a boil. Add rice and stir. Reduce heat to a low simmer. Cover and cook 15 min. (don't open lid until done.) Let cool.

Pre-heat oven to 450. Season salmon with a drizzle of olive oil and salt.

Put salmon in a greased Pyrex or baking pan lined with greased tin foil and bake for about 14 min. or until done. Alternate cooking method is to place salmon in a pan, just barely covered with water and boil uncovered for about 14 minutes. Let salmon cool. Peel off skin if any.

In a Bowl: Mix in all ingredients together, and then place the bowl in the freezer for about 8 minutes. Shape cakes (about the size of little burger patties) on a greased baking pan. Flatten down with a wooden spoon and bake at 450 for about 15 - 18 minutes. Take out and flip. Turn oven down to 350 and put them back for 5 more minutes until brown on top. Let cool before serving.

Note: I love topping mine with an egg cooked over medium for breakfast or as a snack, topped with my vegan hollandaise sauce. My dog loves his any way he can get it!

K9 NOTE: *Minimal Modification.* A bite can help reduce barking. It's hard to bark with a mouth full of salmon rice cake!

STEEL-CUT OATMEAL

- 1 part steel-cut oats
- 3 parts water
- Touch of salt
- 1 or 2 dates or 1 tsp. brown sugar
- Banana, sliced
- Cranberries, dried
- 1 tbsp. rice or goat's milk (optional)

DIRECTIONS: Put oats, water, and salt in a pot. Allow a couple of inches of room at the top of the pot so the oats don't boil over. Bring to a boil on medium high-heat. Turn heat down to low, then simmer the oats for 20 minutes uncovered, stirring every few minutes. While it's boiling, chop 1 or 2 fresh (seedless) dates for sweetness and add to oatmeal. Add a little brown sugar to yours; not the dogs. Top with banana slices or dried cranberries.

K9 NOTE: *Minimal Modification.* Dates are non-toxic to K9's but must be fed in moderation as some dogs are sensitive; just a few small crumb size bites. Never let your dog eat a date pit.

PUP PARFEIT

- Yogurt (non-fat)
- Blueberries
- Honeydew, cubed
- Cantaloupe, cubed
- Apple, sliced
- Sunflower or pumpkin seeds, shelled
- Honey
- Tofu (optional)

<u>DIRECTIONS</u>: Place yogurt in a parfait glass or dog bowl. Add fruit as desired. Sprinkle the top with sunflower seeds and drizzle with a little honey.

K9 NOTE: *Minimal Modification.* You can also add a touch of salmon oil to your dog's serving. Do not give honey to young puppies; only a small amount for adult K9s.

TOFU SPINACH SCRAMBLE

- Canola oil spray
- 10 oz. water-packed, firm light tofu, drained
- 3 cups spinach, chopped
- Pinch of sea salt & black pepper
- 2 free-range omega-3 eggs

<u>DIRECTIONS</u>: Spray skillet with canola oil. Add crumbled tofu and cook over medium-high heat, stirring occasionally for three minutes or until dry and golden. Add the spinach and cook for one minute or until tender. Season with salt and pepper. Whisk eggs and add them to the skillet; scramble together and serve.

K9 NOTE: *Minimal Modification Required.* Spinach in large quantities can be dangerous for your K9! Share a small bite; moderation is key!

TOFU FRUIT SMOOTHIE

- 2 cups fresh blueberries
- 1-2 bananas
- 3-4 oz. tofu
- 1 tbsp. honey or maple syrup
- 2-3 tsp. vanilla flavoring
- Water for dogs; fruit juice for humans

<u>DIRECTIONS</u>: Blend ingredients thoroughly, adding just enough water or juice to bring to desired consistency. Serve immediately. If you like a thicker consistency, use frozen blueberries and bananas. You can add dates for extra flavor.

K9 NOTE: *Minimal Modification.* If you are going to give your dog dates, give sparingly without pits. Share a small amount with your furry friend. Remember, moderation is key!

BONUS!

NOT SO DOG FRIENDLY…
SOME OF MY DELICIOUS FAVORITES!

These are some of my favorite recipes that I love to cook and share with friends and family! However, I *do not recommend* sharing bites with your K9 unless you read them through thoroughly. Some can be modified a bit, but these are mainly human recipes below and not meant for K9's.

CAPRESE SALAD

- 4 oz. Buratta mozzarella cheese, cubed
- Basil leaves, fresh, torn or chopped
- 2-3 medium tomatoes, sliced
- 1 tbsp. extra virgin olive oil
- 1 tbsp. balsamic vinegar
- 1/8 tsp. Kosher salt
- ¼ tsp. pepper
- Bamboo skewers, small

DIRECTIONS: In a small bowl, combine balsamic vinegar, oil, salt and pepper. Whisk and set aside. In another bowl: toss mozzarella with basil leaves and mix with vinegar and oil mixture. Assemble onto skewers by folding basil leaves in half, add mozzarella and tomatoes. Brush with balsamic vinaigrette and serve as an appetizer.

K9 NOTE: *Modification Required.* Dogs can eat small amounts of basil but it must be chopped into small bites. I would also replace balsamic vinegar with apple cider vinegar. Mozzarella cheese is fatty and rich, so less is more. Tomato leaves and stems are toxic, but the meat of the tomato is not. Still, from my experience, dogs don't do well on tomatoes. I would only share one small bite with Fido, and remember to keep the skewers out of your dog's reach.

SHIRAZI CUCUMBER-TOMATO SALAD

- 3-4 tomatoes, sliced or chopped
- 1 Italian cucumber, sliced or chopped
- 3 tbsp. olive oil or 1 lemon, juiced
- ½ tsp. salt
- ¼ tsp. pepper
- 2 scallions, chopped (optional)
- 2 radishes, sliced
- 4 cup parsley, chopped
- ¼ cup fresh mint, chopped
- ¼ cup fresh dill weed, chopped

DIRECTIONS: In a medium serving dish, toss in everything except the lemon juice, oil, salt and pepper and mix. Then add the lemon juice and oil and mix some more. Serve immediately.

K9 NOTE: *Modification Required.* Never give a dog onions, chives, or scallions. K9s can have 1 mint leaf chopped, 2 slices cucumber chopped, and ¼ radish chopped. This dish is dog friendly, but I would not give tomatoes to Fido because they are a nightshade food and although the heart of the tomato isn't toxic, dogs do not do well with tomatoes. One or two small bites of cucumber topped with a chopped leaf of parsley, mint, or dill minus the scallions are all I feed my little dog when I make this dish for myself. Some dogs like radishes, most do not. Moderation!

WATERCRESS & FENNEL SALAD

- Watercress
- Fennel
- Parmigiano-Reggiano cheese
- Pine nuts (*not for dogs; see K9 Note on nuts)

DIRECTIONS: Cut off long stems of the watercress and wash well. Wash the fennel thoroughly. Using the fennel ball (the part on the bottom), peel off a layer or two, just like you would with an onion. Slice and chop into medium-size chunks. Pan-fry pine nuts for about one minute on medium heat (careful as they burn fast). Add pine nuts, sprinkled at the end.

DRESSING
- Olive oil
- 1 tsp. Dijon mustard
- ½ lemon, juiced
- Salt & pepper

DIRECTIONS: Whisk together and drizzle over salad.

K9 NOTE: *Modification Required.* Parsley and fennel are okay. It's best to skip the pine nuts for you pooch, but if your dog eats one or two they should be okay. I usually give my dog one bite of fennel and one slice of Parmigiano-Reggiano cheese only.

BRAISED BRANZINO

- Fish (½ lb. per person)
- 3 tbsp. extra virgin olive oil
- 1 small white onion, chopped
- 6 oz. black olives
- 1 cup white wine (Sauvignon Blanc)
- Flat leaf parsley, chopped
- Salt & Pepper

<u>DIRECTIONS</u>: Clean, wash and dry fish. Season with salt, pepper, and Italian seasoning. Wash, peel and chop the onion together with the parsley. On medium heat, fry onion and parsley in oil in a large flat-bottom pan until the onion becomes translucent. Place fish in the pan; gently stuff the fish with some of the parsley and onion. Turn fish over after five minutes, taking care not to break apart. Add olives and wine, cover and cook for ten more minutes. Wine should be absorbed and reduce and sauce should have thickened. Remove fish from pan, pour sauce over and serve.

K9 NOTE: Not dog friendly, but one of my favorites!

CORN ON THE BBQ

- Corn
- Butter
- Salt
- Garlic powder
- Paprika

DIRECTIONS: Carefully peel the outer corn husks halfway back and pull out the strands of corn silk (without taking the husk all the way off). This works best if you do this under running water (the water also helps the corn from burning while grilling). Put the husk back around the ear of corn. Cook the corn in the husks on the barbeque for about 20 to 30 min. making sure it doesn't burn. When serving, peel back the husks all the way, then carefully cut about an inch off the bottom end of the corn, removing the husk, and roll the corn on a plate of butter and spices.

You can also roast corn in the oven. Again, buy corn with the husk on, and then just clean any dirt off the outside (try not to destroy husk). Place corn in a pre-heated 350-degree oven on bake for about 30 to 40 minutes. Peel back husk and roll the corn on a plate of butter and spices.

K9 NOTE: Corn that is not ground up is not easily digestible and not recommended for dogs; they can choke on the husks. I once pulled the cob out of a dog's throat and saved their life when I was a vet tech. Skip this one for your K9.

EGG BURRITOS

Ingredients (Humans):
- Ground buffalo, beef, chicken, turkey (or leftover Taco or Chili meat)
- Eggs (two per person) or 50-50 mix; eggs to egg whites
- Flour tortillas
- Cheese, shredded

- 1/2 tsp. goat's, plain rice, or coconut milk
- 1 tbsp. onion, chopped
- ½ red chili pepper, chopped or ¼ Serrano pepper or 1 tsp. Ortega chilies, canned
- Tomato, chopped
- Olive oil
- Butter
- Hot sauce (optional)
- Salt & Pepper
- Chili powder
- Oregano
- garlic powder
- paprika
- Herbs of Provence (for poultry)

DIRECTIONS: Brown meat or poultry in a cast-iron skillet on med-high with a touch of butter and olive oil. Add onions and chili (unless using canned, then add later). Turn heat down to medium-low. In a bowl: mix eggs and a teaspoon of milk and a dash of salt; mix. Pour in to the same pan and simmer. When done on one side, flip for an omelet or just scramble. Serve in a flower tortilla for a burrito.

K9 NOTE: *Not* dog friendly. See K9 version below:

K9 VERSION: Hard-boil an egg and sauté or use a non-stick skillet to cook and add a little buffalo, a pinch of cheese, and mix in with your dog's dry kibble for a surprise reward for good behavior. Or make a dog-friendly breakfast burrito using a mandolin to finely slice a large sweet potato or yam into large flat pieces. Bake using cooking oil spray or sauté in a non-stick skillet. Let cool and add a dog bite size of egg, plain meat or poultry, a pinch of cheese, and a drop of non-flavored, low-fat yogurt and roll into a tiny burrito for Fido.

STEVE'S FAMOUS CHILI

HUMANS ONLY!

- 3 lbs. venison, buffalo, or filet mignon, cut into bite-size pieces
- 1.5 lbs. version, ground or coarsely ground beef
- 1 tbsp. Kosher (or a bit less of sea Salt)

- ¼ tsp. black pepper
- 2 red chili pepper (fresh) diced
- 2 green chili peppers (fresh) diced
- 1 Habanero chili (fresh) diced extra small
- 2 cloves garlic, minced
- 3 tbsp. salad oil
- ½ cup green bell peppers, chopped
- ¼ cup red bell peppers, chopped
- 1/1/2 cup yellow onions, chopped
- 2 cups celery, chopped
- 1 tsp. red wine vinegar (with garlic preferred)
- 2 tbsp. red hot sauce
- ½ tsp. oregano, dried
- 2- 15 oz. cans tomato sauce (or homemade)
- 1 beefsteak tomato, chopped
- 1 can stewed tomatoes
- 4 to 5 tsp. chili pepper powder
- 2 tsp. Ancho chili pepper powder
- ¼ tsp. cayenne red pepper, ground
- ½ tsp. thyme, dried
- 1 tsp. sugar
- 5 - 7 tbsp. maple syrup
- 2 tbsp. paprika
- 2 - 30 oz. cans chili beans
- 1 - 15 oz. can kidney beans, mashed slightly
- 1 can Ortega chili, diced
- 1 tsp. mustard seasoning
- 4 - 5 tsp. green taco sauce
- 1 bottle Negro Modelo beer
- 1 tsp. minced onion, dried
- 1 tsp. minced garlic, dried

- ¼ tsp. powdered garlic, dried
- ¼ tsp. onion powder
- ¼ tsp. cumin, ground
- ¼ tsp. coriander, ground
- ¼ cup V-8 juice (optional)

*Ingredients are an estimate; I always make it different depending on the heat tolerance of guest's palates. Most people don't use filet for chili -- they use cheaper cuts that are tougher and chewier, but I say why not use the best cut for chili? That's why people love my chili. Weather it is Antelope, Venison, Buffalo, or even beef filet, whenever possible, I will use filet. To save money, you can do half filet/half coarsely-ground cheaper cut.

DIRECTIONS: Chop meat into cubes. Season with salt and pepper. Lightly brown peppers, celery, and onions on med-hi heat. Transfer peppers, onions, and celery to a big chili pot and place on simmer. Brown meat in the same pan to get the flavors and add to chili pot. Turn up heat to high and stir in everything else, saving the fresh tomatoes for the last 10 min. of cooking. Boil and stir periodically for about 20 min., then turn to med-low for about ½ hr. and keep stirring and tasting. Add more seasonings as needed. Then turn down to a low simmer for the last ½ hour. You want the sauce to reduce into a thick chili. Save a small can of tomato paste if you need to thicken. Serve with fresh raw onions, shredded cheddar cheese.

K9 NOTE: *Not* dog friendly. For dogs: only meat, finely diced celery, and plain beans are okay. Beans are not toxic but they may cause gas and need to be properly prepared.

STEVE'S CARNE ASSADA FAJITAS

HUMANS ONLY!

- Flour tortillas
- 2-3 lbs. flank or skirt steak
- 3 tbsp. soy sauce
- 1 lime (zest) minced
- 1 orange (zest) minced
- ½ cup fresh orange juice
- 4 tbsp. fresh lime juice
- 3 tbsp. garlic, finely minced
- 1 ½ tbsp. balsamic vinegar
- 1 tbsp. sugar
- 1 tbsp. dried rosemary, crumbled
- ¼ cup extra virgin olive oil
- 1 tsp. cumin seeds, tossed and ground
- 1 tsp. Kosher salt
- ½ tsp. black pepper, freshly cracked
- Green onions, whole
- Avocado, sliced (optional)
- Hot sauce

<u>DIRECTIONS</u>: Mix all ingredients in a bowl (except steak, green onions, and avocado) to create marinade. Marinate steak in fajita marinade 1-2 hours. Grill green onions and steaks on the BBQ. Glaze with fajita marinade. Serve on warmed tortillas with sliced avocado, chopped cilantro, lime juice, and a bit of hot sauce. Make into a burrito and enjoy!

K9 NOTE: *Not* dog friendly.

YASMINE'S CORNISH GAME HEN

- 2 Cornish game hens (or Quail; bone-in)
- 2 quince or 1 green and 1 red apple, chopped
- 1 cup Madera
- 1 tbsp. brown sugar
- 2 tbsp. vegetable oil
- 1-cup chicken broth or stock (only for quail)
- 1 tbsp. brandy
- Drippings (from cooked hens)
- 1 tsp. lemon zest
- Cucumber or cilantro (garnish)

<u>DIRECTIONS</u>: Chop fruit and place in large Pyrex. Add 1-cup Madera, 1 tbsp. brown sugar. Mix together. Place in pre-heated oven at 350 – 400 degrees for 30-45 minutes, stirring occasionally. In a large ovenproof skillet, add oil and butter and brown the hens on the stove. Place the hens in the oven. Cook hens approximately 30 minutes or until done. Remove from oven and place in another Pyrex and cover with foil to keep warm. Serve with cooked fruit and rice. Pour with hen gravy (below), garnish with cilantro or cucumber. Goes well with green beans. Delicious!

K9 NOTE: This is *not* a dog-friendly dish but I do give my dog a bite of hen breast without sauce or bones, and a bite of apple or quince (not cooked in the sauce/gravy) and rice. Quince is safe for K9 consumption but the seeds may contain cyanide which is poisonous to dogs as well as humans. This can be a small dog bite as a reward for a down/stay at the far end of the room.

HEN GRAVY

- ½-1 cup chicken stock
- 1 tbsp. brandy
- Lemon zest
- Apple, chopped
- Flour

<u>DIRECTIONS</u>: Using the drippings from the skillet you cooked the fowl in - add lemon zest, 1 tbsp. brandy, ½ -1 cup chicken stock to sauce pan and boil down to reduce. It should be a little thick. Strain and set aside. You don't need the stock if you cook the game hen as it is fattier and has plenty of juices, but you will if you use quail. Serve Game Hens with cooked fruit and rice. Pour gravy over and garnish with cilantro or cucumbers. Delicious!

K9 NOTE: *Not* dog friendly.

MIDDLE EASTERN KABOBS

(Hold the Skewer!)

This was originally a kabob recipe, but I found that they fall off the kabob too easily, plus the skewers didn't fit well on the BBQ, so I recommend making them into oblong-shaped patties, but still serving them as a BBQ platter.

HUMANS ONLY!

- 1 1/2 lb. beef (20% fat), ground
- 1/2 lb. lamb, ground
- 1 egg
- 1 onion, chopped
- ½ onion, cut in quarters (per person)
- 1 tsp. salt (to taste)
- Pepper (to taste)
- 1 tsp. Sumac
- ½ - 1 tsp. paprika
- Dash cayenne pepper
- 1 tsp. yogurt
- 1/2 bunch fresh cilantro, chopped (garnish)
- Pablano pepper (one per guest)
- Tomatoes on the vine (1 or 2 per guest)
- 1 eggplant
- Lavash bread
- 1 tbsp. butter
- 5 saffron strands

DIRECTIONS: Season meat with egg, yogurt, finely-chopped onion, and spices. Gently knead meat mixture and dry spices together with your hands, but don't over work the meat. I find that Kabobs fall off the stick and fall thru the BBQ, so I recommend making them into oblong-shaped patties and cooking on the grill without the stick. Set aside meat for 15 minutes on wax paper (placed on a tray so they don't stick). Slice eggplant and put into a Pyrex oven-proof dish. Drizzle with olive oil, a touch of salt and Italian seasoning (optional). Bake on 300 for 30 min., turning once.

On a hot BBQ: grill the onions and Poblano peppers (20 min.) and whole tomatoes (10 min.), then meat patties. Let the meat sear for at least 2 ½ min. before turning. Turn meat as minimally as possible without burning it, and never smoosh the meat into the grill. The meat tastes best medium-rare. Take everything off the grill when done but keep warm on a big platter. Dip the meat in a sauce made of melted butter and a few strands of saffron. If you are serving it as a kabob, throw the Lavash bread on the grill the last minute to heat. Serve with a side of rice and Shirazi Salad.

K9 NOTE: *Not* dog friendly. Fido can't eat onions and the peppers, tomato, eggplant or spices won't agree.

MIDDLE EASTERN KABOB BURGERS

<u>DIRECTIONS</u>: Using above ingredients, make a round-shaped patty and prepare the meat the same way. Serve on a toasted bun with one slice of eggplant, a slice of tomato (heated slightly) a slice of BBQ onion, a bit of BBQ Pablano pepper, and a touch of butter sauce.

K9 NOTE: Not dog friendly. Fido can't eat onions and the peppers, tomato, eggplant or spices won't agree. You can use plain meat, egg, yogurt, a touch of salt, and sumac to make your dog a small patty.

BBQ SALMON SALAD WITH HONEY-MUSTARD SAUCE

- Wild, fresh salmon with skin (½ pound per person)
- Asparagus
- Baby Romaine lettuce or mixed greens
- Tomatoes, sliced
- Avocado, sliced
- Black olives
- 2 - 3 green onions (per person)
- 1 - 2 yellow squash, sliced long
- Olive oil
- Salt and pepper
- Honey mustard sauce (see recipe)

<u>DIRECTIONS:</u> Marinate the asparagus, yellow squash, and green onions for about 15 minutes with a drizzle of olive oil, a touch of salt, pepper, and Italian seasoning and BBQ for about 8 min. BBQ the veggies the same time you do the salmon.

Wash and dry salmon; remove pin bones if any. Rub lightly with a few drops of olive oil; season with salt and pepper. Marinade the salmon in the Honey Mustard Sauce (below) for ½ hour to 45 min.

Barbecue the salmon, skin-side-down, for 4 minutes each side. When you smell the skin almost burning, flip over. Try to do minimal flipping as the skin may stick to the grill but will protect the other side of the salmon from burning. Some people recommend cooking fish skin-side-up so you get nice grill marks, but I recommend skin-side-down. If you have skinless salmon, set some sliced lemons on the grill and place the salmon on top of the lemon slices to protect from sticking and to add flavor. Brush the salmon with a bit more Honey Mustard sauce about one to two minutes before removing it from the grill. Place BBQ salmon, squash, green onion, and asparagus on top of the dressed salad with avocado, tomatoes, and black olives.

K9 NOTE: *Not* dog friendly.

HONEY MUSTARD MARINADE / BASTING SAUCE

- 4 tbsp. Dijon mustard
- 6 tbsp. honey
- Salt & pepper
- ½ lemon, juiced
- A few drops Yuzu (optional)
- A few shakes dry Italian seasoning (optional)
- 2 tbsp. olive oil
- 1 tbsp. white wine or sake (optional)

DIRECTIONS: Mix all ingredients together and hand whisk or stir in the olive oil last and pour it slow as you whisk.

K9 NOTE: Other than one little bite of cooked salmon, this sauce is *Not* Dog Friendly.

SALMON & HEIRLOOM TOMATO SALAD

- Wild fresh salmon (½ pound per person)
- Mint, chopped
- Smoked salmon or lox, torn into bite-size pieces
- Mixed greens
- Heirloom tomatoes, a variety of colors
- Artichoke hearts (for dressing)
- Salt & pepper
- Several tbsp. olive oil
- 1 tbsp. Dijon mustard
- ½ lemon, juiced + a few drops

DIRECTIONS: Wash and dry salmon; remove pin bones if any. Rub lightly with a few drops of olive oil; season with salt and pepper.

Barbecue salmon, skin-side-down, 4 minutes on each side. When you smell the skin burning, flip over. Try to do minimal flipping; the skin may stick to the grill. That's okay. It will protect the other side of the salmon from burning. If you have skinless salmon then set some sliced lemons on the grill and place the salmon on top of the lemon slices to protect from sticking and it adds flavor.

Make the salad with a combination of a lot of mint, mixed greens, fresh heirloom tomatoes, artichoke hearts, lox or smoked salmon. Dress the salad with lemon vinaigrette before topping with BBQ Salmon.

K9 NOTE: Not dog friendly. Only feed your dog 1-2 small bites of Salmon (not smoked salmon or lox as it's too salty) topped with one leaf of finely-chopped mint. It's great for Bruno's breath.

JACK DANIELS BBQ SAUCE

One of my favorite BBQ sauces for chicken & ribs!

HUMANS ONLY!

- 1 cup Jack Daniels
- ½ cup dark brown sugar, firmly packed
- 1 cup organic ketchup
- 1 tsp. Worcestershire sauce
- ¼ cup apple cider vinegar
- 1 tbsp. lemon juice
- 3 cloves garlic, minced
- ½ tsp. dry mustard
- Dash A-1 sauce
- Salt & pepper (to taste)
- Dry Italian seasoning optional

DIRECTIONS: Combine all ingredients in a bowl and mix well. Great to use as a glaze for chicken, ribs etc.

For chicken: Wash and dry chicken; season with salt & pepper, and sometimes I add a bit of dry Italian seasoning as well rub on a bit of safflower mayo. *Don't use the JD BBQ Sauce yet!* Then marinate while you start your charcoal. Place chicken on a hot BBQ. Grill chicken until done, and then baste the last few minutes of cooking with Jack Daniels sauce. If it starts to burn, have a spot on the grill to move it to that is not as hot. Baste with sauce the last two min. It will flame up, so watch for burning. Remove from grill and place in a Pyrex or bowl. Brush with more sauce before serving. This sauce is doggone good! One of my favorites on chicken and ribs!

K9 NOTE: *Not* dog friendly. Never feed this sauce to your dog. If you give your dog one little bite of breast meat from the center of a chicken breast and you are sure that it's a clean piece without sauce or bones then that's fine.

PEACH & BURBON BBQ SAUCE

- 1 jar Dijon mustard
- ¼ cup peach jam
- ½ cup bourbon

DIRECTIONS: In a saucepan, dissolve peach jam over low heat. Stir in mustard and bourbon until mixture is smooth. This can be used as a glaze and finishing sauce. Great for pork or turkey!

K9 NOTE: *Not* dog friendly. Never feed this sauce to your dog. A small bite of the finished product from the center of the meat should be fine for Fido. No bones, fat, or sauce…only a bite or two.

PINEAPPLE MARINADE

- 1 cup pineapple juice
- 1/3 cup soy sauce
- 1 tbsp. cilantro, chopped
- ¼ cup dry white wine
- 1 cup pineapple, crushed
- 1 tbsp. honey
- Dash cayenne pepper

DIRECTIONS: Combine all ingredients in a bowl (adjust cayenne to your taste). Marinate chicken overnight; fish for several hours. Also can use as a glaze when grilling. Great as a marinade for chicken, swordfish, scallops, etc.

K9 NOTE: This marinade is okay once the wine is cooked into the chicken or fish and the alcohol burns off; never let your dog have uncooked sauce that contains alcohol. Save one bite of pineapple and one leaf of cilantro and a drop of honey for Fido. Soy sauce is too salty for a dog; wine is toxic; and too much cayenne is just mean to give to a dog.

STEVE'S SALSA FRESCO

(Serve with Halibut)
- 3 red bell peppers, chopped
- 2 cloves garlic
- 12 basil leaves, torn
- 1 tbsp. red wine vinegar
- Salt & pepper (to taste)

<u>Directions</u>: Wash peppers, remove seeds and chop. Grill bell peppers on the barbeque or in the oven on broil, let cool and chop. Add garlic, basil, red wine vinegar and salt and pepper. Mix well. This is delicious served over barbequed halibut (see recipe).

K9 NOTE: Do not serve salsa to dogs. Avoid peppers and large amounts of garlic.

MAMA JANE ESSA'S STEW

HUMAN VERSION:
- 1 onion, chopped
- ½ green pepper, chopped
- 2 zucchini, chopped
- 2 granny smith apples, chopped
- 1-16 oz. tomato sauce
- Paprika
- Salt and pepper
- Vegetable oil

<u>DIRECTIONS</u>: Sauté in oil the onion, peppers, zucchini, and apple. Add tomato sauce and simmer for 30 minutes. Add paprika, salt and pepper.

K9 VERSION: Make a separate batch for your K9. Mix rice, chopped apple (no stems, seeds or core) and a few bites of steamed zucchini to your dog's kibble.

K9 NOTE: *Modification Required.* Dogs can't have onions and skip the paprika, tomato, and green pepper.

STEVE'S FAMOUS TACOS

Yield: 8 - 10 Tacos

HUMANS ONLY!

- 1 ¼ lbs. Buffalo or Beef, ground
- 1 dozen corn tortillas
- Canola, safflower, or corn oil (1 -2 tsp. for meat and several tbsp. for tortillas)
- 1 tbsp. dry chili powder
- 1 tsp. dry Ancho chili powder

- A pinch dry cayenne pepper
- 1 - 2 cloves garlic, chopped (or pinch garlic powder)
- Dash paprika
- Pinch dry cumin
- 1 small Habanero chili, diced fine
- ¼-½ green or Serrano chili, diced fine
- 1 tbsp. olive oil
- 1 white onion, chopped
- 4 - 5 limes
- 3 avocados, slightly mashed
- 3 tomatoes
- 1 bunch cilantro, chopped
- 1 handful mixed greens
- 1 can black olives, sliced (topping)
- 1 can green Ortega chilies, diced (topping)
- Cheddar cheese, grated
- Hot sauce (topping)

DIRECTIONS: Pour 2 tsp. oil in a pan on med-high. Season the meat before you put in the pan and even more as it starts to brown. Add the fresh chili peppers to the pan while you brown meat for about 2 min., then turn down to med-low and cover for about 6 - 7 min. Remember… Habaneros are very hot, so just a little pinch is all you need.

Chop tomatoes, onions, cilantro, and two avocados and place each in their own bowl. Saturate everything (except meat and tortillas) with lime juice which will keep the avocados from turning brown. In separate bowls or plates, prepare: Ortega chili, sliced olives, cilantro and lettuce blend, cheese, and hot sauce.

In another skillet: add an inch of oil. Put each tortilla in the pan and fold during first 10 seconds of cooking so it is in a shell formation. Flip once or twice until soft and crispy, but not burned. Remove from pan and pace on paper towels. Put shells on a plate and the meat in a serving bowl. Guests can create their own tacos!

K9 VERSION: Use a yam or sweet potato for the taco shell -- slice sweet potatoes thin (using a mandolin if you have one). These will serve as the tortilla shells. Boil or in a non-stick skillet until soft, then spoon plain cooked meat (boiled, steamed, or non-stick skillet) with no spices or sauce, and a pinch of cheese into yam shells.

K9 NOTE: *Not* dog friendly. ***Modification Required.***

K9 ILLNESS

Since dogs can't talk (that we know of) it's important to pay attention to the signs of illness. Some are obvious, while others take keen perception on the part of the owner. When it comes to your dog's health, it's important to understand the signs of illness or injury – especially since your dog can't tell you what is wrong! The eyes can tell you a lot; you want to make sure your dog's eyes are bright, alert, and responsive. Basic warning signs of injury or illness include: diarrhea, vomiting, listlessness, not eating for prolonged periods, going potty in the wrong place, excessive panting, growling or snapping when touched, etc. It is also good to be familiar with other modalities such as Natural Medicine, Traditional Chinese Medicine and Holistic practices. I'll leave it up to you to decide what is best when it comes to medicinal treatment for your pet. If your dog exhibits signs of illness, contact your Veterinarian immediately.

Allergies. Many dogs have food allergies and sensitivities (just like people) so if you suspect your dog has allergies, do not attempt to diagnose without professional Veterinary assistance. Environmental allergens are more common than food allergens. I've been told that food allergies account for 10 percent of all allergies in dogs. Many times, flea allergies are mistaken for food allergies. With flea allergies, your dog may be licking the root of his tail raw; with food allergies, you may see signs of chronic ear infections, skin rash, hives, itching, red paws and bald spots from obsessive licking. Food intolerance is when a dog's digestive system is unable to digest a specific ingredient.

A food allergy is a negative response by the immune system; usually due to a protein in the diet. The most common proteins dogs are allergic to are dairy products, beef, wheat, eggs, soy, chicken, and peanut butter. Peanut butter commonly contains mold which can fuel yeast growth in K9s. Your dog's ears may get red, stinky, and itchy or they may get hot spots from giving them just a small amount of peanut butter.

The way to diagnose food allergies is through an elimination diet. Your Vet will usually take your dog off all the foods they've been eating and put them on a food that they've never had before (with a different protein that they have never had before). Once the dog has improved, you can start reintroducing foods that the Vet thinks caused the reaction in the first place. If there is an allergic reaction, it usually takes a few days to a few weeks to discern the allergen. Anaphylaxis is a serious allergic reaction that is rapid in onset and may cause coma or even death if left untreated. Symptoms include: diarrhea, defecation, urination, vomiting, itchiness and hives, excessive drooling, weakness, difficulty breathing, pale gums, elevated heart rate, and seizures.

Anorexia (eating too little) is a disease that affects K9s as well as humans. Some dogs that eat too little and are overly anxious can become anorexic. It seems smaller breeds, like Yorkies, have more anxiety and frenetic energy causing them to eat less and burn excess calories by running and jumping all day long! Pay attention to your dog's food intake. If you see a problem or notice them losing too much weight, consult your Veterinarian.

Appetite & Thirst. An increase in appetite (but no weight gain) or drinking and urinating more than usual can mean your dog has diabetes (diagnosed with a blood test). Increased appetite, thirst, and weight gain can mean your dog is hypothyroid or has adrenal issues. The stool may range from soft to watery, often has a greenish-tinge to it, and occasionally contains blood. Infected dogs tend to have excess mucus in the feces. Vomiting may occur in some cases.

Canine Cancer. Dogs diagnosed with cancer require healthy food and vitamins along with adequate sleep to boost their immune system. Sufficient amounts of protein and Omega fatty acids need to be given daily. Without necessary nutrients like protein and fats, the body will take it from the muscles, resulting in muscle wasting and kidney and liver failure. High-glycemic foods like refined sugar and high-fructose corn syrup raise blood sugar levels, which contribute to cancer cell growth, so it's best to remove these entirely from the diet.

According to Veterinary cancer specialist, Dr. Gregory K. Ogilvie of Colorado State University's Department of Clinical Sciences, the following diet percentages are recommended to combat K9 cancer:

- 37% animal protein
- 32% fat
- 21% carbohydrates
- 3.5 Omega-3 fatty acids
- 2.5% DHA fatty acids
- 3.4% Arginine (amino acid)

Consult your Veterinarian to make sure your dog is healthy enough for a high-protein, high-fat diet (especially for those suffering from pancreas, liver, kidney, or spleen issues). Many Vets recommend feeding dogs with cancer a diet comprised of carbs and digestible proteins including:

- Canned sardines (best)
- Beans
- Egg whites
- Chicken (white meat)
- Skim milk
- Cottage cheese
- Lean beef, lamb, hamburger, ground turkey

If your dog is undergoing chemotherapy, try blending the meal to make it easier to consume and add low-sodium beef broth to make it moist and tasty. Chemo can result in loss of appetite, so it may take a day or two for your dog to feel like eating. Nutrition during treatment is essential. Membrane stabilizers such as Omega-3 fatty acids, gamma-linoleic acid, and coenzyme Q-10 may help shrink tumors and reduce inflammation. Fish oil is a good source of Omega-3, 6, & 9 fatty acids. Other essential nutrients to fight cancer and build immunity are antioxidants: Vitamin E – 400 iu. per day, Selenium – 100 mcg. per day, Beta-carotene, Green tea extract (decaffeinated) 50 - 100 mg/day, Grape seed extract, Quercetin, Turmeric. Ask your Vet to ensure proper daily doses, as some may not be recommended, depending on the course of treatment.

Choking. Dogs can choke on bones, toys, or household items. Signs of choking include: difficulty breathing, loud breaths, struggling, gasping, etc. Inspect their mouth…if you see an object; try to remove it with your finger (if it's easy to reach). If you can't remove the obstruction, try the Heimlich maneuver. If the dog stops breathing, administer CPR and get them to the Vet ASAP! If you don't know canine CPR, make sure you check with your Vet or find a class and get lifesaving training. Check out the poster from www.Sunny-DogInk below:

WHAT TO DO IF YOUR DOG OR CAT IS
CHOKING

Sunny-dog Ink
Helping YOU to Help Your Pets! ™

STEPS TO HELP A CHOKING PET:

Anything on the floor or in paw's reach can end up INSIDE your pet! Always supervise & provide appropriate sized toys and chews.

 ### STEP 1

Give pet a moment to cough on his own.

STEP 2

Take a look inside mouth before attempting to grasp object. Proceed only if you can do so safely realizing objects may be lodged in tissue and must be carefully Removed. Also…a nervous animal could bite!

STEP 3

For smaller animals, lower their head bracing between your knees while seated and with the palm of your hand, deliver gentle but firm blows between the shoulders to expel object. On a conscious larger pet, pick up hind legs to lower dog's head (think "wheel barrel" position) taking care to not bump dog's head on the floor.

 ### STEP 4

Begin **Abdominal Compressions** (aka *Heimlich-like Manuever*) on medium-to large dogs by placing fist in soft part of belly behind last rib and pulling up against your own chest 3-5 times. You must brace your chest against animal's back. If not effective, repeat, or try **Side Thrusts** by placing heel of one hand on either side of dog's chest and squeezing air out of lungs. Place an unconscious pet on his side and thrust from one side of the chest only, alternating with Rescue Breathing and looking inside mouth to remove object.

Use fingertips in place of fist for small pets.

STEP 5

Once object has been removed, check vitals, administer CPR if needed and immediately follow up with your Veterinarian.

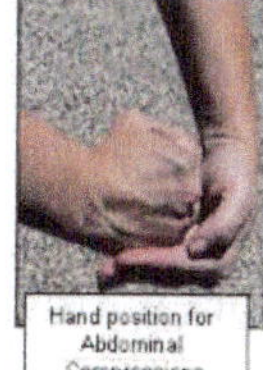
Hand position for Abdominal Compressions

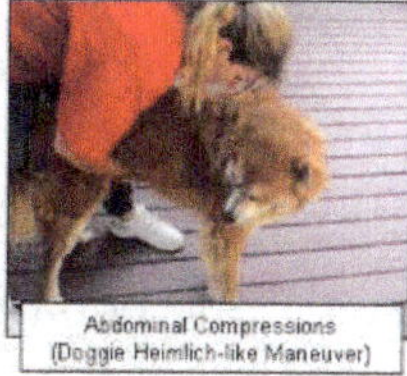
Abdominal Compressions (Doggie Heimlich-like Maneuver)

Side Thrusts.

Side Thrusts on UNCONSCIOUS pet

Coughing/Excess Panting can be a sign your dog may have heart, lung or respiratory disease. Coughing can also mean they have something stuck in their throat. If dogs are not regularly vaccinated for kennel cough (a contagious common cough) with a vaccine called Bordetella, it can cause severe coughing. When in doubt, go to the Vet.

Constipation can be relieved by adding (1 tbsp. med-large dog; 1 tsp. for small dogs) of pure canned pumpkin to your dog's food. If your dog's constipation is not alleviated, straining, lethargy, appetite loss and possibly even vomiting may occur. Your Vet may recommend the following treatments:

- A stool softener or other laxative agent
- Fiber (canned pumpkin, wheat bran or a product such as Metamucil)
- x-rays or an enema
- An increase in exercise

Below is a list of possible causes of constipation in dogs from the ASPCA's website:

- Not enough fiber in his diet
- Lack of exercise
- Blocked or abscessed anal sacs
- Enlarged prostate gland
- Excessive self-grooming can cause large amounts of hair to collect in the stool
- Ingested gravel, stones, bones, dirt, plants or pieces of toys, etc. caught in the intestinal tract
- Matted hair or a tumor at the anus causing an obstruction
- Side effect of medication
- Hernia
- Orthopedic problem that causes pain when a dog positions himself to defecate
- Neurologic disorder
- Dehydration due to other illness

Coprophagy (eating feces) is a normal exploratory canine behavior. Eating the feces of another dog may help developing intestinal flora. Cat feces, because of the high protein may be sought out by your K9, so make sure to keep litter boxes inaccessible to dogs!

This disorder is uncommon and only found in less than 10% of dogs, so don't be alarmed or punish the pup, rather, be aware if it happens too often and refocus the dog's attention on something else. Call your dog back to you if you anticipate them getting ready to ingest. Also clean your yard every time they go potty; don't let it pile up. Many dogs with this issue get relinquished to the shelter, but it is a behavior or nutrition problem than can be dealt with by your Veterinarian or trainer.

Diarrhea. Persistent diarrhea could indicate colitis, pancreatitis, foodborne illness, distemper, or diabetes… to name a few. It can sometimes be eased by adding rice or yogurt to your dog's food or fasting for one meal. Be sure they get plenty of water to keep them hydrated. When you do give them their next meal, keep it light. Most Vets recommend the way to ease diarrhea is to skip a meal, then serve a light meal of rice and boiled chicken breast. When a dog has diarrhea or is vomiting, I check to see if the eyes are bright, alert and responsive; if they're acting like themselves or lethargic. I also check the color of their gums, belly, and ears. I examine the feces for foreign objects, blood, parasites, etc. If I sense anything out of the norm, I go to the Vet right away. Take a small fecal sample with you in case they can't get any from my dog during the exam.

Ear Mites. If you think your dog has ear mites go to the Vet. I have used mineral oil, calendula oil and even olive oil to clean irritated surfaces of the ears. The oil can block the spiracles of ear mites, causing them to asphyxiate and die. If your dog has ear mites, they will be scratching like crazy. Ear mites are contagious to both other dogs and people. Clean the ears every three days to remove as much debris as possible. Since Mite eggs hatch every four days, it's best to clean and treat the ears every three days (3 to 4 times) to resolve ear mite infestations.

Fleas. There is no need to spray or dip your dog in chemicals when there are plenty of natural flea repellents in your kitchen like rosemary, citrus, cedar, eucalyptus, tea tree oil, lemon, clove, and fennel seed oil. These ingredients come in various formulations of shampoos, soaps, oils, sprays, and collars, or you can blend your own potions. Garlic (check with your Vet for the correct dosages and see the benefits and dangers of garlic in this book) and nutritional yeast can be added as a supplement to your pet's food. These repellents give your dog a body odor which repels fleas. A teaspoon of apple cider vinegar in a pet's food or water each day may help repel fleas. You can also dilute the vinegar 50/50 with water, pour into a spray bottle and use as a repellent. All flea control procedures must be repeated weekly for about two months to be sure that newly hatched fleas are killed. It is important to keep rugs, upholstery, and bedding clean and vacuumed regularly and to use a flea comb on your pet. It is also a good idea to spread towels or blankets down where pets lay and then wash the towels weekly.

TIP: Cut up a flea collar and put it in your vacuum bag to kill flees in the vacuum and prevents them from hatching and infecting your pet! To help combat fleas, place a few drops of peppermint oil, warm water, and a pinch of Epsom salt in a spray bottle. Shake ingredients until the salt is dissolved.

- o   Rosemary Flea Dip: Boil one to two cups of fresh rosemary and let it sit for 30 minutes. When cool, discard the rosemary, then fill the tub with a little warm water and mix; soak your dog for ten minutes or pour when cooled directly on your dog until he's soaked, then let him air dry. Then you can add Lavender Essential Oil to your dog's neck and the base of the tail. Apply just a few drops. (Avon's Skin So Soft can help repel fleas.)

Foodborne Pathogens. There are some Vets who advocate a raw food diet for dogs, but use caution as dogs can get bacterial salmonella or E. coli from consuming raw diets. They can also get salmonella from a dirty Kong toy, or humans not washing countertops, etc. It's important for you to wash your dog's food and water bowl as they can get contaminated.

Loss of Appetite can be indicative of cancer or digestive disorders, or even depression. (See more in Chapter 1: My Dog Is a Finicky Eater). Many dogs won't eat if they are full, so you better check with the rest of your family, neighbors, and even dog walkers to see what else your dog is getting into. There is also concern when a dog won't eat that they may have eaten something that they shouldn't have that may be blocking them up. If your dog refuses to eat for more than a day or vomits more than once or twice, an acute condition may be present that needs medical attention. If the protesting of food persists, always check with your Vet. They may need to take x-rays to check for an intestinal obstruction.

Listlessness. If your dog seems weak or listless for more than a day or two or if they are unable to urinate or defecate, contact your Veterinarian immediately. This is not normal behavior and your dog may need medical attention. Since (most) dogs cannot talk, it's up to you to interpret their symptoms and get them the proper medical attention when needed, especially if they are lethargic.

Lying Down/Standing Up. Difficulty lying down or standing up can be signs of arthritis or spinal disc problems. In large breed puppies, like labs, they can get what's known as "growing pains" or Panosteitis (pano), an inflammatory condition that affects the long bones of rapidly growing young dogs. It causes a sudden onset of lameness and limping.

Motion Sickness. If your dog is not used to traveling or is prone to getting car sick, it actually helps to *not* let them see out the window during the ride. Try putting your dog in a down/stay on the passenger seat floorboard…this seems to keep them calm and reduce motion sickness. Most of the time, your dog is sick because of travel stress, not motion sickness. If your dog is not used to traveling or is prone to carsickness, drive calmly without stress… Play soothing music in the car and make the destination of your trip for the dog a positive one. In addition, it's best to not feed the dog before traveling and always make sure your dog has gone potty before you travel! True motion sickness is physiological; it has to do with the inner ear and balance, the eyes, and getting signals mixed up. So if your dog needs assistance or throws up while traveling in the car, ask your Veterinarian about medications to prevent motion sickness.

> ❖ Use a calming cap on your dog. A calming cap is like putting blinders on a horse; the dog can still see out of it, but it cuts out just enough vision to make most dogs chill in the car. If your dog doesn't have a good "stay" yet, start working to get it solid because a well-trained dog should be able to do a down/stay anywhere, even where you want him to sit in the car.

* **Keep a leash on the dog in the car with the end of the leash on your lap.** Dogs seem to behave better when a leash is on.

* **Try placing your dog in a crate and secure the crate with a seatbelt, rope, or bungee cord so it won't tip over.** This is probably the safest way to travel with your pooch. Try placing a lightweight towel over the crate so they can't see out, making sure they have enough air to breathe. Dogs respond to your mood or emotional state. If you drive calmly, play classical or spa music on the radio, and make the destination of your trip a positive one, the dog will react better. It's best to not feed before traveling, but if you have to, feed a light meal and always make sure your dog has gone potty first!

* **To help your dog relax on the ride, I recommend using lavender mist or over-the-counter remedies like *Rescue Remedy* (add two drops in the dog's water prior to traveling), or a synthetic pheromone spray or calming collar.** Synthetic pheromones are what nursing mothers release, which is believed to calm puppies. Try having your dog wear a Thunder shirt or an Anxiety Wrap (if it's not too hot), both of which are used to relax dogs.

* **Herbs and essential oils like peppermint, ginger, fennel, dill, cinnamon, and even coconut oil can be used to soothe the stomach.** Another tip for anxious dogs is to spray lavender mist or dab lavender oil on your dog's bed. I also practice massaging with oils a few minutes a day, focusing on the dog's wrist, the area below and lateral to the knee, and along the spine. Then when you're ready to travel, put some on their collar. The scent of lavender on their collar combined with massage will ease them into relaxation and creates a positive association to travel using their keen sense of smell.

Nausea. To ease nausea, feed a meal of lamb or chicken with no spices or additives (35-50%); pasta, rice, potato (30%) and mild bland veggies (30%).

PICA is the abnormal craving and ingestion of inappropriate non-nutritive objects like dog toys, dirt, rocks, glass, etc. Causes can include extreme nutritional deficiencies or even brain lesions. PICA is rare. Obsessive-compulsive disorders (OCD) manifest with this condition. Many puppies, especially labs, can become obsessed with eating wood chips, rocks, etc. Some senior dogs become scavengers due to nutritional imbalances, like a lack of minerals, and rocks have what they need. Dogs with PICA issues can ingest substances that may require surgery, so monitor your dog with this problem and seek Veterinary advice.

Poisoning. Signs of poisoning include: salivation (excessive drooling), vomiting, diarrhea, difficulty breathing, red skin or eyes, unconscious, ulcers in or around the dog's mouth, shock. If you think your dog may have been exposed to a toxic chemical or poisonous material, contact an emergency hospital or the **ASPCA Animal Poison Control Center: 888-426-4435.**

Polyphagia (excessive eating or compulsive consumption) can be the result of behavioral or medical conditions. This behavior can occur when a new dog is introduced to the home. The first dog feels a threat to his food source and overcompensates. Diabetes also creates polyphagia because of an imbalance in glucose levels.

Skin Conditions. Hypoallergenic diets are recommended for dogs with chronic skin conditions, gastrointestinal issues or immune disease. Make sure to include nutritional needs with balanced protein, fat, carbohydrate and fiber. Shampoos and skin conditioners containing tea tree oil, aloe vera, coconut oil, jojoba oil, vitamin E, chamomile, calendula, oatmeal, and eucalyptus can all help to sooth and heal dry, irritated, and broken skin. Dietary supplements of essential fatty acids are also helpful, as those nutrients protect against many skin ailments.

UTI. An increased need to urinate can mean your dog has a urinary tract infection (UTI).

Vomiting. Persistent vomiting could indicate kidney, liver or brain disease. If a dog has Parvo, they will have both vomiting and bloody stools with a horrible distinctive smell.

Vomiting, along with weakness and disorientation could mean your dog has eaten a poisonous substance. If you notice symptoms, take your dog to the Vet immediately.

Weight Loss. Sudden weight loss could be a sign of cancer or digestive disorders or it may be from exercising to hard or poor quality diet disorders such as diabetes, Addison's disease, or hypothyroidism… to name a few.

Do all dogs stink?

There is a common misconception that all dogs "stink" and that a stinky dog is normal. Some dogs do have a strong smell, but in fact, most healthy dogs do not have much odor. However, if your dog lives outdoors, (which I don't recommend) or if they are dirty and roll in the mud, by all means give them a bath. If you see fleas, they should be bathed immediately with a natural flea shampoo. Soak your dog with lather for 10 minutes before you give a thorough rinse. A dog with normal skin should be bathed every one to three months. If your family is allergic, go ahead and bathe more often. If they smell strange, even after a bath, there could be an underlying health issue.

Gas is another reason your dog might stink. Gas is a normal, but if it gets out of control there may be underlying reasons, so it's always a good idea to check with your Vet. It could be that your dog is eating too fast and swallowing large amounts of air. Problems with GI-tract infections and diseases and can also contribute to stinky gas.

When the smell of gas is strong, it could be the result of bacteria not completely digested in the stomach and small intestines. Excessive gas is usually caused by the dog eating a food that doesn't agree with them. Fennel seed works to relieve gastric discomfort. Use one teaspoon of fresh or dried fennel in eight ounces of boiling water, steeped until cool. The tea can be fed, two-to-four tablespoons (per 20 pounds body weight) or added to drinking water. In general, this herb is safe, but should be used with caution in pregnant or lactating animals. Maybe the dog did well on the food for a while, but sometimes their body changes with age and the food may need to be changed also. Some dogs might do well on one food and others may do better on other foods.

Slow-Feeder Bowl

For dogs that inhale their food, I recommend using a Slow-Feeder bowl. These bowls can also decrease the chance of a dog getting bloat.

DOG BITES Rx

HOLISTIC VETERINARY MEDICINE

Holistic Veterinary Medicine includes a host of herbs that are used to treat canines for a myriad of health issues. This method uses Homeopathic Remedies to organically treat ailments as a result of poor diet, vaccinations, drugs, stress, and other maladies interfere with the healing process during an illness or after an injury. The remedies come in dropper bottles with the number of drops to be taken noted on the bottle. Liquid potencies sometimes use alcohol as a preservative, but the quantity is minimal and will not affect your dog. You want to get a few drops in the mouth – it's not important whether or not your dog swallows the drops, as long as they touch the gums. If you find your dog's reaction to the taste makes it difficult, try putting a few drops into a bowl of spring or filtered water (due to the proliferation of chemicals in tap water). Delivering remedies with food can neutralize the effects, so avoid adding it to their food; it's recommended to wait at least 15 to 30 minutes after a meal. Homeopathic Remedies can also be dispensed as tiny pellets, tablets, pills, teas, creams, salves, gels, sprays, tincture's, or as Essential Oils containing vitamins, antibiotics and antiseptics.

ESSENTIAL OILS:

- ❖ **Anise**: warming and stimulating
- ❖ **Arnica**: Anti-inflammatory, arthritis, bruises, sprains
- ❖ **Basil**: uplifting and refreshing; sinus
- ❖ **Black Pepper**: stimulating
- ❖ **Calendula Oil**: Antiseptic germ fighter, skin and ear problems
- ❖ **Catnip Oil**: repels mosquitoes; mite control
- ❖ **Cinnamon**: antiseptic and digestive aid
- ❖ **Cloves**: antiseptic and warming agent
- ❖ **Coriander**: warming and stimulating agent
- ❖ **Eucalyptus**: head clearing; bronchitis
- ❖ **Fennel**: indigestion
- ❖ **Ginger**: warming and digestive aid
- ❖ **Hypericum**: relieves nerve pain
- ❖ **Lavender Oil**: refreshing, relaxing, reduces anxiety; high blood pressure
- ❖ **Lemon Oil**: refreshing and stimulating
- ❖ **Lemongrass Oil**: toning and refreshing
- ❖ **Peppermint Oil**: topical anesthetic effect; cooling and refreshing; sinus
- ❖ **Red Raspberry Leaf**: Relieves nausea, diarrhea, and gingivitis
- ❖ **Rosemary Oil**: invigorating and refreshing antioxidant. Aids cancer, cardiovascular disease, G.I. disorders
- ❖ **Rosemary Extract** is a natural antioxidant and works to repel fleas
- ❖ **Sage Oil**: decongestant, circulatory
- ❖ **Tarragon Oil**: warming and stimulating
- ❖ **Tea Tree Oil**: relieves itch and associated infections (*Practitioners caution that tea tree oil is toxic to cats and small dogs.)
- ❖ **Thyme Oil**: antiseptic

  *(This list doesn't include all essential oils)

TRADITIONAL CHINESE MEDICINE

I have found that, for many K9 health conditions, Traditional Chinese Medicine (TCM) practices including: acupuncture, herbal medicine, acupressure, and food therapies are highly effective in treating K9 illness. In Traditional Chinese Medicine, the five senses: sight, smell, hearing, taste, and touch are used to diagnose and treat. The practice states that imbalances must be diagnosed and treated before it becomes a disease. According to Dr. Sheryl Schwartz D.V.M., author of **FOUR PAWS, FIVE DIRECTIONS: A GUIDE TO CHINESE MEDICINE FOR CATS AND DOGS**: acupuncture was used 3,500 years ago when an elephant was treated for a stomach disorder. TCM has been used ever since to treat a host of canine ailments, including: arthritis, heart-lung-kidney, digestive, hormonal, allergic, and reproductive issues. While Western medicine treats acute illness (and should be used in an emergency) it can be limited in its approach to chronic maladies, which is why many prefer a more holistic approach.

TCM practitioners call connections between forces in nature and specific internal organ systems the *Five Element Theory*. The five elements include earth, metal, water, food, and fire. Each is directly connected to an organ system in the body:

- **Earth** > digestion; spleen, pancreas, and stomach
- **Metal** > respiration and elimination; lungs and large intestine
- **Water** > plumbing it is comprised of kidneys and urinary bladder
- **Wood** > toxic processing; liver and gallbladder
- **Fire** > circulation of blood, hormones and food; heart, small intestine

These elements create a correlation to the flow of the physical world with the physical body. This flow is a circular rhythm known as the *Creation Cycle*. The Chinese believe that the *Creation Cycle* occurred when fire burns… creating the earth. Then the earth gave rise to the mountains, which contain metal, and the metal separated, making way for the water. The water flowed to the wood of the trees and the trees, vulnerable to burning, kindled a fire; thus the *Creation Cycle* keeps flowing in constant motion.

YIN & YANG

Yin and Yang are principles of opposites: night & day; hot & cold. In TCM, the body's well-being is determined by the interaction of these polar opposites. If the body has any imbalance, it has the potential to cause an illness. Yang energy creates tension, stimulation, warmth, dryness, strength, activity, and regression. For instance, if your dog tends to be aggressive, she may have too much yang energy and you may want to cool her tension by adding yin-type foods to her diet. Yin energy creates ease, calm, cool, moisture, and inactivity. If your dog is too cold or urinates frequently, especially at night, adding warming yang foods will help counter these cold traits. Foods recommended in Traditional Chinese Medicine, according to Dr. Schwartz, help maintain long-term yin/yang balance in the body.

FOODS: Warm or Cool?

Some foods are warming, causing increased energy or aggression; while others are cooling; causing a sense of calm. Both are essential in allowing the body to function optimally. If your dog is aggressive or overheats easily, feed him foods that are cooling and calming such as celery or pork liver. Cooling foods also decrease inflammation and lower body temperature. They can also relieve skin conditions like heat rashes. Although food therapy may not show immediate results, it is important for prevention.

Warming Foods: dried ginger, lamb, chicken, oats…
Cooling Foods: seaweeds, celery, leek, beef liver,
pork liver, plum vinegar, rye, burdock root…
Neutral Temperatures: pork, rabbit potato, rice and corn…

AYURVEDA FOR K9's

Ayurveda is the oldest holistic system of natural medicine. It has three main goals: enlightenment, achievement of perfect physical health, and elimination of disease. The metabolic body and mind are called the Tri-dosha: Vata, Pitta and Kapha. The word Dosha (protective) is used for diagnosing a body out of balance or in a "disease-producing state." I advocate the practice of Ayurveda for dogs and found an excellent article: **DOGS NATURALLY MAGAZINE**: (May/June 2012) by Tejinder Sodhi, DVM. and have included highlights Dr. Sodhi suggests for his patients.

VATA PETS = Ether + Air

Vata controls blood flow, elimination, breathing, and the movement of thoughts. Health issues in Vata pets include hypertension, earaches, anxiety, irregular heart rhythms, muscle spasms, constipation, diarrhea, nervous stomach, and arthritis. Vata pets are physically slender and small-framed. The eyes may be small, dry, and active. The nails are rough and brittle. The shape of the nose is bent and in some cases turned-up.

Attributes of Vata pets include:

- Mental speed; quick to learn, quick to forget
- Excitable, lively personality; full of joy and enthusiasm
- Cold paws; discomfort in cold climates
- Response to fear, worry, anxiety, especially when out of balance
- Dry skin and fur

PITTA PETS = Fire + Water

Pitta controls digestion, nutrition, metabolism, body temperature, the luster of the eyes, intelligence, and understanding. Typical physical problems include rashes, skin cancer, ulcers, hot sensations in the stomach or intestines, vision problems, anemia, and jaundice. These pets are usually medium build.

Attributes of Pitta pets:

- o   Medium physique, strong, well-built
- o   Focused, good concentration
- o   Assertive, competitive; leader of the pack
- o   Strong digestion/ appetite
- o   Stress causes Pittas to react with irritation
- o   Hot weather; heat makes them very tired

KAPHA PETS = Water + Earth

Water enhances biological strength and resistance in the body. Kapha (water) lubricates the joints and helps heal wounds. It also provides vigor and stability; energy to the heart and lungs. Physical problems include respiratory problems, allergies, and atherosclerosis.

Attributes of Kapha pets:

- o   Affectionate and loving; faithful
- o   Physically strong with a sturdy, heavier build
- o   Slower to learn, but never forgets
- o   Overweight; sluggish digestion
- o   Averse to cold, damp weather

The most common herbs and spices used in Ayurveda for K9s include: fresh ginger for Vata pets; cumin and coriander for Pitta pets; and turmeric for Kapha pets. Dr. Sodhi says that if you provide your pet with good nutrition that balances their doshas, you will have a happy, healthy member of your family!

GIVING MEDICINE TO YOUR DOG

There is an art to giving a pill ("pilling") to a dog. First, hold your dog's upper jaw toward the ceiling, taking hold of his nose very gently. With your other hand, pull down on the lower jaw gently. Place the capsule or tablet in the center of the tongue, as far back as you can safely position it. If you need to, hold your dog's mouth closed and rub under his chin until he swallows. If you don't feel comfortable sticking your fingers in your dog's mouth, the easiest way to give your dog a pill is to try tucking the pill inside a Pill Pocket, a piece of cheese, or peanut butter.

Topical Ointments & Creams: Apply a thin layer of cream or ointment to the affected area. A good time to apply this is right before you feed them or just before you take them for a walk. This way, they have something else occupying their mind and hopefully, they won't lick the ointment or cream off right away. Some dogs need to wear an Elizabethan Collar (also known as an E Collar or cone). The collar works to keep them from licking the affected area.

SBK9U FIRST-AID KIT

- ✓ National Animal Poison Control: 1-900-680-0000
- ✓ Veterinarian emergency number:_______________
- ✓ Medications your pet is regularly taking
- ✓ Antibiotic cream
- ✓ Betadine disinfecting solution
- ✓ Hydrocortisone cream
- ✓ Benadryl
- ✓ Hydrogen peroxide
- ✓ Hemostatic powder
- ✓ Arnica
- ✓ Syrup of ipecac
- ✓ Rescue Remedy
- ✓ Saline solution

- ✓ **Ace bandage or Vet-wrap**
- ✓ **Medical tape**
- ✓ **Nonstick pads**
- ✓ **Cotton padding or other bandage padding**
- ✓ **Towels to wrap around an animal**

If your K9 has eaten a toxic plant and has any of these symptoms: vomiting, diarrhea, abnormal urine (color, smell, frequency, consistency, quantity) excessive salivation or weakness, hallucinations, coma, or seizures, have the plant name or the description of the plant available and call **Animal Poison Control Center (ASPCA) 1-888-426-4435** (Petoxins App on the Internet) or go to your nearest Veterinary Emergency Hospital.

To induce vomiting: If you can't get to the Vet right away, give your K9 3% Hydrogen Peroxide (1 Tbsp. per 15 lbs. of body weight) with an eye dropper, a syringe, or a turkey baster by dribbling the liquid onto the back of his tongue or into his cheek pocket until swallowed. I have also made a paste out of salt and water and dabbed it under their tongue. If your dog cannot tolerate salt (due to underlying health conditions), do not use this method. Collect vomit and take it and the poison in a container along with your pet to the Veterinarian ASAP!

HOW TO KEEP YOUR PUP FIT & HEALTHY

Purebred or mixed breed? Whether your dog is a herder or a hound, the fact is… K9s are domesticated and don't live in the wild; it's up to you to make sure they walk, run, and play to keep their bodies fit. Dogs innately hunt and forage for food, so because you are providing their daily meals, they must get out of the house to exercise. Healthy adult dogs need two 30-60-minute exercise sessions every day! All dogs are different, so it's a good idea to check with your Vet for specifics on how much to exercise your dog.

➢ Puppies younger than 18 months should not take part in vigorous exercise routines because their bones are still growing and the stress of a difficult routine could lead to hip and joint issues.

➢ Overweight and senior dogs should get a Vet's OK before starting a vigorous exercise routine.

➢ Breeds with short or flat noses (brachycephalic breeds) like Pugs and Boxers can have trouble breathing when exercised vigorously; especially in warmer climates, so keep the exercises less vigorous and the session shorter.

> ➢ Dachshunds, Bassett Hounds, Corgis, and other breeds with short legs and long backs can develop back problems, so check with your Vet before beginning an exercise routine.

If you use food as a reward during a workout, use it sparingly. Keep food treats very small during exercise (about the size of a pea or a blueberry) and limit the total amount of food. Don't feed your dog a large meal's worth of food during active exercise or he may fall victim to a potentially fatal stomach condition called bloat. Great Danes, Bloodhounds, and Weimaraners are especially susceptible, but the condition can afflict any breed. (See more on Bloat in chapter 4: Water and Your Dog's Health.)

Exercise Benefits:

- Keeps a dog healthy and happy
- Improves chances of living longer
- Helps reduce digestive problems
- Brings a fearful or timid dog out of his/her shell
- Boosts a dog's mood; improves cognitive function in senior dogs
- Curbs behavioral issues like aggression and hyperactivity
- Bonding. Exercising with your dog provides an opportunity for you to bond with your pet while both of you get the benefits!

Q: What Type of Exercise is Best for Dogs?

Some dogs may be happy with a simple walk around the block; while others may require something more active. Dogs will live at least two additional years if they're kept in excellent physical condition. The Journal, **OBESITY**, says that you are more likely to lose weight and keep it off if you exercise with your pet. If you stop to think about it, your K9 may be the most loyal exercise buddy you will ever have! Many experts agree that canine exercise is better when it involves human interaction. A dog left in the backyard on its own is more likely to just snooze than engage in activity. Try exercise that meets your dog's needs taking into account age, size, and fitness level as each breed will require different types of activities. Here are a few owner/pet exercises I recommend giving a try! The following exercises are best executed with a pet that knows a solid foundation of manners, such as SBK9U's Dog-mandments (see Training).

SBK9U EXERCISES: Owner & Pet

> **3-PACED WALK:** You and your dog walk for 30 seconds; then jog for 30 seconds; then sprint for 30 seconds; and repeat.

Benefits: Aerobic conditioning; boosts metabolism and burns more calories; increases cardiovascular function.

Brooks Tip: It helps if your dog knows how to heel and walk properly.

> **DOWN/STAY:** Put your dog in a down/stay while you do a set of jumping jacks. Your dog must remain in a down/stay. Or try sprinting to a tree and call the dog's name to come. Say "stay" and repeat. Or say down/stay and run back to the dog so they do not always want to jump up out of the stay.

Brooks Tip: Try running, jumping, or doing squats while your dog remains in the down/stay.

➤ **WEAVING GRAPEVINE:** You perform walking lunges while your dog weaves through your legs. Step forward into a lunge and guide your dog through your legs; reward with a treat. As you progress, reward every two lunges, then every four. Increase the number of lunges between treats as your dog improves.

Benefits: Teaches your dog self-control and improves agility. You are working your glutes and quads while your pooch works out.

➤ **SHUFFLE:** You walk sideways while dog heels at your side.

Benefits: Increases range of motion, and based on pace, can increase cardiovascular endurance and agility.

Brooks Tip: Your dog must know how to walk without pulling.

➢ **TUG-OF-WAR:** Using a knotted rope long enough for you to hold one end, and your dog to bite the other (so your dog doesn't bite you by mistake), gently pull on your end, while your dog pulls on the other.

Benefits: Tug-of-War is a favorite game for most every dog and can strengthen their jaw and upper body. Playing tug-of-war expends energy and burns calories, but use caution; only play tug with dogs that are not overly aggressive or dominant.

Brooks Tip: Make sure your dog is not aggressive or has a tendency to bite. Your dog should be trained to release with "drop it" on your request and not miss the toy and bite your fingers. Try using a longer toy if the dog is getting your fingers. Remember, as the human, you should always initiate and control the game. Never lift your dog off the ground with the rope in his teeth.

Note: Some trainers caution that playing tug-of-war will make dogs more aggressive. If you are worried, or if your dog has aggressive issues, or you have any fear or trepidation, *do not* play tug. But if you feel safe with your dog and you can control the game, it can be a great reward for good behavior. I have found that teaching a dog a controlled game of tug on a walk for instance, actually keeps them focused on me rather than lunging at a jogger or other dogs.

Be careful when exercising your dog not to overdo it as this can lead to injury or heart problems. Tired pooches will exhibit excessive panting, drooping tongue, staggered walking, and muscle tremors. Sometimes they will lie down and not want to move. Pay attention to the signals and allow them to rest. Schedule time every day just for you and your dog to exercise…start slow and work up in intensity and duration as you and your pooch make progress. Change-up activities you do to keep your dog from getting bored.

> **RETRIEVE:** Chasing a moving object is directly associated with the natural tendency canines have for hunting prey. They love the thrill of the chase, the triumph of the catch, and bringing the object back so they can chase it again and again. Retrieving is an excellent form of both mental and physical stimulation.
>
> Throw a toy, ball, or a stick and yell, "Go get it". When your dog runs to get it and brings it back, say "drop it" and throw again. Before you throw, you can ask your dog to sit or do a trick, then release on your terms and throw again. Chances are you will tire before your dog!
>
> **Benefits**: Works the entire body; aids cognitive function.
>
> **Brooks Tip**: If your dog won't retrieve, find something they show interest in and practice with the leash on. Throw it a few feet. When they get it in their mouth, call them back to you or gently real them back into you without letting them lie down and get their feet on it. Put them in your lap and praise. If they still don't drop it, ask for a "sit". Most dogs will drop it when they sit or try exchanging it for another toy or treat. This teaches them to retrieve and drop.

If you can't find a toy that your dog likes, try putting treats in a water bottle or pill bottle (poke a small hole in it so they can smell it) and throw the bottle. When they bring it back, open it up for them and feed them a bite. Once your dog graduates from the leash and has a concept of retrieve, try it in a hallway with the door closed, and they will be more apt to come back to you. Also try placing a doggie bed next to you. Most dogs want to come back and lay on the bed.

Note: Sometimes I teach the dog to drop something from his mouth by playing with a tug toy. I will let the dog get a good grip and I will pull back with steady pressure so the tug toy is tight. Then I will unexpectedly and gently go into the dog's mouth with the toy and make the toy limp. That's usually the exact time that the dog will try to re-bite it for a better grip, and that's the time I will say "drop" and take it out.

MAKE IT FUN! *Playing with toys can burn calories too!*

Chewing is a natural canine stress reliever. Puppies need to chew because they are teething, so try to give safe toys to chew, rather than your hands or shoes. Chew toys like a stuffed Kong™ are designed to work the jaw and upper body. They also provide mental stimulation as your dog works the toy with a goal in mind: to get the food inside. This activity keeps your pooch busy trying to extract every *dog bite* of a hidden treat.

1. **SAFE TOYS**: These are toys they can't destroy like Nyla-bones, Kong™ toys, or something large enough that they can't rip to shreds and ingest. Safe toys can be left out or rotated. If they are rotated, they have more value and create an element of surprise, and so the dogs don't get bored with them.

2. **YOUR TOYS**: What I call "your toys" are toys that are *unsafe* to leave out unsupervised. These include things dogs can RIP, CHEW, SHRED, or INGEST. I will only use this type of toy to play games with my dog, using caution to put them away when I am finished. I will also use this type of toy on a walk. I might let the dog carry it for a while, or I might hold it for a while so the dog is focused on me. I might play "tug" on a walk when we see another dog approaching so I become more exciting than the other dog! I will put it in my dog's mouth when the doorbell rings just for a few minutes, but I will not let my dog lay down with it, get their paws on it and start ripping it to shreds. I might also play a controlled game of "retrieve". But I won't leave this type of toy out as a safety precaution.

3. **NATURAL CHEW TOYS:** Bones, rawhide, pig's ear, bully stick, antlers, etc., are types of chew toys or rewards. They are not really toys, they are food. I like to give my dogs natural chew toys for relaxing in a spot while I'm watching a movie or working at the computer. I love it when my dog is basking in the sun, chewing on a natural chew toy (and not destroying the yard). Many dogs will start digging up the yard to bury chews. You want to keep an eye on him so he doesn't go off and bury it or take it to hide under the bed. You need to supervise. When they get too small, I take them away to avoid swallowing or getting lodged in their throat. If you have more than one dog, be careful not to let the dogs fight over the bone, as this is considered a high-value item for most dogs. Be especially careful around close quarters like under the table, trapped behind a coffee table, in a hallway, by a bed, etc. These are areas where dog fights are more apt to happen. Dogs can get possessive over bones. (See more in the chapter on Aggression). If you and your Vet agree that natural chew toys are right for your dog, give them American made, non-basted, natural chews rather than ones from other countries like China due to dangerous recalls.

4. **INTERACTIVE TOYS:** If you Google "interactive toys", you will find types of toys dogs love and can use to hunt for food, throw their own treat in the air, or play on their own for a period of time. Watch YOU TUBE videos of dogs playing with interactive toys or try filming one of your own!

Even digging can be a form of exercise. Why do dogs dig? Well, some dogs dig to find a buried (bone) treasure; others to stay cool, or to escape due to separation anxiety, or even mate with another dog. I allow dogs I'm training to dig in certain areas of the yard, but in areas where I don't want them to dig; I supervise them well so they can't practice digging in the first place. I also train to make sure they have a good recall. As soon as I see them digging in the wrong spot, I call them to come. Then I praise them. Then, when they're not looking, I bury small garden rocks (or their poop in the place they were digging as a deterrent). Digging can make a pup dog-gone tired too!

If you live near a lake or pool that allows dogs, swimming provides a terrific aquatic workout. It's excellent for arthritis and provides cardiovascular exercise that keeps Fido fit. If a dog is going to swim in a pool, they need to be trained on where the steps are so they can get out easily without anxiety. Place a cone or marker at the steps so they can see where to exit.

How about trying doggie yoga, called Doga! This is great for mind and body too! Exercises to build your dog's balance include using a doggie balancing disc or a treadmill.

If you have a dog that is obese or hyperactive, a treadmill can be useful, but unless you are highly experienced with dogs on treadmills, I do not recommend this mode of exercise. Dogs must be supervised on all equipment to prevent injury. I've heard horror stories from clients whose dogs have gotten tangled on a treadmill and fallen, even while their owners were standing right there! My thinking is…if you have to supervise your dog, why not take them on a walk and add a few more blocks to your routine? I had a client that had two large dogs and a baby in a stroller – she insisted on walking them all at the same time. Her secret to wear the dogs out was getting the dogs tired on the treadmill first. This made her walks little more enjoyable!

There are dozens of activities dogs love for exercise. See if you can add to this list:

- **AGILITY**
- **DANCING**
- **DANCING**
- **FRISBEE**
- **HERDING**
- **JOGGING**
- **PLAYING PIANO**
- **RUNNING**
- **SCHUTZHUND (PROTECTION SPORT)**
- **SOCCER**
- **SWIMMING**
- **TREIBBALL (A DOG HERDING SPORT)**

- **TRICK TRAINING / JUMPING THROUGH A HOOP**
- **WALKING**

K9 NOSE WORK: SNIFFING & SEARCHING GAMES

I also encourage you to look into doing Nose Work with your dog. K9 Nose Work is a fun search and scenting activity for virtually all dogs! This easy-to-learn activity and sport builds confidence and focus in many dogs and provides a safe way to keep dogs fit and healthy through mental and physical exercise. K9 Nose Work starts with getting your dog excited about using his nose to seek out a favorite toy or treat reward that is hidden in one of several boxes. You then expand the game to entire rooms, exterior areas, and vehicles. As your dog grows more confident with his nose, target odors are introduced and competition skills are taught.

Chapter

KIDS, K9's & SPECIAL OCCASIONS

PARTIES: *Who Let The Dogs Out!?*

Whether you are entertaining at home or going to a friends'…if you plan to include your dog (and who wouldn't?) you will want to make sure your dog has a fun, safe party experience. You never want to worry, "Who let the dogs out?" Always have a plan. It's a good idea to keep your dog on a loose leash and control greetings. However, never put a potentially aggressive dog on a tight leash or restrained in any way when visitors arrive as the frustration of being restrained may bring on aggression. It's like holding a drunk guy back in a bar… the more you hold him, the more he lunges forward and the more aggressive he may get!

It's always exciting for you to greet your guests and your dog is eager to greet them as well. What I suggest is to bring your dog out for a brief time, then put the dog in a secure area. For one, it's nice if a dog has a little independence. Second, dogs need to learn to be alone and relax. But the main reason is, K9's can become anxious or excited in a party atmosphere and for this reason, need to be monitored. It's also difficult to keep track of a guest who might unknowingly feed your dog toxic foods, overfeed or even leave the front door open.

Q: Are there going to be other dogs at the party?

You might say, "I always tell my friends to bring their dogs when I'm hosting and they tell me the same. Our dogs can hang out together while we humans visit -- it's a party, after all!" That's great in theory, but if you are going to "let dogs be dogs," then you'll need some ground rules. It's best if all the dogs have a basic listening foundation, are potty trained, and know:

> - Come: to come when called, quickly, even if distracted
> - Stay: to sit or lie down and be still until released
> - On Leash: Be on a leash without pulling

KIDS & K9s

Young children learn about the social world by watching others and modeling what they have observed. So it should come as no surprise that if you want children to learn how to treat pets, adults must be vigilant about modeling safe, appropriate relationships with dogs. At the age of three, children discover a range of social behavior including empathy, manners, and responsibility, to name a few… Remember, young children are still internalizing these concepts and shouldn't be expected to recall or even understand why they are important. It's up to you as parents to practice proper dog/human etiquette, so your children will follow your lead!

Adults should never use intimidating, dominant training techniques, especially around children. Never leave a young child alone with a dog, unsupervised. Alert adults should always be supervising. Try not to yell and limit the use of the word "no." Parents can model empathy by teaching kids to be the dog's advocate and learn to be their dog's 'helper'. Look for and reward your dog for good behavior, and remember that positive reinforcement works on kids as well as dogs!

***

There is a scene from the film, *Marley & Me*, in the family's kitchen, where Jennifer Aniston and Owen Wilson are dealing with their two kids, one of which is a screaming baby. Jennifer hands the baby to Owen because clearly, she's overwhelmed. Their older child is playing at the table when Marley jumps up, knocking things over… My advice in a situation like this is a small child should never be unattended with a dog in the room without an adult present and actively supervising. A dog could knock the child down without meaning to do anything wrong. I would also caution to always have an adult supervising a young child with a pet.

For festive gatherings, when children are present, a good rule of thumb is to have one adult per young child on watch with no other responsibilities. Babies and young children should be kept away from dogs, especially at parties, unless you're one-on-one actively supervising. You may find that if a dog growls or has outbursts of aggression, they usually happen under kitchen tables or chairs, behind coffee tables, doorways, hallways, water or food bowls, dog beds, toys, or their human. These are often areas where a dog might feel trapped or doesn't have a way out. Or maybe there's a resource that they're guarding or a piece of food that fell under a table?

Growling and aggressive outbursts usually happen when your dog feels trapped and there's no open area for them to be free and run to get away from what they consider to be trouble. If the dog is in a predicament and growls at a child or adult, don't react by scolding the dog and correcting the behavior, because a growl is a warning. Respect it and learn from it. If you get rid of the growl by beating it out of your dog, the dog may not growl anymore, he just may bite you next time instead!

When a dog is an attention hound or jealous, especially over humans – say I'm petting one dog and another comes over for attention, I instantly stop petting the first dog and walk away. I will usually only pet one dog at a time unless I know the dogs well, they are well mannered, there are no jealousy issues, or I'm actively working on a training exercise to teach self-control.

Observing K9 body language is essential.

Everyone should learn K9 body language and how to watch for signs of a dog under duress. A stressed dog may turn away, yawn, pin their ears back, shiver and shake, tuck or raise their tail high, raise their hackles, or grin (which may look like they are smiling). They might exhibit what's called "whale eye" where you see the big whites of their eyes showing. Some dogs under stress will even urinate or defecate.

Observe the proximity or what's called the "threshold" of a dog with a child.

Pay close attention to body language as they get closer or further away from a child, or even an adult for that matter. If you sense trouble, say the dog is interested in a piece of food near a child that fell on the ground and you're in a confined area, that's when you need to have a solid recall and say, "come" to call the dog back to you and get them away from the child. Practice recall with all sorts of distractions and in many different environments. If your dog is ignoring your request to "come", try to distract them. You can drop something on the floor. Then redirect the dog or the child, whichever seems safer at that moment. If that doesn't work, make a loud noise, clap your hands, drop something on the ground, and if your dog listens to "sit / down" better than "come", ask them to do an emergency "sit / down".

Use four or five bowls instead of one.

Here's what to do whenever entertaining your dog with friends' dogs:

Place three, four, or five water bowls, rather than one or two, out for the dogs. If you need to feed them, be safe and do it in a separate area. Then pick up the bowls when they are done. Dogs can become territorial and get aggressive on their own turf, especially when it comes to food and even water! Be proactive and use common sense and good management!

After a bit, I usually move them to a safe environment *away* from the action with the humans. This can be where you put each dog in his own kennel, or one outside; one inside, or one in a room with the door closed – don't forget to put a sign telling people not to open the door and put a secure lock on the door, out of the reach of children. My dogs are actually grateful for the time out, and when I check on them later, they are usually taking a well-deserved nap!

Party TIPS:

- If your dog will be a guest in someone else's house, potty training is a must. If this skill has not been mastered, get a pet sitter to stay in your home or find a kennel boarding facility until you successfully potty train your dog.

- Dogs get excited when new faces show up at the house. To combat jumping on guests, the best thing to do is to teach a solid "sit" or redirect them to play with their favorite toy.

- Positively reinforce your dog by pairing rewards at times your dog shows self-control.

- Look for opportunities to capture your dog doing something good, then mark and praise it. Don't wait for them to be bad before you react.

- Keep holiday plants such as mistletoe, holly, and poinsettias out of reach, since they can be poisonous. If you discover that your dog has ingested part of a plant, contact your Veterinarian or a poison control hotline immediately. **ASPCA's Animal Poison Control Center** can be reached 24 hours a day: (888)-426-4435. (Check out the ASPCA's Petoxins App.)

- Make sure your dog wears an ID collar and is micro-chipped in case she slips out the door while guests are coming and going.

- Don't think they're fine because they've been fine all night. They might be stressed or over-stimulated. At the end of the party is when they might act cranky, so check on them.

WHEN GUESTS COME & GO ...

Many dogs remain stressed even after the guests leave and that's when the trouble sometimes starts. The dogs might nail you when someone turns to leave a party. I've been training dogs for over 20 years and have only been bitten badly maybe two times; one was in the face by a Treeing Walker Coonhound. I was fairly new at being a dog trainer when I got a call from a very worried client named Angela. Her new Treeing Walker Coonhound, Poncho, who had only been with her two weeks, had behavioral issues and would exhibit extreme alarm barking whenever Angela's boyfriend came to the door. Poncho would flip out when guests came over and Angela wanted to have a party for her child's birthday, but was afraid and rightfully so.

When I arrived, Poncho tried to attack me the second I got out of my car! The dog was supposedly secured in the yard. Later, as I was sitting in the kitchen getting behavioral history from the owner, Poncho broke through the window and charged toward me. I instantly spilled the contents of my treat pouch on the ground – which happened to be hot dogs. Luckily, it was enough to distract the dog so Angela could grab him.

I ended up getting just enough of the dog's trust to work with him and coach the owner. Just when I thought everything was going smoothly and I got my confidence up by getting Poncho to perform a few behaviors – when my back was turned to leave at the end of the lesson, the dog attacked. He bit me right under the eye. It was like I was punched in the face. Aggressive dogs can attack when your back is turned or when you move to leave, so always keep an eye on them.

For the next lesson, I came back with a plan to help Poncho. Clearly, this behavior needed to be modified immediately. My training goal was to make Poncho more comfortable when guests arrived. First was strict management. I showed Angela how to secure him in safe places when she couldn't watch him. I explained that using a muzzle, keeping a leash on much of the time, and many other management techniques are essential for safety. We didn't want Poncho to practice these bad behaviors, so we used a lot of management. Then I showed her how to work on a basic foundation of Dog-mandment manners like come and stay.

I had Angela place her slippers, jacket, and the dogs' favorite toys on the porch. I would come over and enter wearing Angela's items so I *smelled* familiar to Poncho. I would also enter carrying Poncho's favorite toys into the house, then toss them on the floor and ignore him. Next, I would enter and drop some boring dry kibble on the floor then just walk away and ignore the dog. I didn't want to try too hard to be Poncho's friend… just let the dog approach me on his own terms. I didn't want to bring in A-list treats as they might get the dog too excited. Next, I called Angela on the phone just before I arrived, rather than ringing the doorbell. This way, the doorbell would not incite the dog. Angela even replaced her doorbell with one that had a choice of sounds so she could change the ring of the doorbell to something softer and different. The goal was to change her dog's emotional feelings from fear of guests to a feeling of joy whenever guests arrived.

It wouldn't be long before Poncho would start looking forward to when people came over. I also told Angela not to react when he barked at the ringing doorbell…to just wait until the dog stops barking and then praise or reward the cessation of barking. Soon the duration of barking decreased. Sometimes, all it takes to stop a barking dog is to put a toy in the dog's mouth…but Poncho required a bit more effort.

The next thing we worked on was behavior modification. I had Angela sit on the couch with her boyfriend while I sat across the room holding the dog on a slack leash with treats nearby. When her boyfriend got up to leave the room, Poncho would get anxious and growl. I then asked him to simply stand up and then sit back down. This put Poncho in an alert state but if he were to walk around the room, Poncho probably would have lunged. I explained that the growl was a warning and to "respect the growl" rather than try to correct it.

This time, when I had her boyfriend stand up and sit back down, Poncho didn't get as agitated. This was a good "threshold" to start making better things happen. The next time I had him stand, Poncho scored some tasty *dog bites* (the good kind!) delivered by me at the other end of the room. I delivered them when her boyfriend would first stand up so Poncho realized that when this guy stood up this meant "good things happen". More importantly, I would deliver the treats when Poncho stopped intensely staring at him and instead looked away. The next step was to have Angela's boyfriend walk around the room slowly…just a few steps at a time. Poncho quickly learned that at the other end of the room where I was sitting, amazing bites of food would fall on the ground whenever this guy moved around the room!

Next, I had Angela and her boyfriend hug and then wrestle for fun… Poncho learned that going to his bed and digging into some grub was a lot better than pushing people off the couch. When I wasn't there to hold the leash, I asked Angela to tether Poncho for safety (never tie an aggressive dog if they are in a teased state as the frustration can heighten the aggression). Now that Angela's dog was learning new behaviors, I reminded her that instead of just yelling "no no no!" asking Poncho to go to his bed and relax actually was a much better plan. Poncho learned that guests were not a threat and eventually we had friends walk him to help build a bond.

Once Poncho got a little calmer, I had Angela wait to feed him until guests came over so she could feed in creative ways right before the doorbell would ring. We did this training over several sessions. I thoroughly explained, and made sure she understood, to *never* leave Poncho unattended with anyone without actively supervising. If she couldn't comply, I thought it would be best to find a new home for the dog, because he was truly big and scary. It turns out that Poncho had some medical problems that may have contributed to his aggressive outbursts. Months later at a follow-up visit I was happy to see Poncho was now a well-behaved member of the family!

***

If you're unsure about a dog at someone's house, don't necessarily believe it when the owner tells you their dog is "okay with strangers". Use your own gut instinct. You may need to ask the host to put the dog away in a closed room – the host will need to put a sign on the door letting people know not to go in there or use a crate or baby gate. This is a great time to give the dog a Kong™ toy stuffed with yummy *dog bites*! To help mellow the dog out in another room, I suggest you turn on soothing spa music or burn lavender oil in a safe place. You can also try spraying a synthetic pheromone called DAP (Dog Appeasing Pheromone) or one to two drops of Rescue Remedy directly in their mouth or in the water bowl to help Fido chill.

If your dog is too stressed or just doesn't know how to chew the Kong, you can turn them into Kong lovers using the exercise below in Separation Problems: Verdine White, *Earth Wind & Fire.*

DOGS DON'T KNOW IF YOU'RE FAMOUS

I am featured as a dog training expert in the Blu-Ray DVD of *Marley & Me* (2008) a comedy-drama about the mischievous dog Marley, based on the best-selling memoir by John Grogan. The film stars Jennifer Aniston and Owen Wilson, but I think the real stars are Brownie and the 21 other dogs who played Marley in the film spanning 14 years of his life!

The story is about a couple contemplating becoming parents who decide to adopt a dog first, and can't resist a yellow Labrador retriever puppy named Marley. Behavioral problems ensue, so they take little Marley to a dog trainer (Kathleen Turner as Ms. Kornblut) who firmly believes "any dog can be trained" but when Marley refuses to obey her commands, she expels him from her class. The misadventures of Marley become a successful column in *the Philadelphia Inquirer*, offering antics and anecdotes that thousands of dog owners and dog lovers can relate to…

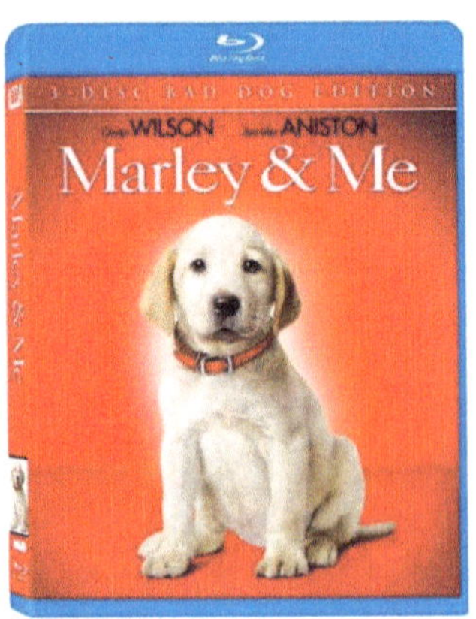

Look for Steve Brooks in *Marley & Me* (Blu-Ray DVD) Dog Training Trivia Track: (Picture-In-Picture) featuring Steve's tips on dogs, behavior modification, and training with positive, reward-based methods. It worked for Marley in the movie and it can work for your dog too!

CELEBRITIES & THEIR FOUR-LEGGED FRIENDS

As a Certified Professional Dog Trainer at **STEVE BROOKS K9U**, I have had the pleasure of training Hollywood celebrities' four-legged friends for 20 years including: Sheryl Crow, Robert Downey Jr., Cheryl Tiegs, Verdine White (*Earth, Wind, & Fire*), William Fichtner, and music producer, Rick Rubin, to name a few… I want to share with you a few stories about celebrity clients whose dogs I have trained. Keep in mind, the dog doesn't know their owner is a celebrity and yours won't either. They will love you all the same, unconditionally!

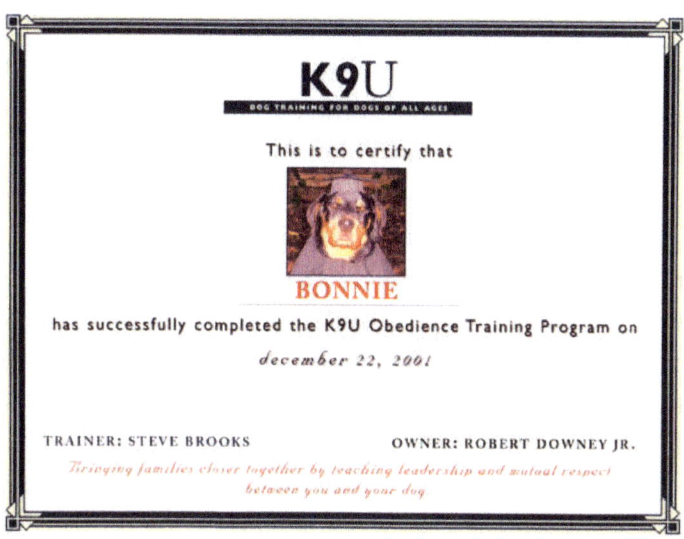

RUNAWAY: Robert Downey Jr.

Robert Downey Jr. had a sweet Rottweiler named Bonnie. He brought her over to train with me for my 21-Night Jump Start Training Program. This is where I first train the dog, then train the family so they can maintain training. Robert loved his dog and explained that one of the problems with Bonnie was that she would run away from home. I talked to him about ways he and Bonnie could build a better bond and how to improve their relationship so Bonnie wouldn't want to run away anymore. One of the first safety precautions I took when RDJ dropped Bonnie off for training was to add an "If Lost Call" SBK9U ID tag on Bonnie. Even though I've never lost a dog in all my days of boarding and training, I always do it as a safety precaution.

When RDJ picked Bonnie up, I spent the day training him on how to maintain everything I had taught her. I explained that when people pick up their dog from a board and train program, it works best if everybody involved in the dog's life comes to the demonstration lesson. Unfortunately, his girlfriend wasn't able to come. A few days after Bonnie went home, I got a call from a frantic woman in Studio City…she came home from the store and freaked out when she found a giant Rottweiler on her bed! When she saw the SBK9U tag, she immediately called me. I realized it was indeed Bonnie.

The woman told me she was unloading groceries from her car and left her car door open. A whole roasted chicken was still in the car and it seems Bonnie got a whiff and rummaged into the bag and ate some chicken, then wandered into the house and decided to crash on the woman's bed – all while she was going to and from her car! It turns out RDJ left Bonnie with his girlfriend while he was filming and Bonnie broke out of the yard and ended up in the neighbor's house down the street. I told the neighbor I would be right over… When I reunited Bonnie with RDJ, Robert was really grateful and said he owed me his life, etc. I wouldn't go that far… but he is an A-list actor whom I admire, so I really appreciated his heart-felt gratitude! I discovered that Bonnie was awesome and took to my training, graduating with flying colors!

The issue with many celebrity dog owners is that due to their busy schedules, the dog has many different people walking, feeding, and caring for them, which is always a challenge. Dogs do better when they have consistent role models and when everybody in their life is on the same page when it comes to maintaining training.

BOLTING: Sheryl Crow

I got a call from singer, Sheryl Crow, who was concerned because her dogs wouldn't come when called and would bolt out her front gate at the entrance of her driveway. Sheryl had two very rambunctious sibling shepherd-mix puppies named, Oscar and Lucy. At the time, the dogs had zero manners and were quite a wild pair! Like so many celebrities I work with, Sheryl told me that due to her busy schedule recording and touring, the dogs had many different people walking, feeding, and caring for them and that it was indeed a challenge.

Sheryl decided to drop the dogs off for my 21-Night Jump Start Training Program where I first train the dogs and then train the family after I have laid out the ground work. When Sheryl dropped Oscar and Lucy off for training, I told her the same thing I told Robert Downey Jr., that it would help if everyone involved in the dog's life could come to the training demonstration lesson so they could all be on the same page. I was hoping that everyone who interacted with the dogs would be present at both the demonstration and the follow-up lessons, but it was only Sheryl and she did great with the dogs. We scheduled a follow-up lesson the next day at her house because I wanted to work with her staff. I tell all my board and train clients that dogs are not robots… they need a relationship they can count on and need to trust you. They also need consistency in order to excel in training.

Sheryl Crow's property was in the Hollywood hills next to Runion Canyon, a famous destination for hikers and dog walkers in Los Angeles. The estate was massive and several of her staff members had their own guest house up against the hillside. Basically, the dogs were free to run for acres and acres; from house to house. While it sounds great to have all that space and freedom, there was actually way too much freedom for the dogs. They were clearly lacking structure and consistency, although there was no shortage of love! Sheryl was very nice and her Shepherd mixes, Oscar and Lucy, and even her older dog, Scout, were as sweet as can be. It was clear that Sheryl loved all her dogs very much!

The dogs learned all of the basics, solid as a rock. I worked on a rock solid recall, which is getting the dogs to come when called, every time and with enthusiasm. On my property, the dogs were pretty good at recall, but I knew we would have to work on it at Sheryl's property as well. Bolting was one Sheryl's main concerns. So Sheryl and I practiced just sitting on the porch holding long leashes with the dogs wearing a harness – we just waited and held onto the leashes tight as the dogs pulled toward the direction they wanted to run. We didn't pull back, we stood our ground; just sitting there like posts in the ground and waited a few minutes… Once they stopped pulling (all on their own) and gave up ever so slightly and turned their heads back to us to see why we *weren't* reacting, we marked the fact that they gave up with a click and a very enthusiastic 'good dog'! Immediately, we surprised them with half a cheeseburger that I had hidden by Sheryl's front door. I wanted the dogs to realize that good things happen; tasty *dog bites* are usually available on the front porch and that coming home to the front porch was the best place to be.

We eventually taught Oscar and Lucy to "come" mainly using the games, "Steal the Doggie" and "Wait, Why Don't You Hang Out?" as well as "How To Get Your Dog To Come In Mid-Run" (as talked about previously in this book). Sheryl and I got Oscar and Lucy to *want* to come back home in mid-run and discover that the front porch was the best place to be. I would reward them with amazing treats and praise. Sheryl was very pleased that now she could get them to *flip a U-turn in mid-run*. Sheryl was excited that her dogs learned new behaviors that she could reinforce at home. I still never got to work with all the other people that worked for her and lived on her property, but at least they listened to her when she shared training tips. Sheryl then referred me to music producer, Rick Rubin...

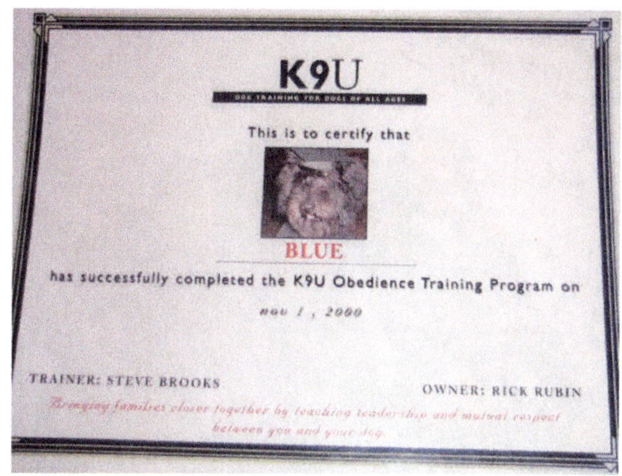

ON-LEASH AGGRESSION: Rick Rubin

Rick Rubin is a music producer who works with dozens of well-known recording artists in his Hollywood Hills studio. At one of our lessons, Rick was immersed in recording a session with Country legend, Johnny Cash. Needless to say, Rick was a busy guy and his dogs got much of their attention from Rick's staff, which was great because they were social with most people. Rick said a major problem was that whenever a UPS truck or equipment deliveries showed up, his 100-pound Briard named Blue, would bark like crazy and disturb his sessions. Blue was also starting to show signs of aggression with one of the recording engineers who was there every day working with Rick in the studio. By using positive reward-based Behavior Modification methods (like the one talked about in this book, Desensitization: Reduce Anxiety), I was able achieve great success with not only Blue, but his two older dogs (Pulis) named Monday and Chompa!

At the time, I mentioned to Rick that I had just finished recording my own music CD, *K9 Fusion*. It's real music played by real dogs (except for the drums, which as the only human in the band, I was honored to play). I gave a copy to everyone and the engineer even passed along a copy to legendary great, Johnny Cash! Another celebrity who enjoyed listening to *K9 Fusion* was Verdeen White of *Earth, Wind, & Fire…*

SEPARATION PROBLEMS: Verdine White

Verdeen White, bassist for the band *Earth, Wind & Fire*, had a Pit Bull named Duchess. One day…a lovely woman dropped Duchess off for the 21-Night Jump Start Training Program. At the time, I had no idea who this lovely woman and her son were. She just told me that she wanted all the commands taught in Swahili. I told her I would be happy to do so and created a list of training words they wanted to use in Swahili.

As they were leaving, they spotted *K9 Fusion*; the CD I recorded of real music played by real dogs (except for the drums, which, as the only human in the band, I was honored to play). I gave them a complimentary copy as they left, not knowing they were the wife and son of a musical legend! When they picked Duchess up three weeks later, the woman said "I gave your CD to my husband" – who just happened to be Verdeen White – the original (and current) bass player of *Earth, Wind & Fire*. She said they listened to it over and over again in the limo on their way back from Las Vegas and loved it! I did a follow-up session at their apartment in Hollywood and marveled at the gold records on the walls… I even asked Verdeen if he would like to jam with me sometime. (It never happened, but at least he was kind and enthusiastic.) The good thing is that the whole family was involved in the at-home training lessons which in my opinion are a remedy for lasting success.

One of Duchess' issues was anxiety. He could not stay comfortably in a room alone and was too stressed out to even chew a tasty stuffed Kong™ toy. I trained him to realize that it was safe to be in a room alone and I taught him to be a Kong toy junky using a John Rogerson technique (that I modified a bit). The goal of this exercise is to teach the dog to be left alone in a room, be calm, and to love a Kong… even with distractions like someone at the front door. By the end of Duchess' stay with me, he gained confidence and was soon happy to be alone for periods of time with the help of the following exercise:

Phase 1: I would spend 20 minutes of smothering Duchess with love. Immediately after the 20 minutes of love, I would tether him to a door, giving him a pre-stuffed Kong™ toy full of amazing sticky stuff. I would sit two feet away from Duchess and ignore him for 20 minutes. He was getting sick of my love and would start to enjoy his Kong toy. Next, I would calmly pick up the Kong and take it away until the next day's session.

- Repeat once a day for 10 days.

Phase 2: I spent 20 minutes smothering Duchess with love (like in Phase 1). After 20 minutes, I immediately put the dog behind a baby gate in the next room. Then gave him the stuffed Kong and sat about 10-20 feet away, where he could still see me behind a baby gate. You can also use a sliding glass door or screen. After 20 minutes, I calmly took the toy away.

- Repeat for 10 days.

Phase 3: Give 20 minutes of love. I put him on my lap, held him, and didn't take my attention off him. I smothered him with love. This time, immediately after the love smothering, I would put him in a bathroom or bedroom with the door closed and give him his tasty stuffed Kong™ toy. After five minutes, I opened the door. (Avoid getting excited that they were able to stay alone in the room for five minutes). I increased the time in the room each day in 5-minute increments until I got to 30 minutes in the room alone. Goal: they will become a Kong™ toy junky and be okay with being alone in a room without you!

- Repeat until the dog can remain calm in a room for 30 minutes.

If you can get a dog to stay in a room alone with the door closed for 30 minutes you may just fix some pretty serious separation problems. If, during those first five minutes, the dog starts scratching at the door, you can try to ignore it or lay a sheet of shelf paper on the floor in front of the door with the sticky side up. Most likely, your dog won't want to stand on the sticky paper and will prefer to dig into the stuffed Kong that he has become accustomed to.

Duchess had an affinity for my Salmon Pate (but you can use anything sticky like cream cheese, honey, yogurt, peanut butter, chicken breast, etc.). See if you can get creative and make stuffed toy dissecting time the best part of your dog's day! You don't want to overfeed; you can just dab a little bit of sticky stuff inside and pack it mostly with their regular food.

FRIGHTENED & WON'T EAT: Cheryl Tiegs

A dog will perform better during training if they have a little bit of food in their belly. The goal is to get them to eat Vet-recommended regular meals first before you start giving them the good stuff. If you start with the good stuff, you have nowhere to go. But if they won't eat you have to change your strategy. What you have to do in cases like this is get creative.

I've had thousands of dogs board and train with me over the years, and let me tell you, I've seen my share of dogs that are frightened and just won't eat. When a dog doesn't want to eat it's scary… Whenever this occurs, I get a list of their favorite foods from their owners and work to build trust. I remember training Cheryl Tiegs' lab named Truffle, who simply wouldn't eat. Labs are usually food hounds and vacuum cleaners when it comes to food, but Cheryl's dog was a rescue that was scared to death.

The day Truffle was dropped off at SBK9U; I went to help get her out of the car… As soon as the door opened, Truffle dove out of the car and I caught her in mid-air like a football. If I hadn't caught her she would have landed on a busy street full of traffic.

Poor Truffle was shaking like a leaf on a windy day. She wouldn't even look me in the eyes for a few days and wasn't the least bit interested in food. So I had to get creative…

The first thing I tried (which usually works) was to moisten dry kibble with anchovy oil and a touch of anchovy. Anchovies are full of salt (too much is bad for dogs) so I'm talking about crumb-size pieces. Truffle would lick the anchovy crumbs off the kibble and spit the kibble out. Next, I did the same with Tuna. Then I tried mashing in just a crumb of turkey and a crumb of string cheese between two kibbles like a mini sandwich. When even that didn't work, I tried mixing kibble in a plastic bag with stinky cheese and steak overnight so the kibble would pick up the odor. That usually gets them to eat but not Truffle.

I tried five different brands of kibble and all sorts of food that I had around the house. She still wouldn't eat, and we were going on two days now. Believe me this is not that abnormal. It's hard for me to sleep at night knowing a dog hasn't eaten all day, so sometimes I just give in. I didn't even care if she worked for it, I just needed her to eat anything, but she was too scarred. When I'm trying to get a dog like this to eat, I don't put too much in the bowl at once. It helps not to overwhelm them. Just put a little bit in the bowl at a time. You can even measure or count the kibbles so you know if they ate anything at all or how much.

Eventually, Truffle ate (on the second or third day). She began to trust me and realized that I was trying to help her. By the end of Truffles' stay with me, she was rocking out for just the plain dry kibble. She learned all the basic Dog-mandments, including several tricks, and graduated from SBK9U with a ton of confidence!

LORI ALAN

JEALOUS HOUNDS: Lori Alan

Actress Lori Alan, (*Sponge Bob Square Pants*, *Wall-E*, *Toy Story*) is a very loving, attentive dog owner. I remember she was really into her mixed breeds, Harry and Frankie. She called me all the time to discuss behaviors and share stories of their latest antics. Sadly, Lori recently lost Frankie due to Leukemia and I wanted to dedicate this story to his memory. Lori is extremely grateful for the training I have provided over many years and recently told me I am one of the most important people in her and her dog's life! The truth is her dogs inspired me!

Harry and Frankie were the sweetest dogs who loved everyone and always wanted to please. They loved being around people and doing a trick for a treat. Like many dogs in need of training, they had trust issues with little children, especially Frankie. He once growled at a toddler at one of Lori's parties that I attended. A party environment can be a bit much to handle for most dogs. Frankie never bit anyone…but a growl is a warning and should be respected. Many times, a growl without biting shows great self-control. When Lori's dogs growled at a guest (and because of all the prior training we did) Lori was able to just calmly say "come" and the dogs listened. In this case, training worked because Lori was a good student, did her homework, and practiced!

STINKY DOG: William Fichtner

Everyone hates it when a skunk sprays their dog, right? Especially when their entire house is suddenly overpowered by that horrible stench that's almost impossible to get rid of. Unfortunately for actor, William Fichtner, (*The Lone Ranger, The Dark Knight*) his dog, Daisy, was out of control when it came to chasing critters in the yard and was constantly getting sprayed. That's when I got the call to rid Daisy of her stinky habit!

Skunks are nocturnal so the chances of your dog encountering an "odiferous funk" from a skunk increases after dark.

Even though there is a host of cleaning remedies on the market, you may find you have supplies in your kitchen that can clean Fido just as well! I've used all kinds of stuff to rid dogs of that stinky skunk odor including distilled vinegar, tomato juice, Scope mouthwash, and Dawn dishwashing soap (I do the tomato juice between each step). I always end with a nice smelling regular dog shampoo (preferably oatmeal based).

Before you begin the cleaning process you will want to arm yourself with several old towels, an apron, and rubber gloves to keep the stench from getting on you. Dogs usually get sprayed in the face which is why I first rinse their eyes with a saline solution. I've also used Benadryl to help my dog when he could barely open his stinging eyes after being sprayed in the face. Even though I've been told by many Vets that Benadryl is safe for dogs, I still encourage you to ask your Vet before giving your dog medicine.

STEVE BROOKS' K9 SKUNK REMOVAL

SUPPLIES:

- Saline solution (for the eyes, if needed)
- 1-2 large bottles of tomato juice
- 1 bottle white distilled vinegar

- Mild dishwashing liquid (Dawn)
- Scope mouthwash
- A nice smelling oatmeal dog shampoo to ease itching
- Old towels or rags
- Rubber Gloves
- Apron
- Lavender candles to help mellow out everyone

INSTRUCTIONS:

1. Place your dog in the bathtub (wearing gloves) rinse your dog with warm water.
2. Rinse their eyes with saline solution if they were sprayed in the eyes.
3. Pour a generous amount of tomato juice and rub into the fur; soak for about 5 minutes then rinse thoroughly.
4. Pour a generous amount of distilled vinegar all over coat; soak for about 5 minutes and rinse.
5. Then do a second rinse with tomato juice.
6. Lather their coat with dishwashing liquid, let it soak for a few minutes then; rinse with warm water.
7. Then do a third rinse with tomato juice.
8. End with a nice smelling dog shampoo.
9. Repeat these steps the next day! The smell will come back a little bit when you wash the dog the next day but once they are dry the smell will start to dissipate.

Once you rid your pet of the stench you will want to make your yard a "skunk-free zone". First, make sure there are no holes in the fence. Next, sprinkle a few rags with ammonia and human hair placed in some panty hose and scatter around the yard. This seems to rid both pesky rodents and skunks. If the skunk is living under your house, leave one opening and place a radio with loud music at the other end to scare them away. For more information, check out my chapter in **DOCTOR'S BOOK OF HOME REMEDIES** (20th Edition).

So now that you know how to rid your dog of skunk stench, you may want to learn how to stop your dog from chasing after a skunk in the first place. In order to stop Daisy from running after skunks or squirrels, I suggested the family work on recall with Daisy (using the methods in Chapter 2). I also talked to them about being a little more proactive and managing things around the house – like making sure to scope out the yard at night before they let her out. I used a fishing pole and tied a squirrel toy to a fishing line and had them play chase games in the yard with their dog. The goal: playing a game with humans becomes more exciting than a skunk or a squirrel!

Another way to modify this behavior is to let the dog sit in the yard on a leash and stare at the squirrels. They can be pulling at the end of the leash… it's okay, let them. Don't react. Wait for the dog to give up, look back at you, or relax a little bit…then the *second* he gives up staring at that squirrel, praise and treat. The dog will soon learn that giving up on the squirrel pays off. I bet there's a healthy food that your dog will go nuts for and you can use as a surprise as long as you don't give up and keep experimenting. …After bathing Daisy, we had tomato juice left over so we made Bloody Mary's!

ON-LEASH AGGRESSION: William Peterson

Actor, William Peterson, and his wife Gina brought several of their wonderful dogs to train with me over the years. They rescued and fostered an adorable two-year-old Pit Bull named Joe Pete. At first, Joe Pete was extremely dog-aggressive and could not be walked on a leash without lunging and attacking other dogs. During our first training session, I tested to see how aggressive he was by placing him in front of a mirror… As soon as he saw his image in the mirror, Joe Pete immediately tried to attack the dog looking back at him–clearly unaware that it was his own reflection. I let him growl at himself for about five minutes before he relaxed a little bit. Despite the grim prognosis, I did not give up on Joe Pete. I devised a plan to muzzle him on walks and reward him with a squeeze tube (looks like a toothpaste tube) that I got at a camping store.

First, I packed the squeeze tube with my homemade Salmon Pate (later using peanut butter, cheese whiz, or cream cheese). I chose a tube because it was easy to administer by squeezing it through the basket muzzle and into the dog's mouth. This was essential because there weren't many rewards out there more interesting than going ape over every dog he saw on a walk. After a few sessions, Joe Pete was able to calmly face his own reflection in the mirror and even pass dogs on the street without a hitch.

Practical Tricks & Treats

It's a good idea to teach dogs new tricks to keep their brains and bodies agile. The novelty of a new route on a walk or learning a new trick can recharge brain cells. I love teaching dogs of all ages fun tricks… like how to dance, play the piano, or even open the fridge to bring me a cold beverage! I always tip my doggies well with a dog bite treat and advise you do the same! You may be familiar with "play dead", 'walk on two legs", or "speak" but I have expanded on these tricks to create many that you may never even heard of! And let me tell you, it's really fun for dogs of all breeds to learn and practice these advanced tricks.

"You CAN teach an old dog new tricks!"

I taught my mixed-breed soul mate Love Dog, Sven, all of his best tricks when he was a senior. He learned tricks like "how to turn on and off appliances", "play the piano", and yes, even "open the fridge" to bring me a cold beverage…

➢ Open the Fridge & Retrieve a Beverage

Open the Fridge begins by playing a controlled game of tug-of-war with your dog. This means you start the game with self-control on the dog's part. Play tug with a fairly long rope. Tug gently from side-to-side instead of straight up as it is safer on their neck. Practice playing tug with the rope or dish towel you will be tying on the fridge door. Use the item you will want your dog to retrieve from the fridge to practice your retrieve. You can use the plastic six-pack beer or soda holder and play retrieve with just one beer on it or a beer can cooler sleeve or even a small plastic water bottle or film container with some treats in it.

Then when you're ready (on your terms) ask for a "sit". Most dogs will drop the rope when they sit. You can also work on a "drop it" as talked about in the retrieve section on pg. 209. Start and stop the game on your terms; don't let it get out of control. Teach all the components separately first. Start by teaching to Retrieve: work on retrieving with your dog as a separate exercise with the item that you want your dog to retrieve. I use Tupperware, a film container or plastic water bottle filled with yummy treats! You will also need to have trained your dog:

#1. Sit/Stay. #2. Send Out. #3. Hold. # 4. Recall. #5. Drop item in your hand.

Now that your dog understands each component separately, you're ready to start teaching Opening the Fridge as a complete trick.

1. Start by playing a controlled game of tug-of-war by the refrigerator.

2. Tie a rope to the fridge.

Keep your hand on the rope up by where it's tied and play tug with your dog. If your dog can't open the fridge by pulling right away, help your dog open it and have an amazing tasty dog bite treat easily available for your dog to eat. As the door opens, grab the container (that you have previously set inside the door) and quickly open it and deliver the treat from the container. Reward any effort to pull at first; then start putting the item you've been practicing the retrieve game with on the bottom shelf of the fridge and have your dog retrieve.

3. Place dog at the far end of the kitchen.

4. Put toy, food item or beverage in the fridge.

5. Go back to your dog and send them off to retrieve saying, "Go get me a beer" or "go get it". The first time your dog opens the refrigerator door on their own, instantly drop a high-value treat in their mouth, on the ground, or on the shelf of the fridge.

6. As the dog is opening the fridge…slowly back up so that eventually, the dog can do a full sit/stay, send out, pull fridge open, return with beverage, and drop in your hand. When they drop the beverage in your hands, open the drink and have an A-plus treat ready to surprise them!

Now you have to teach your dog to close the fridge…

➢ **Close the Fridge**

Close the Fridge

1. Hold a target stick on the door where the dog can reach it easily.

2. Each time he touches it and the door moves (even a little) click and treat.

3. Start waiting until he pushes the door closed. Click and treat.

4. Do this until he closes the door each time. Click and treat with a high-value dog bite treat when he gets it right.

5. Add a word like "close" when he closes the door. Repeat several times until

your dog can do it when asked.

Don't forget to take the rope off the door when you're not around or you might end up with a plump puppy! Be happy with little baby steps your dog offers you, ignore bad behavior, and acknowledge and praise good behavior. Keep the sessions short, angle the fridge, and play with the length of the rope so it's easy for your dog to open the door.

➢ Turn on Lights

The way to train your pooch to turn on the lights is to start by teaching them to touch a target stick (as described in this book) or to touch your hand.

1. When they touch, mark it with a click or "good dog" and deliver a C-list treat.

2. Next, place a piece of tape or a round sticker on the end of your finger or on the end of the target stick. When they touch the tape, they will now get the treat.

3. Once that's down, have them touch the stick right *next* to the light switch or appliance button.

4. Now, transfer the tape to the switch or button. If the dog touches the tape, they will quickly get a C-list treat.

Do this several times and deliver the treat every time your dog (ever so slightly) touches the tape. You want the dog to expect the treat every time. I liken this to waiting for an elevator. You wait… it doesn't come fast enough and you get frustrated. You start hitting the button harder. Well, that's what needs to happen with your dog. He needs to hit the switch a little harder to make it turn on. Fido will be expecting the C-list treat every time…

5. Now, you are going to hold off on delivering the C-list treat. When your pooch gets frustrated, they will hit the switch harder. Just when the light or the appliance turns on, Jackpot! You surprise your dog with an A-list treat.

➢ **Play the Piano**

Uni at the Keyboard

"Play the Piano" is a practical trick because I have gotten many dogs over their fear of noises and fear of walking on unfamiliar surfaces by teaching this fun trick. It helps if the dog has a good sit/stay and knows how to shake or give a paw before you teach them how to play piano. I like to use a small electric piano placed on the floor. Before I even turn it on, I toss treats near the piano or place their food bowl next to the piano so they are comfortable just being around it. I turn the keyboard on a low volume and tap a key, then drop a treat to make sure they are not afraid of the sound.

1. I put my dog in a sit/stay in front of the piano and work on giving paw, wave, give me five, shake, or whatever you have taught them.

2. I hold a treat with one hand by my chest or face and with the other hand, I try to get them to "give paw" and have them miss my hand and hit a key by accident. I encourage them to take a step forward (or sideways) by way of a target stick or my hand. If I can get them to touch a key, I immediately deliver an A-list treat.

3. I'm happy with one paw hit on the key for a treat at first… but then I will not deliver until I get two or three hits on the keys. Then I wait until I can get 5 or 6 hits on the keys before I deliver a treat.

4. You can get them to move around on the keys by use of a target stick or

targeting your finger.

Controlling the game is key. Start on your terms; stop on your terms. Don't set your criteria too high at first. Start slow and be happy with baby steps. Work on this just a few minutes a day. Once things connect and the dog really realizes that "If I hit this key, I get a treat," you are on your way to success!

➢ **Find the Treat**

This game is a great way to teach your dog to use his sense of smell to find something. It's also a great way to stimulate a senior dog or tire out a puppy. Find the Treat allows you to bond with your dog by sharing tasty *dog bites* with them!

1. Stuff a Kong™ toy with smelly treats. Show your dog the Kong and encourage him to sniff it.

2. Hide the Kong toy in an easy-to-find spot while your dog sits and stays.

3. Release the dog and say, "Find the treat".

4. Let him eat the treat and say, "Good dog!"

5. Then do it again, but this time, hide the Kong in a more difficult to find spot. This way, your dog has to use his sense of smell to find the Kong and get the treat.

About the Author

STEVE BROOKS (CPDT-KA)

As a Certified Professional Dog Trainer (CPDT-KA), a credential granted by the Certification Council for Professional Dog Trainers (CCPDT), Steve Brooks completed rigorous tests on humane training practices using the latest scientific knowledge related to dog training. He offers workshops and seminars and attends conferences across the United States and is also a proud member of the Pet professional Guild (association for force free pet professionals). Steve Brooks is a professional member of the Association of Pet Dog Trainers (APDT). Steve is a Family Paws Parent Education Licensed Presenter, Licensed Dogs & Storks Presenter, and Licensed Dogs & Toddlers Presenter. Steve was one of the first non-Veterinarian experts CPDT/KA invited to attend the Post-Graduate Institute for Applied Clinical Behavioral Medicine at the North American Veterinary Conference in 2005, led by Dr. Karen Overall.

Steve Brooks' appearances on national and international television mean humans around the world can participate in creative, customized Reward-Based Canine Training. Broadcasters spanning the globe from Canada to Japan to Australia have profiled him with appearances on Fox News (San Diego, Los Angeles), NBC News (Palm Springs), *Animal Planet*, National Geographic Channel, CBS' *World's Funniest Pets*, TBS' *Ripley's Believe It Or Not*, *Inside Edition*, and many more…where he gives advice on canine training and safety. Steve is also a contributing writer for *Fido Friendly* Magazine.

Steve also appeared as a dog training expert on the Blu-ray DVD for the film, **Marley & Me**. His new book, **DOG BITES**, filled with expert techniques and training tips, is now available! Steve Brooks was born in Hollywood, California and lives with his wife Yasmine, their cat Fuago, and their dog Uni, in the Silverlake area of Los Angeles.   Visit: www.SteveBrooksK9U.com

Acknowledgements...

Steve would like to thank his late Love Dogs: Sven and Legali, and his current pup, Uni (pictured above), as well as every dog he's ever met and had the pleasure of training! He would also like to acknowledge the humans with whom he trained, studied, and was inspired and influenced by to create his own practice as a Certified Professional Dog Trainer at Steve Brooks K9U and write this book, *DOG BITES*:

- **Dr. Karen Overall**
- **Dr. Ian Dunbar**
- **John Rogerson**
- **Roger Abrantes**
- **Raymond Coppinger**
- **Jean Donaldson**
- **Karen Pryor**
- **Peter Beeman DVM. to name a few...**

Additional Photo Credits:

- **Sean Vincent Biggins: p. 242 & 243**
- **Chris Weeks: p. 19 & 20**
- **Kelvin Jones: p. 57**
- **Yasmine Essa Brooks: p. 7, 99, 176**
- **Neil Amigone: p. 30, 33, 34, 45 & 239**

Resources...

AAFCO Pet Food Committee
Minnesota Department of Agriculture Dairy and Food Inspection Division
625 Robert Street North, St. Paul, MN 55155-2538 www.aafco.org

FDA Center for Veterinary Medicine
7500 Standish Place, Rockville, MD 20855 (301)594-1728 www.fda.gov/cvm/

Pet Food Institute
2025 M Street, NW, Suite 800, Washington, DC 20036 (202) 367-1120

THE HANDBOOK OF BEHAVIOR PROBLEMS OF THE DOG AND CAT
by Landsberger, Hunthausen, & Ackerman

THE HANDBOOK OF APPLIED DOG BEHAVIOR AND TRAINING: VOLUME 1 & 2
by Stephen R. Lindsey

THE DOG VINCI CODE by John Rogerson

CLINICAL BEHAVIORAL MEDICINE FOR SMALL ANIMALS by Dr. Karen Overall
THE HUNTING BOOK OF GASTON PHEBUS

MINE by Jean Donaldson

The Journal **NATURE** (featured in *LA TIMES* January 23, 2012)

THE WHOLE DOG JOURNAL: "Diet and the Older Dog"

FOUR PAWS, FIVE DIRECTIONS: A GUIDE TO CHINESE MEDICINE FOR CATS AND DOGS by Dr. Sheryl Schwartz D.V.M.

DOGS NATURALLY MAGAZINE (May/June 2012) by Tejinder Sodhi, DVM.

Animal Poison Control Center (ASPCA) 1-888-426-4435

The Journal **OBESITY**

SUNNYDOGINK.COM: "WHAT TO DO IF YOUR DOG IS CHOKING"

Steve Brooks is a master at creative, positive, science-based reward training methods that can be used effectively with teeerrrific results without force or threats.

Steve's philosophy of "dog training for the real world" holds that every dog should know a set of real-life manners using positive reinforcement without the use of threats or force.

Steve Brooks is a Member of the following:

CPSIA information can be obtained
at www.ICGtesting.com
Printed in the USA
FSOW03n1349191114
3519FS